Working with Computers

Computer Orientation for Foreign Students

Working with Computers

Computer Orientation for Foreign Students

Michael Barlow

ATHELSTAN

Printed in the United States of America

ISBN 0-940753-07-3 (cloth)
ISBN 0-940753-08-1 (paper)

Library of Congress Card Number 86-83418

Thanks to Sandra Ward of Meyer Memorial Library, Stanford University
for her helpful comments on library research.
Photographs on pages 8, 25, and 40, courtesy of Apple Computer Inc.
Photograph on page 10, courtesy of Xerox Corporation

Athelstan
P.O. Box 6552-W
Stanford, CA 94305
U.S.A.
(415) 285-0734

Contents

CONTENTS

Preface

As a foreign student, you have a lot to put up with: strange food, unfamiliar customs, and a different language. And since on top of this you have to cope with classes and assignments, you may be reluctant to take the time to learn how to use computers. However, you will be much better equipped to successfully complete your academic studies if you spend some time and energy mastering the basics of using a computer.

Working with Computers has two aims: first, to teach you how to use computers, and secondly, to show you how to make use of computers to complete your academic work efficiently.

No prior knowledge of computing is assumed. As you work through the book, you will learn more and more advanced techniques. Each new concept is explained, building on more basic concepts introduced previously. If you forget what a term means, you can look it up in the glossary, which contains all terms appearing in *italics*.

Part I of *Working with Computers* introduces the basic operation of computers. It also covers the major areas of computing that are relevant for academic work: *word processing, data bases, spreadsheets,* and *communications*, with the most emphasis placed on word processing. For each of these topics you will learn how to use the programs and how such programs will help you in your academic work.

Chapter 1, **Introduction**, provides a first look at the computer and discusses some common computer anxieties. This chapter introduces the different parts of a computer for students who have not had any previous computer experience.

Chapter 2, **Working with large computers**, and Chapter 3, **Working with microcomputers**, briefly describe the two main types of computers in use today. Chapter 2 explains how to get started on a *time-sharing* computer: how to get an account, *log on*, and give commands. Chapter 3 describes how to *boot* a microcomputer and *load* software programs so that you can start your work.

Chapter 4, **Basic editing**, provides a survival guide to writing with a computer, introducing the essential features of word processing programs.

Chapter 5, **Files and operating systems**, describes a set of basic functions that are needed to carry out routine tasks. These functions include various aspects of file-management: naming, copying, moving, and printing *files*. This chapter also gives some advice on how to cope with disasters such as the accidental deletion of files.

Chapter 6, **More on editing**, describes powerful features of word processing programs such as 'search and replace' commands; inserting, deleting, and moving blocks of text; and controlling the layout of your text.

Chapter 7, **Communications**, tells you how to take advantage of computer *networks* to send electronic mail, transfer files from one computer to another, and get access to a wide range of computer services.

Next is Chapter 8, **Data bases and spreadsheets**, which discusses the use of *data base programs* to store, retrieve and organize information. It also introduces you to the use of spreadsheets to store and manipulate numerical data. A simple analysis of a set of test scores is presented to show how spreadsheets are used to perform calculations on data.

Chapter 9, **Advanced editing**, returns to the topic of word processing. In this chapter, advanced word processing techniques are covered, including: moving text from one file to another, defining *macros*, and taking advantage of *spelling checkers* and *formatting programs*.

Part II of *Working with Computers* concentrates on specific academic tasks. For each of these tasks, you will learn what is expected of you at college or university and how computers can help you meet these expectations.

Chapter 10, **Library research**, discusses how to find research material in a library using a *card catalogue*.

Chapter 11, **Computers and library research**, covers the techniques of searching an *online library catalogue*. This chapter also discusses the advantages and disadvantages of using computerized searches.

The ability to take good notes and recover information from your notes are essential skills. Chapter 12, **Taking notes and organizing information**, describes techniques for taking notes and getting the best use out of them. Two methods of organization are discussed: one using index cards and the other using a computer.

The next two chapters cover various aspects of academic writing.

Chapter 13, **Writing an academic paper using a computer,** guides you through the steps involved in writing an academic paper: choosing a topic, making an outline, writing a draft and revising your work. This chapter describes how the computer can help you at every stage of the writing process. Chapter 14, **Polishing your paper**, tells you how to produce the final version of your paper. This chapter describes how you can improve your paper in terms of both content and appearance. The topics covered include guidelines for the correct format of papers, assembling bibliographies, and adding diagrams and tables to your paper.

Following most of the chapters, there are some questions and topics for you to think about or for class discussion.

At the end of the book, there are five appendices containing general reference material, followed by an index. Appendix A, **Three editors: WordStar, EMACS and MacWrite**, covers the fundamentals of these three commonly used word processing programs. Appendix B, **Three operating systems: DOS, UNIX and the Apple Macintosh System/Finder**, describes three major operating systems in use on today's computers. Appendix C, **Computer commands**, provides a list of common computer functions. For each of these functions, you can enter the command appropriate for the computer and word processor you are using.

Appendix D, **Answers**, contains selected answers to the questions at the end of each chapter. Appendix E is an extensive **Glossary** containing explanations of technical terms. All the words which appear in the text in *italics* can be looked up in this glossary.

Throughout the book, illustrations are used to exemplify or clarify material covered in the text. In addition, warnings and helpful hints appear enclosed in rectangular boxes. Cautionary notes and common mistakes are indicated in boxes containing an exclamation point:

> **!** This symbol warns you about common pitfalls.

Boxes containing an asterisk are more positive; they include hints that nudge you towards a more sophisticated use of the computer:

> ***** Watch for this symbol for useful computer and writing tips.

Part I

Computer Basics

1

Introduction

This is a not a book to be read from start to finish. And it is certainly not a book to be read all at once. The best way to use this book is to alternate between reading the book and actually using a computer.

For this introductory chapter we will assume that you have had no real contact with computers. If you are familiar with the basic workings of computers, then you should just skim through the beginning of the book until you reach material that is new to you. One way to get an idea of how much you know is to look at the questions at the end of each chapter.

If you don't know much about computers but you are sitting in front of one and are eager to discover what the different parts are, then you should jump ahead to Section 1.2.

1.1   Computers and foreign students

Computers have as much feeling as a piece of chalk, yet they inspire extreme emotions in people—everything from fear and loathing to infatuation. It is not clear which of these extremes is worse as far as academic work is concerned. It would be unfortunate if fear prevented you from taking advantage of the power of computers; but possibly even more unfortunate would be a passion for computers that distracts you from your real aim of completing your studies. It is conceivable that as a foreign student you could spend too much time at the computer, especially if you found that 'communicating' with the computer was easier than talking with other students in English.

A computer is not something to be feared, nor is it warm and fuzzy, like a teddy bear. It is a tool, and like any other tool, it brings within reach tasks that are beyond our natural capabilities. Keeping this in mind will help you keep a balanced perspective: the computer is a means to an end, and not an end in itself.

Fear of libraries

Do you fear going into a library? Do librarians frighten you? Probably not. Perhaps you feel a little uncomfortable going into a new library where you are unsure of the rules and procedures or even the places for entering and leaving. However, you have most likely experienced libraries before and have some idea about how to gain admission, find books and check them out. So any anxieties you may have are probably counterbalanced by the belief that a new library cannot be all that different from the libraries you are familiar with.

Fear of computers

Do you fear computers? The answer depends in part on whether you have used computers before. One problem with computers is that they cannot be used in a casual, disinterested manner, the way that most libraries can. It is unfortunate, as far as the new user is concerned, that computers demand a certain level of attention and knowledge. It is difficult, if not impossible, to learn to use them just by experimenting with the keyboard. However, you will find that the amount of expertise needed to start doing useful work is minimal.

For various reasons, people often have fears concerning computers. They may feel a general anxiety when they are near one, much as some people feel when they encounter a strange dog. This general computer anxiety may become an acute fear when such people are asked to sit down at a computer. Some students may feel that it is almost as bad as being told to sit at the controls of an airplane and take off. Such general anxiety cannot always be abolished immediately, but fortunately it recedes as familiarity with the computer grows.

Let us examine a few common anxieties about computers. (Fearless souls can skip to the next section.)

1. The 'helpless at math' syndrome.
   Mathematical ability is completely irrelevant as far as using a computer is concerned, so we will pass on to other fears.

2. The 'destruction of Moscow' fear.
   This is very common. The computer novice believes that pressing the wrong key on the computer will cause, if not the destruction of Moscow, then at least the failure of the computer (a *crash*), making him or her very unpopular with everyone around. Don't worry. You cannot make the computer crash by

pressing the wrong keys. (If you could, the computer would be *down*, i.e., not working, all the time.) Another thought, which may be only moderately comforting, is that the only person's time you are going to waste by giving the wrong command is your own.

3. Not knowing how to *program* the computer.
   Programming a computer involves writing a set of instructions in a *programming language*. (Remember, words in italics are explained in the glossary in Appendix E.) However, it is not necessary for you to program the computer to get it to do what you want. For tools such as word processors and data base programs, the programming has already been done. You can use these tools, called *applications* programs, without any knowledge of programming whatsoever. Applications programs typically use English-like commands such as **print**, **copy** and **search**. (Throughout the book, **boldface** type is used to indicate words that are typed into the computer.)

4. Feeling silly.
   A tough one. The main advantage here is that you cannot look silly to a computer. It makes no difference to the computer whether you devise an elegant set of commands or whether you sit for hours at the computer pressing the wrong keys. One good way to build your knowledge and confidence is to experiment and practice at the keyboard when there is a more experienced user who is close at hand. You should keep in mind that operating a computer, like driving a car, is very easy once you know the basics.

5. Harming the computer.
   This is related to the 'destruction of Moscow' fear. Typing at a keyboard cannot harm the computer. You should, however, treat the system with respect, since there are certain sensitive parts (for example, the *disks* and *disk drives* on *microcomputers*) which need to be handled gently.

The language of computing

Since everyone has been intimidated to some degree by computers, it is unfortunate that the language of computing sounds so drastic. Serious errors, for example, may be described as *fatal*. Further examples of violent language associated with the computer include the following commands:

- abort

- break

- disable

- expunge

- kill

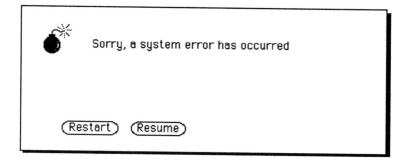

Figure 1. A bomb

Even the Apple Macintosh computer, which set new standards for approachability and 'user-friendliness,' presents the innocent user with a picture of a bomb (Figure 1) when something goes wrong—the pictorial representation of a fatal error.

Don't worry if you don't understand either the literal or the technical meaning of these words. They all have fairly violent interpretations in ordinary English. Why such strong language came to be used is not clear. Possibly, the early computer programmers felt that they were dealing with a powerful machine which merited powerful commands to control it. Perhaps they considered 'finish the job' too weak as a command and preferred the stronger language of 'kill the job.' In any case, when you get used to computers, these words soon become neutral, technical terms, lacking any darker associations.

Some computer terms, such as 'data base' and 'interface,' are used in everyday conversations. Other words and phrases, such as *downtime* and *boot the computer*, remain restricted to computer talk. Downtime, for example, has nothing to do with periods of emotional depression; it simply refers to periods of time when the computer is unavailable to users. And *booting* refers to starting microcomputers (discussed in Section 3.2).

Quite a few computer terms are introduced in this book. However, it is more important that you learn how to use computers, rather than how to talk about them.

1.2   About the computer

Types of computer

There are two main types of computers: large time-sharing computers and microcomputers. When you use a large computer you work at a *terminal* that is connected to the computer by means of a cable. The computer terminal consists of a *monitor* (also called a *VDU* or *CRT)* and a *keyboard* (see Figure 2).

Figure 2. A terminal

Even though you might use a large computer every day, you will probably not see the actual computer system unless you express an interest in doing so. The computer is often kept in its own room, possibly at some distance from where you work. If you do have a chance to look at a computer, you may be pleased to find that it looks something like the computers depicted in movies. There are some rather small, flashing lights, though these days you may not see the reel-to-reel tapes that are often displayed in the movies to indicate that the computer is working.

A microcomputer resembles a terminal in having a monitor and a keyboard (see Figure 3), but it has, in addition, a *system unit*. The system unit, often located under the monitor, may be considered to be the actual computer since it contains a *microprocessor* and certain other crucial components.

Figure 3. A microcomputer—The Apple Macintosh (with mouse)

Mainframes, minicomputers and microcomputers

If you are not interested in the classification of computers, feel free to skip to the next section.

Large computers are referred to as *time-sharing* systems because of a technique that allows the *processor*, a large version of a micro-processor, to jump from user to user very quickly. This technique creates an illusion of constant access to the computer for all the users. However, if a large number of students are using a computer at the same time (often the night before an assignment is due), then the response of the computer slows considerably due to the heavy *load*. Computers, whether large or small, which allow several people to use them simultaneously are called *multi-user* systems.

Another term that is used for a large computer is *mainframe*. Traditionally, mainframes were contrasted with smaller computers called *minicomputers*, which are still quite large and use time-sharing techniques. However, nowadays it is becoming more common to call all time-sharing computers mainframes in contrast to the much smaller microcomputers.

Microcomputers, such as the IBM PC, Apple Macintosh and BBC microcomputer, are designed to be used by one person at a time. Microcomputers are self-contained units and are small enough to fit on the top of a desk.

The distinctions between these three kinds of computers in terms of design (or *architecture*) and size is becoming less clear, partly because the small computers of today are more powerful than the large computers of yesterday.

A new generation of computers, sometimes called *workstations*, which are produced by companies such as Digital, Sun, and Xerox, have recently been making their way into universities (see Figure 4).

With their powerful processors and large graphics monitors, these machines are most often used for engineering design or for simulations, but they are now reaching other academic areas.

Monitors, prompts and cursors

To the computer user, the screen of the monitor serves as a window on the workings of the computer. Letters typed at the keyboard enter the computer and immediately appear on the screen. Occasionally, information flows along a different path and 'messages' from the computer are displayed on the screen.

The image on the screen is an illusion; it is not an accurate representation of what the computer is actually doing. However, a good illusion makes working with the computer easier. A realistic representation of the computer's operation would not be very useful—it would look something like a very fast, automatic abacus.

The Apple Macintosh microcomputer illustrates the metaphorical nature of the screen image. In Figure 5 you can see that in the

Figure 4. Two Xerox workstations

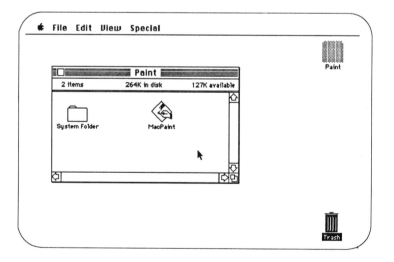

Figure 5. A Macintosh screen

bottom right-hand corner of the screen there is a representation of a trash can. On the Macintosh you can delete files by moving them to the trash can. However, there is no object equivalent to the trash can inside the computer.

A crucial item on the screen is the *cursor*, which simply indicates where text typed at the keyboard will appear on the screen. The cursor is usually a flashing block or line (■ or □ or ___), but on some screens it may appear as ˆ or as an I-shaped indicator. (In this book the symbol □ is used to represent the cursor.)

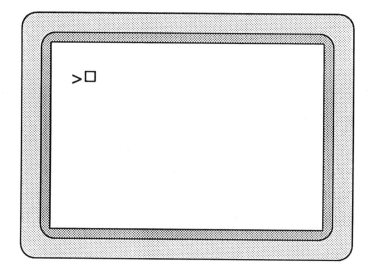

Figure 6. A screen with a prompt and a cursor

The cursor is often located immediately after a *prompt*, as shown in Figure 6. The prompt indicates that the computer is ready to receive a command.

Different computers have different prompts. Here are some examples (Remember that □ represents the cursor):

```
@ □
> □
% □
? □
computer> □
```

The form of the prompt sometimes changes when you use (or *run*) a different program. For instance, the prompt may change from @

to MM> when you run a mail program. How to give commands to a prompt will be discussed in Chapters 2 and 3.

You may have noticed that the Macintosh screen shown in Figure 5 looks very different from the screen shown in Figure 6. The Macintosh does not have a prompt and there is no cursor. Computers like the Macintosh do, however, have an arrow-shaped *pointer*. The two screens shown in Figures 5 and 6 illustrate quite different computer designs. For the purposes of this book a computer of the kind shown in Figure 6 will be referred to as a *prompt and cursor* computer. The main characteristic of the prompt and cursor computer (apart from the screen) is the fact that commands are generally given to the computer by typing at the keyboard.

In contrast, the Macintosh type of computer illustrated in Figure 5 will be referred to as a *menu and pointer* computer. Instructions are given to a menu and pointer computer not by typing commands, but by using the pointer to 'select' a command from a *menu*, or list of choices. How to select commands using the pointer is discussed in Chapter 3.

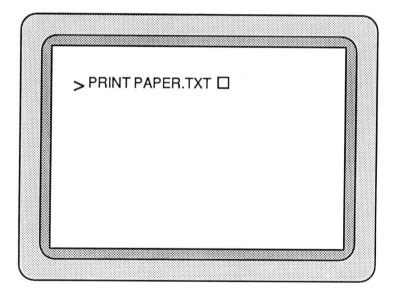

Figure 7. The print command

Figures 7 and 8 show two screens which illustrate how commands to print a document might be given in the two types of computer. Can you tell which kind each one is?

In addition to the pointer, the menu and pointer computers do

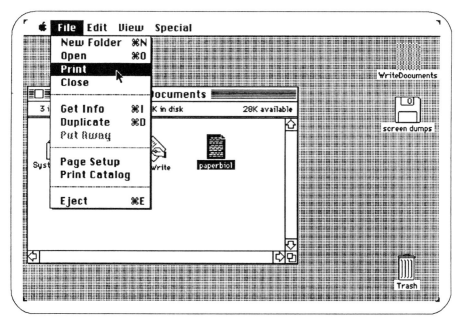

Figure 8. The print command

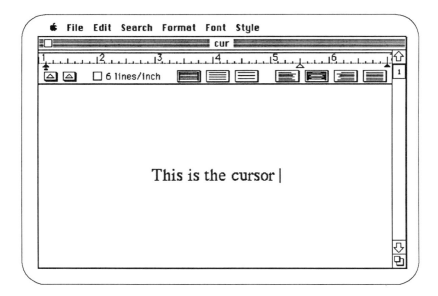

Figure 9. A cursor in a MacWrite file

have cursors when they are used with word processing programs. The cursor, which is shaped differently from the pointer, indicates where text that is typed in at the keyboard will appear on the screen. An example is shown in Figure 9.

If this is confusing, don't worry. How to use these computers will be explained later. If you want to take a break, why don't you go and look at some computers that people are using? Try to see what kind they are. (Hint: The menu and pointer computers have a small oblong box next to the keyboard and connected to the computer by a small cable. This device is called a *mouse*. See Figure 3)

Typewriters and keyboards

Because the computer keyboard evolved from the typewriter keyboard, it has a similar layout. What has been lost in the transition from typewriter to computer is the *carriage return* lever; what has been gained is a few more *keys*, which will be described below.

If you are unfamiliar with typewriters, you will face two problems: First, the computer keyboard won't seem as familiar to you as it will to students accustomed to using typewriters; secondly, you will 'type' very slowly. You can overcome the first problem by simply reading the following pages and practicing at an actual computer keyboard. To solve the second problem, you should learn to 'touch type,' that is, type without looking at the keyboard. You should at the very least learn to type using all your fingers rather than just your two index fingers. (There are special computer programs that help you learn to type.)

Keyboards on different computers vary somewhat, both in the keys that they contain and in the exact position of these keys. The following description of a keyboard should be taken only as a general guide. The keyboard you are using may differ in some details.

This section contains information about a wide range of keys just so that you have a reference guide if you need it. The most important part of the following section is the discussion of *command keys*, in particular, the *control key*.

Letters and numbers

Let us start with what you are most likely to be familiar with: the keys corresponding to the letters and numbers. These are called the *alphanumeric* keys.

```
1234567890
abcdefghijklmnopqrstuvwxyz
ABCDEFGHIJKLMNOPQRSTUVWXYZ
```

On a keyboard the letters are not arranged alphabetically but in the *qwerty* layout shown in Figure 10.

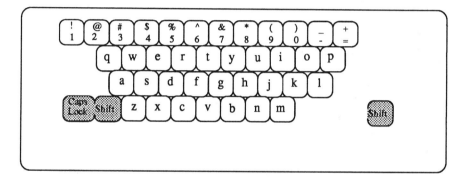

Figure 10. The alphanumeric keys

Pressing one of these keys causes the letter or number indicated on the key to enter the computer and at the same time appear on the computer screen. Letters and numbers are examples of two of the types of *characters* that the computer recognizes.

It will help if you can find a keyboard to work with. To enter a character, simply press and release the appropriate key. You don't have to press hard and you don't have to hold down the key—just tap it. If you hold down the 'a' key, for example, you may inadvertently enter a string of characters like **aaaaaaaaaa**.

Here is your first warning:

> **!** Don't use the letter l for the number **1**, or the letter **O** for the number **0**, since to the computer these represent two distinct types of characters. You should get into the habit of distinguishing them now, to avoid difficulties later.

Holding down either of the two shift keys while tapping a letter key will cause the corresponding capital (or *upper case*) letter to be entered. The shift keys are often found to the left of 'z' and to the right of '/' or ' '.' Holding down the shift key while you tap a number key will enter *symbolic characters* like the following:

@	'at' sign	$	dollar sign
£	pound sign	%	percent sign
^	circumflex or caret	&	ampersand
*	asterisk	()	parentheses
#	sharp sign (hash mark, pound sign)		

You can use the above list of commonly available symbolic characters for reference. Check what symbols are written on the number keys of the computer you are using. If you don't recognize some of the symbols, then it probably means that you will use them rarely, if ever.

If you want to type a series of upper case letters, such as COMPUTER ORIENTATION, you can press the *caps lock* key. Once the caps lock key is depressed, you can enter capital letters without depressing the shift key. To return to the normal way of typing, press the caps lock key again. (Try it out.)

> **!** When the caps lock key is depressed, only the letters will be in upper case. Pressing the number keys will still give you the numbers, not the symbols you get when you press the number keys with the shift key depressed.

Other symbols

In addition to the symbols indicated above, certain punctuation marks are also associated with the number keys, for example, the exclamation point (!). Other punctuation keys are found to the right of the alphanumeric keys, as shown in Figure 11.

The names of the other punctuation marks are as follows:

,	comma	.	period (or full stop)
;	semi-colon	:	colon
?	question mark	[]	square brackets
{}	(curly) braces	<>	angle brackets
-	hyphen	/	slash
!	exclamation point	\	backslash

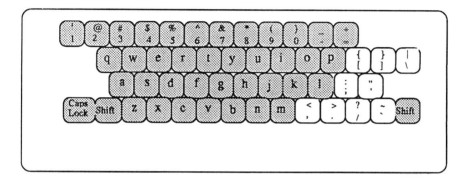

Figure 11. Some punctuation symbols

The slash is used to present two words as alternatives:

`The student should check his/her work.`

Two hyphens can be used to form a dash (--).

`A professor--I cannot tell you who--has been nominated for a Nobel Prize.`

Other symbols include the following:

+	plus sign	=	equals sign
-	minus sign	_	underline character
	(same as a hyphen)		

On a computer, pressing the underline key a few times will give you a line like this: _____. How to produce underlining depends on the word processing program you are using.

Tab key

Pressing the tab key once allows you to enter several spaces at a time. How many spaces are entered when the tab key is pressed depends on your word processing program. The tab character is the first of a family of invisible characters that we will encounter. These invisible characters do not show up on the screen, except as blank spaces. To the computer, however, invisible characters are just as real as visible characters like letters or symbols.

Backspace and DEL(ete) key

All computers have keys which move the cursor one character back (usually to the left). Such keys are often labelled Backspace, Delete (DEL) or ←.

A key for backwards movement can have two different effects depending on the word processing program you are using. Pressing such a key always moves the cursor one character back. In some programs, however, the previous character is simultaneously removed or *deleted*, while in others it remains.

This is a mistaker☐
↙   ↘
This is a mistake☐   This is a mistake☐

The result of using the backspace key depends on the program.

Some computers have separate keys for delete and backspace functions. If your computer has only one backwards movement key, then it is likely to act like DEL and always delete a character.

Space bar

The space bar is the long horizontal bar at the bottom of the keyboard. Pressing the space bar enters one blank space (character).

---

* It is conventional when writing English on typewriters or computers to enter one space between words and two spaces between sentences.

One common mistake new computer users often make is pressing the space bar to move the cursor. You should use the space bar only to enter spaces. To the computer, a space is a character just like 'a' or '1.' The space character is another of the invisible characters.

The tab, backspace and space bar keys are shown in Figure 12.

Return (or Enter) key

The *return* or carriage return key (often marked 'enter' on the keyboard, as in Figure 13) has two functions. One function resembles the action of a carriage return on a typewriter, which moves the paper so that a new line of text can be typed. Thus you can move the

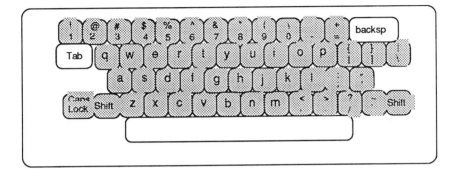

Figure 12. The tab, backspace and space bar

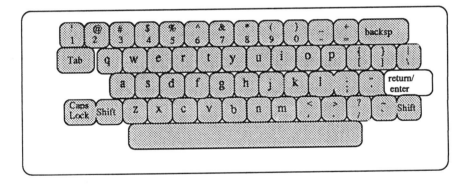

Figure 13. The return/enter key

cursor to a fresh line by pressing the return key. Remember, though, that what you are doing when you hit the return key is starting a new line. This means that when you press return, all the text following the cursor is shifted down the screen by one line. The return is another of the invisible characters. You may see its effects, but you do not see an actual return character on the screen.

The second function of the return key is to enter a command into the computer. (This is why the key is often labelled 'enter.')

After you have typed a command such as **print myfile**, you press
the return key in order to complete the command and send it to the
computer so that the command can be executed.

Command keys

The main distinction between a computer keyboard and a typewriter
keyboard is that the computer keyboard is used to give commands as
well as enter text. Commands are entered using certain special keys.
It would be possible to have a special key for each command; one for
printing, one for copying files, etc. To do this, however, would require
a large number of keys and there would be little flexibility for adding
new commands. One common solution is to have special command
keys that are used in conjunction with the standard alphanumeric
keys.

The control key

The most commonly used and most important command key is the
control key (CTRL), illustrated in Figure 14.

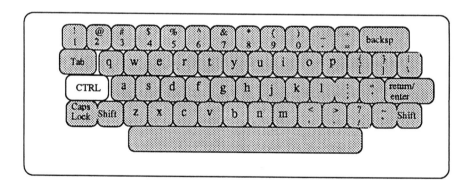

Figure 14. The control key

The control key is used in combination with other keys to give
commands. Control commands are abbreviated as follows: *ctrl a*,
ctrl b, etc. To execute a command like *ctrl a* you do the following:
While holding down the control key with one finger, you tap the 'a'
key with another. Thus CTRL, like the shift key, is held down while
another character is typed.

Each application program will assign a particular meaning to the control characters, a fact that will become clearer as you acquire more experience with computers. For example, three popular word processing programs, WordStar, MacWrite and EMACS (discussed in Appendix A), all happen to use the command *ctrl f*, but for different purposes. In WordStar, *ctrl f* will move the cursor one word to the right; in MacWrite, *ctrl f* is used to find a specified character or word; and in EMACS, *ctrl f* moves the cursor one character to the right.

It is not necessary for you to remember these commands. The main point is that the same control command may do different things in different programs.

Escape key

The *Escape key*, labelled ESC, is usually located on the top left of the keyboard, as in Figure 15. It is used as a command key either by itself or in combination with other keys. Escape differs from control in the way that commands are entered. The control key, as we saw, is held down while the second key is pressed. The escape key, in contrast, is pressed, then released *before* the second key is pressed. For example, to give the command *esc f*, press and release (i.e., tap) the ESC key, then press the 'f' key immediately afterwards.

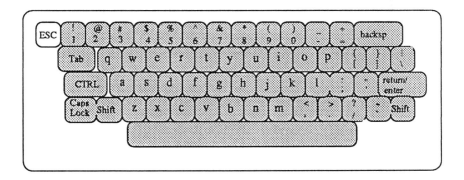

Figure 15. The escape key

Other command keys, similar to escape, are the *ALT* and the *Meta* key. Since these are used less often, they will not be discussed here. However, if your word processing program uses a meta key (like EMACS) and your keyboard does not have a meta key, you can probably use the escape key instead.

Function keys

Some computers and terminals have *function* keys on the left (see Figure 16) or along the top of the keyboard. These keys, which may be labelled 'F1, F2, ...' or 'PF1, PF2,...' are also used to give commands to the computer.

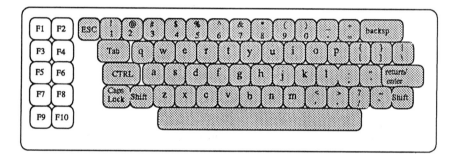

Figure 16. Function keys

Again, the command associated with a particular function key depends on the program you are using. Function keys are often just a shortcut, a convenient way to give a command which could be given in another way. For example, in WordStar, the function key 'F10' is equivalent to *ctrl q ctrl c*, a command sequence that moves the cursor to the end of the file.

Cursor keys

Some keyboards have keys with arrows on them: ←, →, ↑ and ↓. Pressing one of these keys will move the cursor in the direction indicated by the arrow. Holding down one of these keys instead of just tapping it may cause the cursor to move rapidly in the indicated direction.

Numeric keypad

All keyboards have number keys listed along the top row of the keyboard. Since this arrangement is not very efficient for fast entry of numbers, some computers also have a second set of numbers arranged in three rows to the right of the keyboard. Such an arrangement of number keys is called a *numeric keypad.*

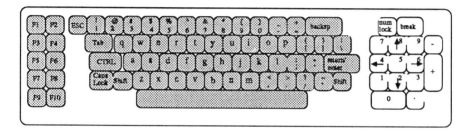

Figure 17. Numeric keypad and cursor keys

In computers like the IBM PC, the numeric keypad and the cursor keys are combined as shown in Figure 17. A *numlock* key is used to switch from one use to the other. The numlock key is similar to the caps lock key which switches letters from lower case to upper case. Keys like numlock and caps lock, which you press once to turn a function on and then press again to turn the function off, are called *toggles.*

Printers

Once you have typed your work into the computer, you can get a printed copy by giving a *print* command to the computer. The computer then sends a copy of your work to a printer and the printer provides you with a paper copy (or *hard copy* or *printout*) of your work.

Fortunately, you don't need to know much about printers. It will be helpful, though, for you to know about some basic characteristics of the main types of printer. There are several kinds of printers including:

1. line printers

2. dot-matrix printers

3. letter quality printers (daisy wheel printers)

4. laser printers

Line printers

Line printers are 'industrial strength' printers; they are fast printers that are often linked to mainframe computers. These printers are not designed for producing good-looking text. Their main purpose is to generate a large volume of printed output, sometimes for hundreds of different users. Typically, line printers do not offer different variations in type style or type size which are available on other printers. The paper that line printers use is wide and may be striped, but their output is good enough if you have no other alternative. You can improve the appearance of a paper produced on a line printer by photocopying it onto standard paper.

Dot-matrix printers

Dot-matrix printers are often hooked up to microcomputers. They produce letters and other symbols by printing a series of small dots to make the shape of a character. The smaller and the more numerous the dots, the better the printed output looks. Better quality dot-matrix printers, such as the Apple Imagewriter (see Figure 18), are called 'near letter quality.'

Letter quality printers

Some printers are based on the same sort of idea as a typewriter. (In fact, some typewriters can be linked to computers to act as letter quality printers.) In these printers, the characters are printed on the paper by a striking action of an element containing an image of each character onto a ribbon. The output looks good, like the output of a typewriter. However, such printers are limited when it comes to printing graphics (diagrams and pictures).

Laser printers

Laser printers, such as the Apple LaserWriter (Figure 19), produce very good quality output and they have the advantage of being able to produce a variety of characters and graphic images, making documents look highly professional.

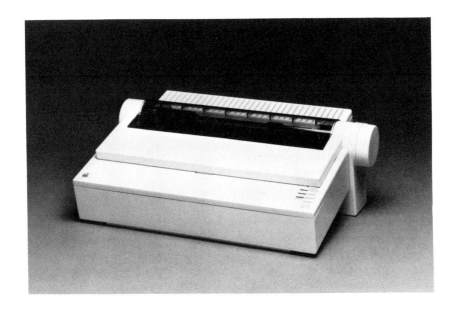

Figure 18. A dot-matrix printer—The Apple ImageWriter

Figure 19. A laser printer—The Apple LaserWriter

Questions

1. (a) Do you think computers are smart?

   (b) Do you think computers are dumb?

   (c) Do you think computers are smarter than you are?

   Explain why in each case.

2. To find out the time on some computers, you must type a command something like **daytime** or **date**. If you were designing your own program, would you choose a different command? If so, what would you choose?

   Would you prefer the command to be: **Please tell me the time?**

3. Write down or discuss some fears that people have concerning computers.

4. Do you know any everyday English words that came originally from the computer domain?

5. Is the computer you are working on a menu and pointer computer or a prompt and cursor computer?

6. Does the computer you are using have a prompt? What does it look like? What does the cursor look like?

7. Does your computer have the following?

   (a) function keys

   (b) a numeric keypad

   (c) cursor keys

8. Experiment with the keyboard you are using. Can you find the following keys? Most, but not all, computers have these keys.

   (a) !

   (b) -

   (c) _

   (d) '

   (e) backspace (←)

   (f) shift

   (g) caps lock

(h) return (or enter)

(i) DEL

(j) ESC

(k) CTRL

9. What character appears on the screen if you press the following keys?

   (a) shift and a

   (b) shift and 1

   (c) caps lock and a

   (d) caps lock and 1

10. What is the difference between the way you give a control command and the way you give an escape command?

11. In general, letter quality printers are better than dot-matrix printers because their output looks better. In what way might a dot-matrix printer be better than a letter quality printer?

2

Working with large computers

In this chapter we will concentrate on large computers. If you are using a microcomputer only, then you might want to skip to the next chapter.

Remember that to work with a large, time-sharing computer (a mainframe or minicomputer), you use a terminal. A terminal consists of a monitor and a keyboard. The monitor displays information from the computer and the keyboard is used to send instructions or text to the computer.

All the computer programs that you need and all your own work will be stored on the computer. You don't have to worry about finding software or storing your work on floppy disks.

To start work on a time-sharing computer you need to know how to do the following:

1. get an account (Section 2.1)

2. log on (Section 2.2)

3. use the operating system (Chapter 5)

4. use applications programs (Chapters 4 and 6–9)

5. log off (Section 2.5)

If you already have an account and you want to get a quick introduction to using the computer, you should look at the sections on logging on (p. 30), giving commands (p. 31) and logging off (p. 35). Why don't you try these commands a couple of times before reading the other sections in this chapter?

2.1   Opening an account

In appearance, computers are quite different from libraries: they look modern and don't have any ivy growing on them. Nevertheless, there are resemblances between the use of libraries and the use of computers, and your familiarity with libraries will help you understand how large computers are organized and administered.

You walk up to the entrance of the library to begin some serious academic work, only to find that you need a library card to use the library services or even to get in the door. Similarly, with a computer, you have to be certified as a 'bona fide' user and informed about the rules and regulations for users before you are admitted. You must get, and perhaps pay for, an account. Setting up an account often involves either seeing a computing services administrator or simply finding an empty terminal and using a special program on the computer to open an account. In either case, to register as a user, you will have to provide basic information about yourself, just as if you were asking for library privileges or opening a bank account.

One novel feature of opening a computer account is that you will choose (or be assigned) a new name called an *account name*, which identifies you to the computer.

You will also need a *password*, which is kept secret from other users. Choose one that is easy for you to remember, but difficult for others to guess, such as the formula for acetic acid or the word for 'hello' in Polish. As a foreign student, you have a head start in coming up with good passwords. The password prevents others from using your account and interfering with your work files. Security is important since the computer may hold days and nights of your work, which you would not want others to tamper with or copy.

If you don't use your account for some time, you may forget your password. If this happens, you must contact the computer system administrator again. You will probably need to show some identification to prove that the account belongs to you.

2.2   Logging on

Once you have a library card, you can work in the library and take advantage of its many resources. Similarly, once you have a computer account, you can begin to work on the computer.

In a typical session at the computer you will probably go through the following steps:

- find a terminal

- log on

- read your electronic mail

- reply to your mail

- use an editor (word processing program) to work on a term paper or class assignment

- print out your work

- log off

For now we will concentrate on the basics of logging on, using a few simple commands, and logging off. Sending mail, editing, and printing will be discussed in later chapters.

First of all you must find some terminals connected to the computer on which you have an account. When the terminal is on and you have a computer prompt (e.g., > or *login:*) you must *log on* (or *log in*). It is necessary to log on every time you start a session at the computer.

To log on, you simply type your account name, press the return key and type in your password (which will not show on the screen). Don't worry if you make a mistake; you can either use the delete key to erase what you typed or you can press return a couple of times and start again.

Some computers are fairly liberal and will accept your account name in either upper or lower case letters (or with extra spaces). Other computers, however, are less tolerant. Computers running the UNIX operating system, for example, make a distinction between upper and lower case letters.

Logging on achieves several functions: it identifies you to the computer and makes your computer *files* (or working documents) readily available. How to create your own files will be explained in the following chapters.

The fact that many users work on a time-sharing system means that you will have to take note of administrative bulletins. For example, when you log on, you may see some messages from the computer system operator. These system messages may announce future events such as downtimes or they may inform the users of *hardware* problems, such as printers that are not working.

2.3 Some basic commands

Eventually, you will be faced with a prompt and a cursor. (Do you remember prompts and cursors? If not, check back to page 11.)

What can you do now? Well, you have a range of programs at your disposal: the equivalent of a clock, a calculator, a mail service, perhaps a dictionary and possibly some computer games. You might even be able to find a list of local restaurants or ice-cream shops. In addition, there are traditional computer programs: word processors, spelling checkers, data bases, statistical packages, and programming languages.

Where do you start? Well, one thing you need to know how to do is end your session by *logging off* (or *logging out*). Try logging off and logging back on again. To find out how to log off, see Section 2.5.

> * Finding out how to log off as soon as you have logged on illustrates a useful general strategy: checking how to exit whatever program you have just entered.

When you have tried logging on and logging off a couple of times, you can return to the question of what you can do once you have logged on. First, it is possible to get information about the state of the computer system. For example, you should be able to find out who is using the computer system at the moment and what *jobs* or *programs* they are running. How to find out who else is using the computer varies depending on the computer operating system that you are using. Common operating systems include UNIX and TOPS-20. Operating systems will be described in more detail in Chapter 5 and Appendix B. For now, you can think of an operating system as a program that reads and interprets your commands. In UNIX, the command to find out who is using the system is **who** or **finger**. You type **finger** and press the return key.

The screen in Figure 1 shows the computer's response to a finger command. As you can see, the information about what users are logged on is organized in columns. On the left is the account name followed by a real (personal) name. Moving to the right we see the job number, which you can safely ignore most of the time. (Note that some users, such as DANIEL, have more than one job running at the same time.) To the right of the job number is the name of the program ('subsystem') being used. Most of the users here are running MM, a mail program. The final column shows the location of the user's terminal.

> * Remember to press the return key after entering a command.

User	Personal Name	Job	Subsys	Location
ALEX	Alex Bronstein	48	MM	LOTS Two
BARLOW	Mike Barlow	56	FINGER	Dialup:
BARWISE	Jon Barwise	16	MM	Reid Hall 12
CHEN	Richard Chen	13	EXEC	Trailer H6
DANIEL	Daniel Flickinger	42	MM	Trailer H1
		51	EMACS	Trailer H2
DIKRAN	Dikran Karagueuzian	6	TELNET	Polya Hall 40
		35	MM	Polya Hall 42

Figure 1. Who is 'on the system'—the finger command

Another much-used system command shows you a list of the files that you have created. The command to list all your stored files is **ls** in UNIX and **catalog** or **dir** (**directory**) in certain other operating systems. In Figure 2, you can see at the top of the screen that the command **dir** has been issued. The computer responds by giving a list of the files in the *directory* of the user 'chung.' At the bottom of the screen you can see the prompt (@) and the cursor. The computer is ready for the next command.

Some of the commands you give to the computer will be control commands. Again, the precise form of these commands varies depending on the operating system or the program that you are using. For example, the most common command used to stop a process (or program) running is *ctrl c* (pronounced 'control c'), which you may need to press a couple of times. The *break key* performs a similar function on some computers. However, it is much better style (and safer) to exit from your program elegantly by using the proper exiting commands whenever you can.

2.4   Getting around

Learning to use a computer is similar to finding your way around a new town. As you know, when you first arrive in a new area, everything is unfamiliar. Only one or two major landmarks stand out in a maze of streets and buildings. As you wander around and explore the new town or neighborhood, you gradually get to know the geography of the area. Then, once you have formed a 'mental map' of the local environment, you are able to get around quite easily.

```
@dir
USER:<chung>


ABSTR.TEX
APPLICATION..1
BIBLIOG..1
CONFERENCE..1
EMACS.INIT.4
FINGER.PLAN.1
LOGIN.CMD.2
MACUSER..1
MAIL.TXT.1
MUG..18
PAPER-AGREEMENT.TEX.1
PAPER-ARABIC.TEX.1

Total of 98 pages in 12 files

@
```

Figure 2. Listing the files in your directory

Beginners using a computer commonly 'get lost' trying to follow unfamiliar instructions. Either you give the wrong command, or else the command is right in some sense, but inappropriate for the particular mode (or state) that the computer happens to be in. The result, in either case, is that you feel disoriented. The computer does not respond in the way you expect and the screen does not look quite right. Worst of all, you don't know how to move back to where you were before you issued the command. If you are lucky, there will be someone around whom you can ask to help you get back on the right track. Otherwise, in situations like these you often feel compelled to start over from the beginning (since that is the easiest point to get to) and start over again along the same path.

Experienced computer users have constructed a 'mental map' of the organization of the computer they are operating. This knowledge allows them to move around in the computer environment with comparative ease. They get lost much less often than novices and they know which commands are appropriate for each part of the software environment.

When you log on you are often presented with a blank screen containing only a prompt and a cursor. Logging on puts you at the *exec* or *top level*. From the top level you can 'call up' or start particular programs. For example you might call up the mail program, send a message, and then quit the program to return to the top level. You can then enter another program, for example, a text editor. When you run a program such as an editor, then you go down one level. At this lower level, you have a different set of commands available (editing commands instead of general operating system commands). When you are finished with the editor, again you quit or exit and return to the top level. This pattern of computer use is shown schematically in Figure 3. (Note that there are other ways of thinking about the organization of a computer; for example, you can think of it in terms of concentric circles or spheres.)

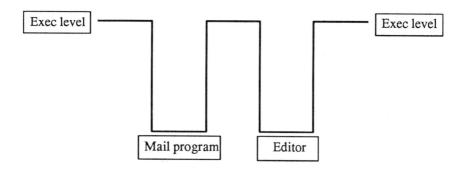

Figure 3. Entering programs from the 'top level'

2.5   Logging off

Logging off simply means ending your session at the computer. To do this you type **logoff** or **logout** and then press the return key to send the command to the computer. Alternative commands used in some systems for logging off the computer are *kill* and *bye*.

2.6   Getting help

There are several ways in which you can learn about how to use a particular computer. These include:

1. classes

2. consultants and other users

3. online help

4. manuals

Classes

There are probably classes or videotapes available on how to use your computer system. These classes are very short, sometimes just an hour long. You can find out the times of these classes, which are often given at the beginning of term, from the computer system administrators.

Consultants and other users

If you have any problems using the computer you should be able to get help from a consultant. A consultant is someone who knows the computer system well and is available to help users with any problems they might have. You may have to learn how to send a message on the computer to the consultants. Alternatively, you may be able to go to a special area or room to get consulting help.

It is also quite usual for new users to ask another computer user about basic commands; most users remember when they themselves were novices and are happy to help you if they can.

Online help

Online help refers to help from the computer itself. The computer may have several means of helping you. Most computers have an introductory tutorial program that teaches you the basics of using the computer. In addition, there are tutorials on specific programs, such as editors or programming languages, and there will probably be a *help system* that describes all the commands and general documentation that you can use. If you want to know about sending messages, for instance, you might be able to get information by typing **help message** or **help mail**.

You may also be able to obtain information by simply typing a question mark. On some computer systems typing a question mark will give you a list of all the options or responses that you may give when faced with a particular prompt. Combining the use of help with the question mark, you may be able to type **help ?** to get a list of all the topics (probably a large number) that the computer has information on. The question mark is most useful when you do not know what commands to use or how to complete a command that you have started.

> ***** Learning to use a computer's online help system will save you time in the long run.

On UNIX systems, you can get help by looking through an online manual. For example, if you want to know all about the mail command, you type **man mail**. The first part of the computer's response is shown in Figure 4.

```
        MAIL(1) UNIX Programmer's Manual MAIL(1)

NAME

        mail - send and receive mail


SYNOPSIS

        mail [ -v ] [ -i ] [ -n ] [ -s subject ]
        mail [ -v ] [ -i ] [ -n ] -f [ name ]
        mail [ -v ] [ -i ] [ -n ] -u user



INTRODUCTION
Mail is an intelligent mail processing system,
which has a command syntax reminiscent of ed with
lines replaced by messages.

The -v flag puts mail into verbose mode; the
details of delivery are displayed on the users
terminal.  The -i flag causes tty interrupt
signals to be ignored.  This is particularly
useful when using mail on noisy phone lines.
```

Figure 4. Help in UNIX—the **man** command

Manuals

When all else fails you can always read the printed manual. Manuals are usually found in places where there is a cluster of terminals. Alternatively, you can buy your own manual from a computer services office or the campus bookstore. Manuals are a useful reference source, but they are often difficult to read since they are not generally written with novice users in mind.

Questions

1. What do you have to do before you can start working on a large computer?

2. What does logging on consist of?

3. What prompt or prompts does your computer use?

4. What are the commands used on your computer system for the following functions?

   (a) logging off
   (b) listing the users who are logged onto the system
   (c) listing the files in your directory

5. Look at the following screen and answer the questions.

   (a) What is Bill Pinter's account name?
   (b) What program is DIKRAN running?
   (c) Where is COWER's terminal?

User	Personal Name	Job	Subsys	Location
AMY	Amy Brown	48	MM	LOTS Two
BARLOW	Mike Barlow	56	FINGER	Dialup:
BRITON	John Wilson	16	MM	Reid Hall
BULL	Bill Pinter	33	MM	LOTS Two
COWER	Richard Cower	13	EXEC	Trailer H6
DANIEL	Daniel Flickinger	42	MM	Trailer H1
		51	EMACS	Trailer H2
DIKRAN	Dikran Karagueuzian	6	TELNET	Polya Hall

6. Find out what happens if you forget to log off the computer you are using.

7. What are the ways in which you can get help or information about your computer system?

3
Working with microcomputers

In the last chapter we talked about large, time-sharing computers and compared them with campus libraries. In this chapter we will turn to microcomputers, and discuss their similarities with small libraries.

Small libraries are much more welcoming than large institutional libraries. Best of all, perhaps, is having your own private library: you don't need a student ID card to get in and you can use it whenever you want. The convenience of a personal library makes up, in part, for its limitations in size. However, you have to do more work yourself: you have to buy the books, reshelve them and keep track of who you lend them to.

Microcomputers are the equivalent of small home libraries. They don't have the range of services of large computers; nevertheless, they are very useful. And just as you will use the main library to supplement your reading needs, so you can use your microcomputer to link up with a large computer to take advantage of its extended services, such as electronic mail and laser printing.

Microcomputers are small computers designed to be used by one person at a time. Consequently, microcomputers are often called *personal computers*. They are very small compared to mainframes; in fact, they can fit right on your desk. There are many different kinds of microcomputers produced by companies such as Apple, IBM, NEC, and Olivetti. Examples of microcomputers include the Apple II (pronounced 'Apple Two'), IBM PC (pronounced as initials, 'I.B.M. P.C.') and IBM PC *compatible* computers.

You have to know a little about the workings of microcomputers in order to look after them properly. The basic configuration of a microcomputer, illustrated in Figure 1, consists of:

- a monitor

Figure 1. A microcomputer—The Apple IIe

- a keyboard

- one or more disk drives

- a hard disk (optional)

- a system unit (containing the microprocessor)

- a printer

The keyboard, monitor and printer were discussed in Chapter 1. In order to use a microcomputer you need to know how to use a disk (illustrated in Figure 2). We will discuss *floppy disks* (or diskettes or simply 'disks') and *hard disks* in more detail at the end of this chapter. For now, all you need to know is that disks are used to store *applications programs*, such as a word processor, or *data*, such as your files.

The disk drive, which is a kind of electronic box that you put disks into, transfers information between the disk and the computer.

The system unit, which normally sits under the monitor, contains the microprocessor and other components involved in the actual computing processes.

3.1 Getting started

To work on a microcomputer, you need to know how to do the following:

1. insert disks into the disk drive

2. *boot* (or boot up) the microcomputer

3. use the operating system (Chapter 5)

4. use applications programs (Chapters 4 and 6–9)

5. remove the disks and turn the microcomputer off

In this chapter, we will go through the basics of each of these steps. You can look at the chapters given above for further information. Before starting, however, you need to know a few important facts about using disks.

Handling disks

The disks and disk drives are the least robust components of microcomputers. The older 8-inch and $5\frac{1}{4}$-inch floppy disks are the most fragile since the magnetic material is covered only by thin cardboard

Figure 2. A $5\frac{1}{4}$-inch disk

and it is completely exposed in the area where the disk drive head accesses the disk (shown in Figure 2). Great care should be taken when handling these disks to avoid touching the exposed magnetic material. You should always pick up and hold the disks by grasping the part with the label, keeping your fingers away from the exposed area. When you have finished using a disk, you should replace it in its jacket or sleeve.

The smaller $3\frac{1}{2}$-inch disks, which are used with microcomputers such as the Apple Macintosh, are protected by a hard plastic cover and are therefore much sturdier.

> **!** Diskettes do not work well if they have been bent, punctured, heated, or magnetized.

Inserting disks

A floppy disk is inserted into a disk drive with its label facing up and towards you. On larger disk drives, such as those found on the IBM PC, you must gently close a little door or lever on the front of the disk drive once the disk is fully inserted.

> **!** Remember, no disk is going to last forever. You should make backup copies of your important files— the ones you don't want to lose.

Booting a microcomputer

When you turn on a microcomputer, it runs some memory tests and then reads a disk containing a *system file*. The computer then transfers information from the disks into its temporary internal memory (called RAM). This is called *booting* the computer. If the system files are not present because there is no *bootable disk*, the computer will give you an error message on the screen.

Using a program

What you can do with the microcomputer once it is booted includes the following:

- word processing (also called editing) (Chapters 4, 6, and 9)
- data base programs (Chapter 8)
- spreadsheets (Chapter 8)

- communications (Chapter 7)

- games

Booting a microcomputer does not give you immediate access to all the programs that you might want to use. Suppose you are using a word processing program, for example, and decide you would like to take a break and play a game. To do this, you must take out the disk containing the word processor you were working on and then insert the disk containing the game you want to play. Thus, using a microcomputer typically requires quite a bit of disk-switching. Hard disks, which hold a considerable amount of data and programs, minimize the need for switching disks (called 'disk-swapping'), but do not eliminate it altogether.

What you see after booting the computer depends on the kind of microcomputer you are using. Recall the two types of computer that we introduced on page 12. If you are working with a *prompt and cursor* computer, then you will see a blank screen with a prompt and a flashing cursor. Alternatively, if the machine is a *menu and pointer* computer, you are faced with a 'desk top.' On the desk top you will see a disk *icon*, that is, a pictorial representation of a disk, and perhaps some file icons, as shown in Figure 3.

Giving commands

How to give commands to a microcomputer depends on both the type of computer you are using and the particular program you are working with. We will give a simple overview here. (You can also look at Section 4.2 on using an editor, Section 5.2 on working with files, and Appendices A and B.)

Giving commands on a 'prompt and cursor' computer

To give commands on a prompt and cursor computer, you simply type the command at the prompt and press return.

> ***** Remember to press the return key after entering a command.

For example, if you want to run the WordStar word processing program, you insert the WordStar disk in a disk drive and type the command **ws** (and press the return key) to load the WordStar program.

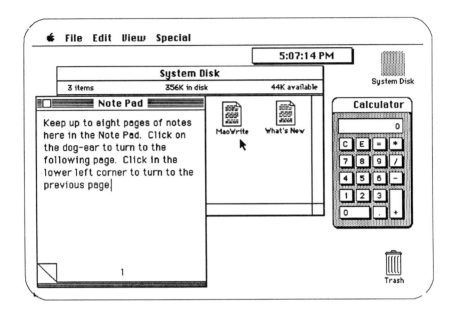

Figure 3. A 'desk top' representation

Most commands can only be acted upon by the computer when the appropriate disk is in the disk drive. For example, if you gave the command **ws** to start working with WordStar and there was no disk containing the WordStar program in the disk drive, then the computer will respond with an error message which will show on the screen. If this happens, you will have to insert the WordStar disk in the disk drive and try again. (Note: if you have a WordStar program on a hard disk, then you won't have these problems.)

Giving commands on a 'menu and pointer' computer

There are two basic steps to giving a command on a menu and pointer computer. These are:

1. Moving the pointer

2. Selecting a command from a menu

Remember that menu and pointer computers have an additional device connected to the computer called a mouse. Try moving the mouse side to side and forward and back on top of the desk or table. You will see that the pointer on the screen moves as you move the mouse. At first, you may find that it is hard to control the mouse so that the pointer is positioned correctly, but you will soon be able to manipulate the mouse with ease.

The mouse

The mouse sits next to the computer, attached to it by a cable. Moving the mouse on the desk or table causes an analogous movement of a pointer on the computer screen. The mouse contains one or more buttons. By pressing and releasing one of these buttons you can give commands to the computer.

Moving the pointer to a specific place on the screen and pressing the mouse button will cause a menu to appear. (Don't release the mouse button yet.) The menu contains a list of commands. As you move the pointer up and down the menu, each command will be highlighted in turn. To issue a command, you move the pointer to the correct place in the menu so that the command you wish to give is highlighted (for example, outlined in black). Then you release the mouse button. If you decide you don't want to issue any of the commands, you simply move the pointer away from the menu and release the mouse button.

To give commands on a Macintosh computer, you move the pointer to the menu bar at the top of the screen, shown in Figure 4. When the pointer is positioned over a word (such as *File*) in the menu bar, you press and hold down the mouse button, which causes a menu to appear (see Figure 5). You can then select a command from the menu by moving the pointer to the appropriate command (such as *open*) and then releasing the mouse button.

For some commands like *open*, you must indicate what program or file you want to open (i.e., start working with). To do this, you move the pointer to a file icon (such as MacWrite in Figure 3) and click (i.e., press and quickly release) the mouse button. The file

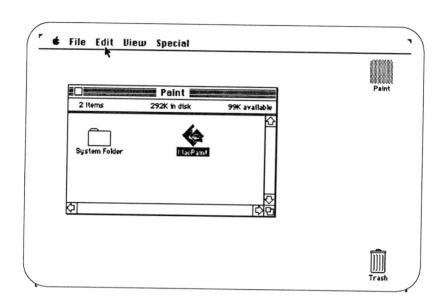

Figure 4. A pointer positioned on the menu bar

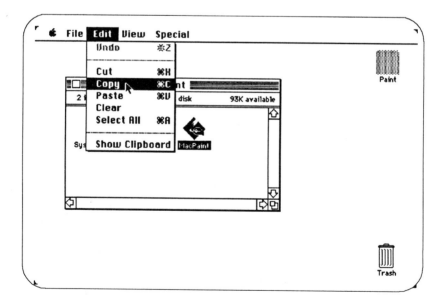

Figure 5. Selecting a command

icon becomes highlighted and you can then give the *open* command described above.

Many commands on menu and pointer computers have the two-step property just described. The two steps involved are the following:

1. select an icon

2. choose a command

> ***** Remember to save your work often: every fifteen minutes or so and every time you take a break.

3.2   Switching off a microcomputer

The steps in switching off a microcomputer are as follows:

1. Save your file

2. Remove disks

3. Switch off

Saving files

Unfortunately, it is very easy to switch off a computer without saving your work. When you type the final sentence in a paper, you get a feeling of relief. You have finished! This is a natural reaction; you can see your work on the screen in its final form. However, it is only on the screen, and not on the disk until you transfer it to the disk by saving it. So you have to be careful and save your work before you relax.

Removing disks

Having saved your work, you can then remove the disks from the disk drives. The fact that there may be words still on the screen does not matter. You just have to make sure the saving operation is complete.

On microcomputers such as IBM PCs, you remove your disk by simply lifting up the levers or flaps on the disk drive, grasping the edge of the disk and gently pulling it out. Remember *not* to touch the exposed area. Put the disk away in its sleeve.

On computers like the Macintosh, you do not manually remove the diskette. Instead you eject the disk by choosing *eject* from the file menu. If the 'eject' option is not highlighted and the eject operation does not work, it means that you have to first leave (quit) the program that you are running. (If you have any problems, you can always turn the Macintosh off, then turn it on again while holding down the mouse button. This will eject the disk.)

Switching the computer off

The final step is to turn off the power switch on the system unit (and with some computers, an additional switch on the monitor). It is not a good idea to leave a microcomputer on for a long time, since they tend to get hot and the screen may wear out. (However, there may be cases in which the microcomputer should be left on— look for instructions near the computer.) If you are going to switch the computer on again after switching it off, you should wait a few seconds before doing so.

A Guide to Bytes

- A byte is the amount of information needed to store one character of text or data. One byte is eight 'bits.'

- A kilobyte (1K) is equal to 1024 bytes

- A megabyte (1 MB) is approximately a thousand kilobytes

A twenty-page paper (double-spaced) takes up about 15K.

3.3　Storing information on disks

Most software is stored on magnetic material of some kind. This is true of both *applications programs* (such as word processors) and *data* (such as your files). The most common form of magnetic storage material for microcomputers is *disks* which include both *hard disks* and *floppy disks*. Floppy disks are not necessarily floppy (flexible) anymore, and so perhaps the term diskette is more appropriate; however, we will use the term disk, which is used to refer to both floppy disks and hard disks.

A Guide to Disks

$5\frac{1}{4}$-inch Disks

$5\frac{1}{4}$-inch floppy disks contain between 300 and 600 kilobytes (K), depending on whether they are single-sided or double-sided. Thus a double-sided disk should have room for a couple of hundred pages of double-spaced text or for one commercial applications program such as WordStar.

$3\frac{1}{2}$-inch Disks

These disks are smaller, but they contain more information, generally 400 to 800 K. The $3\frac{1}{2}$-inch disks have a solid plastic covering and are much better protected than the $5\frac{1}{4}$-inch disks. They also have a metal covering over the part of the disk where the disk drive reads the disk.

Hard Disks

A hard disk is a storage device capable of holding a large amount of information, typically 20 megabytes (MB) or more. The hard disk, which is often located inside the computer, has a dramatic effect on the operation of the computer. It speeds up the computer and gives you instant access to a considerable number of files and programs, greatly reducing the need to switch disks in and out of the computer.

Laser Disks

Laser disks are not yet generally in use for computers, but they are used in Compact Disk players. The advantage of laser disks is the fact that they can store a vast amount of information. For example, the entire contents of the Encyclopedia Britannica could easily fit onto a single laser disk.

The head in the disk drive, which works in a way similar to the head on a tape deck, *reads* from or *writes* to the disk. The floppy disks spin rapidly and the head passes over the disk, very close to the surface. Do not attempt to remove the disk during this operation, as doing so could damage both the disk drive and the disk. (It is not difficult to know when the disk drive is in operation; there will be a whirring or humming noise and some disk drives even have a small red light to warn you when the disk is being read.)

> ***** It is better not to completely fill up your disks with data. Leaving some free space reduces the chance of malfunctions. Some operations, like printing, may need extra space in order to work properly. Try to leave yourself at least 20K free on each disk (or the same number of K as the file you are working with).

If the notch in the side of the $5\frac{1}{4}$-inch disks (shown in Figure 2) is covered by a special tab, then the disk is *write-protected*. (The $3\frac{1}{2}$-inch disks can also be protected in a similar way.) When a disk is 'write-protected,' data can be read from the disk, but the data cannot be deleted or changed.

3.4   Microcomputer peripherals

A device used to enter information or commands into a computer is called an *input device*. The keyboard is the main device for communicating with computers, but some computers utilize other input devices as well. For example, a second kind of input device is a *mouse*.

There are other input devices that are mentioned here for completeness: *graphics pads*, *joysticks*, *digitizers*, and *optical scanners*. These input devices are briefly explained in the glossary.

In addition to the various types of input devices, there are also devices concerned with the computer's output. Two that have already been mentioned are monitors and printers. More specialized output devices include *plotters* and loudspeakers.

All the input and output devices described above are called *peripherals*. The computer itself along with the peripherals is referred to as *hardware* (a mass noun, with no plural). Hardware is contrasted with *software*, which refers to the programs that run on a computer. If there is some sort of problem on a computer, it is important to find out whether it is a hardware problem or a software problem. (In general, problems with the workings of a computer will not be something you have to deal with yourself.)

Questions

1. What are the steps involved in booting a microcomputer?

2. List the steps that you have to follow before you can start working with your word processing program on a microcomputer.

3. Name two input devices.

4. Name two output devices.

5. What is the most vulnerable part of a diskette?

6. Name two ways in which diskettes can be damaged.

7. What kind of disk does your microcomputer use?

8. What is the function of:

    (a) a disk
    (b) a disk drive

9. What are the steps you take when switching off a microcomputer?

4
Basic editing

Word processing, also called text editing or simply editing, is the most widespread use of computers on campus. This is not surprising since being a student often involves a considerable amount of writing and computers can be of great benefit in this area.

Most people find that once they have become accustomed to using an editor, then writing a paper on a computer is much easier than using a typewriter. There are many advantages of using computers, but perhaps the most fundamental one is that it is simple to change what you have written. And since a considerable portion of what is called writing is in fact revising, this is a major advantage.

For you as a foreign student, the revision process is even more important. You know that when you write a paper, it is likely to contain some grammatical and spelling errors, as well as problems with overall organization. Using an editor will make it easier for you to reorganize your paper and to make corrections. In addition, there are programs available which will also help you find some (but not all) of the errors you make.

Needless to say, you shouldn't put too much faith in the computer; the computer can help you, but it will not write the paper for you. You have to know what you want to say and how to say it in a manner appropriate for an academic paper. Furthermore, although knowing how to use an editor is important, there is a considerable gulf between knowing how to use an editor and knowing how to write a paper. In this chapter (and Chapters 6 and 9) we will concentrate mainly on the former—the mechanics of using an editor. In the second part of the book, in Chapter 13, we will discuss how to write an academic paper efficiently using a word processor. The basic steps in editing a file are the following:

1. starting the editor and opening a file

2. entering text (i.e., writing)

3. saving text

4. making changes

5. saving text (again)

6. leaving the editor

If you want to start working at a computer straightaway, turn to Section 4.2.

Computer work habits

Before talking about the technicalities of using a computer for word processing, you should know that using a computer will alter your style of working. Computer working habits may be good or bad just like other habits. It is important for you to acquire good rather than bad computer habits. Bad computer habits often consist of overusing simple commands instead of taking advantage of the computer's power. Conversely, good habits involve an efficient use of the computer—making the computer work for you. When you do this, a little work by you is magnified many times by the computer.

One of the disadvantages of using a computer is that the power and possibilities that it offers may lead to endless fiddling, either with the mechanisms of the word processing program itself or with the contents of your text. Some adjustments are inevitable when you try to perfect your paper. However, beware of falling into the trap of making unnecessary changes. This kind of activity can become a kind of displacement activity, like obsessive pencil sharpening. It is always possible to make more changes. But with a computer, you have to learn to *stop* making changes, so that you can move on to your next task.

Naturally, how people approach the task of writing papers varies. There is no single method that is appropriate for everyone. Moreover, each person works in different ways at different times. What is important is that for each style of writing, there is a way in which the computer can be used most advantageously.

You must organize your work in the way that is most convenient for you. For example, many people find it difficult to work exclusively on a computer. They might write their first draft using paper and pencil, and then type these notes into the computer. Next, they make modifications using the text editor, get a printout, mark changes on the printout, make more modifications using the editor, and so on. Many people find it necessary to make at least some editing changes by looking at a printout (called a *hard copy*), rather than working entirely with the text on the screen. Your habits will probably change as you become more accustomed to the computer; most people find that the proportion of work done directly on the computer gradually increases.

Studies have shown that people read text on the screen 20 to 30 percent slower than they read a printed copy. It is also harder to spot mistakes on the screen. However, since getting a printout takes time, you should limit the number of printouts you produce. (Remember to recycle the paper printouts you produce.) It is usually possible to get a printout of just a portion of your paper (e.g., pages 5 to 9) so that you can check your most recent revisions without printing out the entire document.

4.1 Different kinds of editors

Before going through the mechanics of editing, let us take a moment to consider different types of editors. Obviously, the design of the editor will influence how you work and what kinds of editing work you can do with ease.

Line editor

A *line editor* treats a text as a series of numbered lines. If you want to make an editing change, you must select the appropriate line and make changes to it. Line editors are often included in operating systems (which are discussed in the next chapter) for rudimentary editing at that level. DOS, for example, has a line editor called Edlin and UNIX has Ed. It is unlikely that you will use a line editor for writing papers, though you may use one for writing computer programs.

Figure 1 is an example of a text displayed using a line editor. You can see that the command **list** is given at the prompt (which is an angle bracket, >) followed by the characters **9/19**. This tells the computer to give a list of all the lines in the text from line 9 to line 19. Each line has its own line number, which appears on the left-hand side.

To make changes you must specify both an action (like delete) and a line number. Since using a line editor for writing papers is quite cumbersome, line editors will not be discussed any further.

```
> list 9/19
9.
10.   Fula is the language of the Fulani, the nomadic cattle
11.   owners of West Africa, whose unknown origins have
12.   provided a fruitful field for speculation for those
13.   so inclined, and prompted theories of relationship
14.   to peoples as diverse as the Ancient Egyptians, the
15.   biblical Phut, the Basques and the Dravidians of India.
16.   Now after centuries of gradual movement, mainly in an
17.   direction, from an early habitat which seems to have
18.   been somewhere in what is now Senegal or the western part
19.   of present-day Mali, they are found throughout Africa.
```

Figure 1. A line editor

Screen editor

Another common kind of editor is the *screen editor*. It presents text
in screenfuls rather than lines. The user is able to *scroll* though a
text file, screenful by screenful. Scrolling will be described in more
detail later (p. 63); for now you can think of scrolling as similar to
turning the pages of a book.

An example of a screen editor is EMACS. Figure 2 shows you what
the screen editor, EMACS, looks like. You can see that the text takes
up most of the screen. Below the text (in this editor) is a status (or
mode) line.

The status line gives information about the editor and the file.
This status line shows that EMACS is in Text and Fill mode (described
in Appendix A). The file being edited is called FUL3.TXT and the
percentage given in the status line means that 27% of the file is
above the screen. The asterisk simply indicates that changes have
been made to the file since the last time it was saved.

Below the status line is a blank area where some of your commands are shown (or 'echoed') as they are typed.

Don't worry about the details of this particular screen editor for
now. The main thing you should know is that editing using a screen
editor is like editing on a two-dimensional page. You can move the
cursor anywhere on the screen and you can move from one screen to

```
Fula is the language of the Fulani, the nomadic
cattle-owners of West Africa, whose unknown origins
have provided a fruitful field for speculation for
those so inclined, and prompted theories of
relationship to peoples as diverse as the Ancient
Egyptians, the biblical Phut, the Basques and the
Dravidians of India.  Now after centuries of gradual
movement, mainly in an easterly direction, from an
early habitat which seems to have been somewhere in
what is now Senegal or the western part of
present-day Mali, they are found throughout a wide
band of Africa.


Some Fulani still live the nomadic life inherited from
their forebears, moving with the seasons from wet-
season to dry-season grazing grounds and back again.
EMACS (Text Fill) Main:  FUL3.TXT (79) --27%-- *
```

Figure 2. A screen editor—EMACS

the next by scrolling (turning pages).

Window editor

A *window editor* (like MacWrite) is similar to a screen editor except that the text is contained in a portion of the screen called a *window*. Windows can be moved around the screen and their size and shape can be changed to suit your needs. Editing within a window is basically no different from editing using a screen editor. Powerful microcomputers called workstations, which will appear in the academic environment in the near future, use this kind of editor.

4.2 Starting the editor

If the editor is analogous to the writer's pen or typewriter, then what is equivalent to the paper? The 'electronic' paper is a *file* or document which you edit. The choice of the term 'file' comes from the common office practice of using files to store documents. As a student, you will often store each paper that you write on the computer in a separate file. Or, if you write a long paper, you might store each section of the paper as a separate file.

How do you get started on a new paper? First, you need to 'call up,' or start, the editor. This will give you a blank page that you can then start working on. Precisely how you call up the editor depends on the computer and the program that you are using, but there are two basic ways to do this. On a prompt and cursor computer, you type a command, perhaps **edit** or **ed**. On a menu and pointer computer, on the other hand, you 'select' and 'open' the editor. You select (and highlight) the *icon* representing the editor by moving the pointer so that it is over the icon and then clicking on the mouse button. Once you have selected your editor (e.g., MacWrite), you choose the *open* command from a menu, as shown in Figure 3.

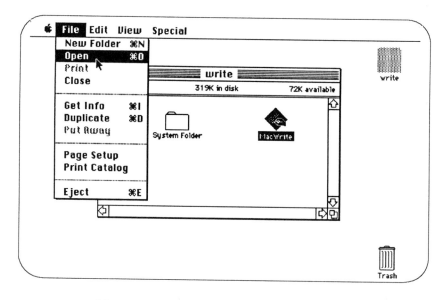

Figure 3. 'Opening' the editor MacWrite

Perhaps you have worked on a file previously and saved it for later revision. How do you call up the text you wrote before? Let us assume that you saved this work in a file called 'biologypaper.' How do you continue to work on the file? On a prompt and cursor computer, you type the command to call up the editor, followed by a space and the filename.

edit biologypaper

Alternatively, you may have to enter the word processing program before you can select a file. This is true for WordStar, for example.

On a menu and pointer computer you 'select' and 'open' the icon for the file called 'biologypaper.'

This may be a little confusing at first. Why don't you find out (and write down) how to use your editor to open (a) a new file, and (b) a file that you have worked on previously. Enter the commands in Appendix C.

4.3   Entering text

Once you have opened a file, you can enter text. To do this, you simply start typing. You don't need to worry about every spelling mistake that you make. You will be able to change what you have written later. You might, however, want to use the delete key to back up and change mistakes that you see as you write. The advantage of changing mistakes just after typing them is that it saves you from looking for them later. The disadvantage is that it interrupts the flow of your writing and may cause you to lose the thread of your thoughts.

> **!**   The knowledge that you can change what you are writing may free you from worrying about the exact form of words and phrases that you use. However, there is a danger that you will write so sloppily and disjointedly that it will be impossible to repair the text at a later date. You need to find a balance between attention to form and attention to content. This becomes easier with practice.

In many respects, entering text is similar to using a typewriter. One difference is the presence of a cursor on the computer screen, which indicates where the next character will be placed. Also, the physical feel of a computer differs from that of a typewriter. This difference in 'touch' may be a little disturbing at first if you are used to using a typewriter, but you will soon become accustomed to the lighter feel of the computer.

Word wrap

A very convenient feature of editors that are designed for writing text (rather than data or programs) is called *word wrap*. This means that when the end of a line is passed (as defined by the right margin setting), the last word in the line will automatically jump to the next line.

This has to be seen to be believed. Word wrap frees you from looking for the end of the line and pressing the return key. You need to press return only at the end of a paragraph.

Adding and removing lines

You can add blank lines by pressing the return key more than once. To remove a blank line you place the cursor at the beginning of the following line and then press the delete key. This technique can also be used to join two lines of text together. Try it. Joining two text lines together may result in a line that goes off the right-hand side of the screen. If this happens you can reform the paragraph as explained on page 65.

4.4   Saving text

Text that is on the screen is easy to change. It can be added to, deleted, replaced or moved around. This is because the text is electronic and temporary. As usual, there is a price to be paid for this convenience. The problem, in a nutshell, is that the image on the screen is not permanent.   If the electricity goes off or if you are disconnected from the computer (for example, when the computer *crashes*), then what is on the screen will be lost forever.

Does this mean that you have to start over again from a blank page? No, not if you saved your text at some point before you were cut off. When you save your file, the whole of the file (not just what is visible on the screen) is stored on magnetic material, either a disk or tape. If the computer crashes or some other disaster occurs, you will just have to start from wherever you were when you last saved your file. You can simply retrieve the version of the file that was last stored in permanent memory.

> ***** Save often. Save whenever you have done more work than you want to lose. Save after every paragraph or after every 10–15 minutes.

The fact that a file exists in two versions, one visible on the screen (in temporary memory) and one on a disk (in permanent memory) is hard for beginning computer users to grasp. Figure 4 illustrates the difference between temporary memory and permanent memory.

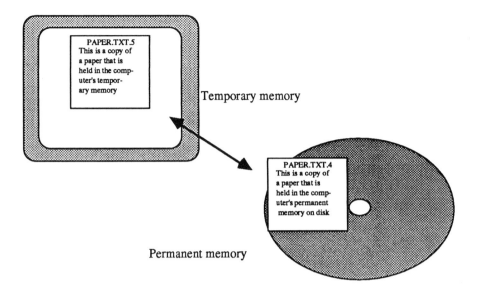

Figure 4. Temporary and permanent memory

> * Save often! This cannot be overemphasized. Make backup copies of your files too.

4.5 Modifying text

Word processing really excels when it comes to modifying text. Modifications can be of two types. They may be *global* changes, that is, changes that affect the whole file. For example, if you wanted to change every occurrence of 'co-operate' to 'cooperate' in your file, then you would carry out a global change. Global changes are described in Section 6.3 on Search and Replace.

For now, we will just talk about local changes. Local changes simply involve inserting, deleting or moving a single piece of text. These changes only apply to the text that is displayed on the screen in front of you; thus local changes are much more restricted than global changes.

There are two parts to locally modifying (or editing) text: (1) moving the cursor to the appropriate place in the file, and (2) making the actual change.

Moving the cursor

Since the page of text shown on the screen is a two-dimensional object, you can get wherever you want on the page by moving the cursor in one of four directions, as shown in Figure 5.

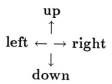

Figure 5. Moving the cursor

Moving the cursor is achieved by commands given to the computer. Therefore, before discussing cursor movement we must briefly consider how to give commands to the computer. You know that you can enter text by simply typing in characters. How then do you enter a command? That is, how do we distinguish text that we want to put into our document from commands that we want to give to the computer? For example, you cannot type **u** to move the cursor 'up'; typing **u** would simply enter the character 'u' into your text file.

There are a number of different ways in which commands can be distinguished from text. A prompt and cursor computer distinguishes commands from text either by making use of a special *command mode* (as in the UNIX editor, *vi*), or more commonly by using a special command key, often the control key. To give a command, you hold down the control key and simultaneously press some other key. Each computer program will have a series of control commands, represented as *ctrl u, ctrl v, ctrl x*, etc.

A menu and pointer computer allows you to use the *mouse* (see Chapter 3) to position the cursor when using a text editor. The mouse is also used in selecting commands from a menu, though control keys may also be used in some cases.

The difference between giving commands and entering text may be subtle. For instance, if you move the cursor forward by repeatedly pressing the space bar, you are actually entering text in the form of a series of spaces. Spaces, to the computer, are text just the same as any other text characters. Instead of entering spaces, you should use the appropriate command to move the cursor forward.

Moving the cursor is such a basic part of editing that there may be special devices to make it easier to give cursor movement commands. For example, your computer may have four cursor keys (each marked with an arrow). Pressing the right arrow will move the cursor one space to the right; pressing the down arrow will move the cursor down one line, and so on.

There are other devices that are used to position the cursor. The most common is the mouse, which has already been mentioned. Others include a *graphics pad* or tablet, a *touch screen*, and a *light pen*.

The computer may have an *autorepeat* capability, which means that instead of repeatedly striking a key, you can just hold it down and after a short pause, perhaps half a second, the key will 'repeat,' causing a series of characters to be entered. This is useful for cursor keys, in particular. By holding down a cursor key, you can move the cursor rapidly in a particular direction.

Scrolling

In addition to moving the cursor around the screen, it is also useful to be able to move the cursor to the next or previous screen in the file. This is called *scrolling*. The term scrolling is used because a file exists as a sort of continuous electronic scroll, rather than as a series of stacked pages. The file can be thought of as extending past the top and bottom of the screen as shown in Figure 6. To make off-screen parts of the file appear, you must scroll forward or backward. The cursor will then move to the next or previous page of text. An alternative way to think about this is to imagine that you must move the actual text to make it appear on the screen. On this view, the cursor and screen remains stationary, while the text moves up or down. Thus, in order to view material nearer to the beginning of the file, you must issue a command which you can think of as either scrolling the screen *up* or scrolling the text *down*.

To sum up what you have learned about modifying text so far: If you want to change something that you have written, you must first move the cursor to the appropriate place. Moving the cursor gets you around the screen, but to get to parts of the file that are off the screen, it is necessary to scroll through the text.

Making changes

Once the cursor is positioned in the correct place, it is possible to make the changes you desire. If you wish to delete text, you must use the delete key or one of a set of commands that will delete a character, word, line, or paragraph as appropriate. You can enter the specific commands used by your word processor in Appendix C.

To insert text, you just start typing. Remember, text will be in-

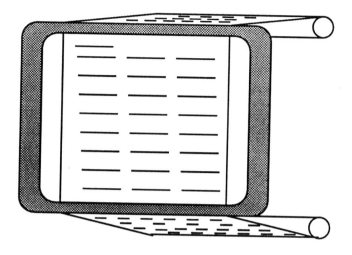

Figure 6. Scrolling

serted wherever the cursor is, and not necessarily where you happen
to be looking. What happens to the original text to the right of the
cursor (if there is any) when you insert new text? If the editor is
in *insert mode*, then text following the cursor will be pushed further
over to the right. Insert mode is illustrated in the example below.
Remember that the symbol □ represents the cursor.

Starting with the following:

> This is a□ book

Typing **computer** in <u>insert</u> mode results in the following:

> This is a computer□ book

If, on the other hand, the editor is in *overwrite mode*, then when
you type text it does not push the text following the cursor to the
right. Instead, the new text replaces or overwrites the old text. The
problem with overwrite mode is that you may accidentally delete
text that you want to keep. Here is an example of the result of
entering text in overwrite mode.

Starting with the following:

> `This is a`⬜` book`

Typing **computer** in <u>overwrite</u> mode results in the following:

> `This is a computer`⬜

Suppose you accidentally rest a book on the space bar. If your computer has an autorepeat mode, then two things can happen. If you are in insert mode, a series of spaces will appear in the text. However, if you are in overwrite mode, then the text will be replaced by blank space(s).

It is safer to remain in insert mode and replace text by inserting new material and then deleting whatever you don't need. Of course, this is a slightly slower way of modifying text.

Reforming a paragraph

When you enter text, the word wrap feature ensures that the text is lined up nicely into regular paragraphs. The changes that you make while revising, however, will upset all this. When you delete a chunk of text from a line, there may be a gap left in the text. On the other hand, when you insert text in the middle of a line, the rest of the line will extend past the right margin, giving an irregular looking paragraph like this:

```
Your editing changes, however, will change all
this.  When you
delete a chunk of text from a line,
there may be a
gap in the text.  On the other hand, when you
insert text, the line may extend
past the right margin, giving a irregular
looking paragraph like this.
```

Some editors (like MacWrite) will automatically readjust the paragraph as you make editing changes. If your editor does not make this adjustment, then you will have to give a command to *reform* the paragraph. Reforming essentially rearranges the text so that it conforms to the current margin settings. When the uneven paragraph above is reformed, for example, it results in the following:

```
Your editing changes, however, will change
all this.  When you delete a chunk of text
from a line, there will be a gap in the text.
On the other hand, when you insert text, the
line will extend past the right margin,
giving a irregular looking paragraph like
this.
```

4.6   Leaving the editor

When you want to finish an editing session, you first give the command to save your work (unless, of course, you decide to discard the changes you have made). Then, once your work is safely saved in permanent form, you give the command to quit the editor and return to the operating system. If you try to quit the editor without saving your work, some editors, such as MacWrite, will present a message asking you if you want to save your changes. Other editors, like EMACS, will simply let you quit, without warning you that you haven't saved your work.

4.7   Printing

Printing is either carried out from within the word processing program itself, or else by returning to the operating system level and giving a print command such as:

print myfile

This is another example in which the different levels of a computer can lead to confusion at first. You can issue a print command from two places: the operating system and the word processor. Also, the form of the command may well be different in the two cases.

Summary

In this section we have covered the basic operation of using an editor on a computer. You need to find out the commands that your editor uses. If you are using WordStar, EMACS or MacWrite, look at Appendix A. If you are using another editor, look at the manual to see how to carry out the basic operations that we have covered in this chapter.

You should try out the commands for the basic editing functions on a computer before reading any further. Let us run through a quick session as a review.

1. Call up the editor and open (create) a file (or document) named 'quicktry.'

2. Type **This is a test.**

3. Save the file.

4. Insert **quick** before 'test.'

5. Save the file.

6. Exit the editor.

This covers the basics of word processing. You now know enough to write a paper. But we won't stop here because you have only learned a small part of what the computer can do for you. In the following chapters, you will learn how to make the computer work harder for you.

Questions

1. How do you call up the editor you are using?

2. How do you edit:

   (a) a new file
   (b) a file you have worked on previously

3. What are the two basic steps in modifying text?

4. What is the difference between moving the cursor and scrolling?

5. Give two different techniques for moving the cursor on a microcomputer.

6. What is the difference between insert mode and overwrite mode?

7. What can you do to protect your work against computer or power failures?

8. What is the difference between temporary and permanent memory?

9. How do you save a file in your editor?

10. What happens when you save a file?

11. How do you leave or quit the editor?

12. Does the editor warn you if you quit without saving?

13. Try printing a copy of a file.

5

Files and operating systems

When you walk into a library, you find that it is organized in such a way that people can find the books and periodicals they want, despite the thousands of volumes that are stored there. Each title is given a number and arranged on the shelves in a particular area. And located in some central area there is probably a map or floor plan telling you where books on different subjects are located. Without some organization, finding a particular book would be like looking for a needle in a haystack. The fact that different libraries organize their books in different ways does not cause too much trouble, because it is expected that the books will be arranged in some logical manner, whether by subject, by author's last name, or some combination of both.

Similarly, a general method of organization is needed for the computer. There must be some way of managing computer operations and keeping track of files (the equivalent of books in the library). For example, you need to be able to create, copy, rename, and delete files. These 'housekeeping' functions are performed on the computer by the *operating system*. The operating system of a computer is a general framework that provides a basic organization within which you can work.

You may not even notice your operating system, because like the organization of the library it is simply 'there' in the background. But whenever you begin a session of work at the computer, you are dealing with the operating system. Whenever you give a command to run an applications program, you give it to the operating system, and whenever you are finished with a program, you return to the operating system before beginning another one.

In addition to its organizing function, the operating system places a considerable amount of information at your fingertips. You can find out the date and time, and look at the list of files that you have created. On time-sharing computers, you can also send messages and see who is logged on at a particular moment. Some operating systems, notably UNIX, provide a very rich environment containing large numbers of *utilities*; such systems allow you to develop your own programs.

This chapter covers the basic tasks performed by operating systems. For details of three particular operating systems (DOS, UNIX, and the Macintosh System/Finder), you can refer to Appendix B.

5.1 Before you start work

Before you can start work, you have to prepare the computer for action. This involves either booting a microcomputer (p. 42) or logging on (p. 30) if you are working on a time-sharing computer. The effect of booting is to load the operating system into the computer's memory; the effect of logging on is to make the operating system aware that you are a current user. Once you complete the procedure appropriate for your computer, the operating system is ready to receive your instructions.

Formatting a disk

One procedure that is relevant only to microcomputers is formatting a disk. If you buy a new disk or if you want to completely erase an old one, then you will need to *format* (or *initialize*) the disk before you can use it. The formatting process puts electronic lines on the disk, dividing it into tracks and sectors. This process enables the computer to write information to the disk (and read it again when needed). Note that a disk formatted for one operating system will not be readable by another operating system.

!   Formatting a disk completely erases any files the disk contained. Take care not to format a disk containing files. You only need to format a disk once.

Once you have formatted your disk, you may be prompted by the computer to enter a name for the disk. The name you give allows the computer (and you) to distinguish this disk from any others you might be using. In addition, it is usual to write the name on a label and attach the label to the disk. With the $5\frac{1}{4}$-inch floppy disks, you should write on the label *before* you attach it to the disk. If you have to write on a label which is already attached to a disk, use a felt-tipped pen to avoid damaging the disk.

5.2 Working with files

A considerable portion of your computer housekeeping time is spent manipulating files. The main file operations include:

1. creating files

2. copying files

3. naming files

4. creating directories

5. printing files

6. deleting files

Before looking at the commands for these functions, you will need to know how to get a list of the files that you have created. As mentioned earlier, the command to list your files is **ls** in UNIX and **dir** or **catalog** in other operating systems.

If you want to display the contents of one of your files on the screen (without using an editor), then on most systems you can give a command such as **cat** (in UNIX), **type**, or **list**, followed by a file name. You will have to check the commands appropriate for your operating system. You can then enter the commands in Appendix C.

Creating files

It is possible to create a file using an operating system command. However, files are usually created from within applications programs such as word processors or data base programs. For example, you can start a word processing program such as WordStar or EMACS and then choose a word processing command to open or create a file. (See Appendix A for details on how to create files in WordStar, EMACS and MacWrite.)

Copying files

You will often need to copy files from one place to another, either from one disk to another or from one directory to another. If you want to copy a file from one computer to another, you will have to look at the section on file transfer in Chapter 7.

Copying files is straightforward. The command on a prompt and cursor microcomputer or a mainframe is likely to be **copy** (or **cp** in UNIX). The copy command needs two file specifications: the first is the name of the file you wish to copy from, and the second is the name of the new file resulting from the copying operation.

Naming files

As an example of what *not* to do when naming files, look at the following list of files (or directory):

```
assign1
bill
bill2
billyltr
conftt
dynmcs.txt
lettr
paper.txt
scratch1
temp
```

What is in the files? It is hard to say, given the titles. When you create a new file, you should choose an appropriate name, one that will make sense to you in a couple of months' time. Otherwise, you will find yourself always having to open your files to find out what they contain. In addition, you might delete a file by mistake because you didn't know what was in the file. To avoid these problems, you should:

1. Be descriptive in giving file names.

2. Be consistent.

When choosing a file name you should make it as descriptive as possible, even if this means using a long name. Often you can use some punctuation in the file name, for example, a period or a hyphen. What kinds of characters are allowed in a file name depends on the system you are using. You can also use abbreviations or omit vowels to reduce the length of the name. You should develop a standard set of abbreviations to use in file names. For example, homework assignments might contain the label **asgn** or **hmwk**.

You can put other information in the file name, such as the course or the professor, as in **asgn-econ12** or **asgn-frdman**. You will also need to keep track of which assignment you are working on. You can do this by using numbers or by entering the date the assignment is due, for instance **asgn-3-econ12** or **asgn-4/5-econ12**.

File names generally consist of two parts: an identifying name and an extension (separated from the identifying name by a period). The above discussion centered on the identifying name. The extension usually consists of a three-letter sequence which indicates the general type of the file. Some commonly used extensions include:

.**txt** a text file

.**bak** a backup file

.**pas** a Pascal file

.**bas** a Basic file

.**bat** a batch file

.**dat** a data file

The exact use of these extensions does not matter here. The main point is that there are some conventions for file name extensions which give an indication of the contents of the file, both to you and to the computer.

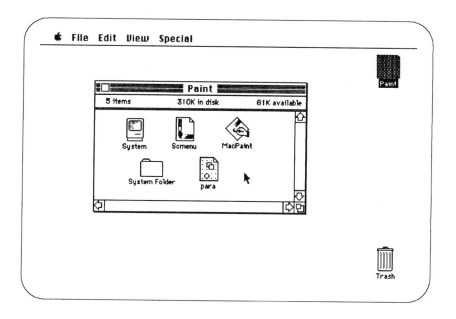

Figure 1. Different file icons for Macintosh files

The equivalent of extensions in Macintosh-like systems is a set of different icon patterns for different types of file. Figure 1 gives a sample of these.

You may also be able to give creative extensions. For example, a common file name is 'read.me.' You could use an extension like .asg to distinguish your assignment files from the rest of your files. There is a slight danger, however, that creative non-standard extensions will get you into trouble, because the computer may be programmed to expect only standard extensions.

It was noted earlier that by giving the command **dir** or its equivalent, you can get a list of all your files (on a time-sharing system) or a list of the files on a disk (on a microcomputer). However, it is often useful to be able to list only a subset of your files, perhaps all your personal or business letters or all your assignments. For example, if your letters are called 'ltr-billy,' 'ltr-jon,' 'ltr-mom,' etc., then you can get the computer to list just these files. All the files start with 'ltr...' and so you can ask for all files beginning with 'ltr' followed by any character or characters. To do this, you give a command equivalent to **dir ltr***, shown in Figure 2. (The @ preceding the command is a prompt.) The asterisk acts as a 'wildcard' character standing for any sequence of characters. (The wildcard character may be different on your computer.)

```
@dir ltr*

  PS:<GONZALES>
ltr-apple
ltr-dan
ltr-ibm
ltr-jose
ltr-marg
ltr-maria
ltr-phil

Total of 7 pages in 7 files
```

Figure 2. Using **dir** with a wildcard character

> **!** The larger the permanent storage available to you, the more important it is for you to organize your files systematically.

In case you need to do some reorganizing of your file system, there is also a command to rename your files. For example, you might want to change a file name from 'billyltr' to 'ltr-billy.txt.' On many computers the **rename** command accomplishes this.

rename billyltr ltrbilly.txt

> **!** When using a rename command, make sure that the new name that you specify is different from existing file names in your directory.

To rename a file on a menu and pointer computer, you select the text under a file icon and type a new name.

Creating directories

How do you avoid spending a lot of time looking for the files you want to work on? In the previous section, the importance of choosing the right file names was discussed. In addition, it is common on large computers or computers with hard disks to group similar files together in some way.

For example, on the Macintosh you can group files by putting them in *folders*. To do this, you choose *new folder* from the File menu, name the new folder, and put a group of files inside by dragging them over the icon representing the folder. A disk containing folders is shown in Figure 3. One advantage of using folders is that your 'desktop' does not get cluttered up with too many file icons.

Another common method of grouping files that is used by advanced computer users is to distribute files in different directories or subdirectories. For instance, you can create a subdirectory called 'letters' for all your letter files. And you can create another subdirectory for assignments for each of your courses. If you create such subdirectories, a command to list your files will show you a list of several subdirectories rather than a list of hundreds of files. You can then choose one of the subdirectories and get a list of the individual files it contains.

On some computers it is also possible to set up a subdirectory within a subdirectory. Thus you might decide to have a general subdirectory for letters and within this subdirectory, create one subdirectory for personal letters and one for professional or business letters. Under this system you arrange your files in a 'hierarchy.'

The UNIX operating system utilizes subdirectories and allows the user to create *paths*, or records of how to get around several levels

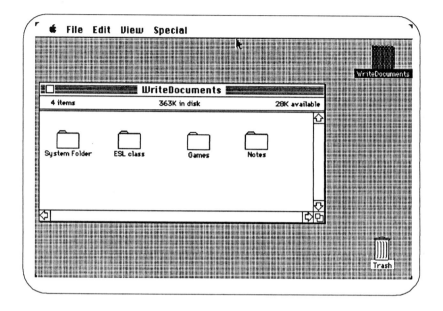

Figure 3. Folders on a Macintosh

of subdirectories to the exact file you want. Thus a file might be identified by a path name such as /letter/business/ibm. Here 'ibm' is the name of a file in a subdirectory 'business,' which is itself in a subdirectory called 'letter.'

If you are using a system that supports subdirectories, you need to know how to create a subdirectory, how to remove (i.e., delete) a subdirectory, how to get from one subdirectory to another and how to move files from one subdirectory to another. These operations are described for the UNIX operating system in Appendix B.

If you use a computer that does not support subdirectories, you can achieve a similar effect by choosing to name your files in a certain manner. For example, if you have two letters, one for Jane and one for Ben, do you name them **janeletr, benletr** or **letrjane, letrben**? The latter is better since it will group the letters together when they are listed alphabetically. In this way you create a kind of 'letter subdirectory.'

Printing files

Printing files can often be done either from the operating system or from within an application. Usually, printing from the operating system simply involves giving the command **print** followed by a file name. On a menu and pointer computer, you select an icon for a file and choose *print* from a menu. There may be other options that you can specify, such as which printer you want to use.

Deleting files

After a while your directory or disk will fill up with files that you no longer need. In order to free some space, you will have to delete some files. Files are deleted by giving a command like **del** or **delete** or **erase** (or **rm** in UNIX) followed by a file name. On the Macintosh, a file to be deleted is dragged onto the trash can icon.

Obviously, you should not be too liberal in your use of the delete command. Deleting files is one of the main causes of heartache for computer users. For some reason, we often accidentally delete files that we really want to keep. We will discuss what to do in the event of such mistakes in the next section.

For more details on operating system commands, see Appendix B. You can enter the operating system commands found on your computer in Appendix C.

5.3   Catastrophes and how to cope with them

Everyone who uses a computer encounters a catastrophe at some time or another. Usually, this involves losing an important file or files, often shortly before a deadline.

---

* The most serious effects of catastrophes can be avoided if:

- you save your work regularly

- you make backup copies of your files.

The importance of making copies of important files can't be emphasized too strongly. Everyone loses some material from time to time. What you have to do is minimize your losses.

If you are using a microcomputer, you should set aside a disk (or disks) that contains backup copies of your main files. These backup copies should be updated at the end of each day's work. If you only have one disk, save your important file on a friend's disk.

If you are using a mainframe computer, you can store backup copies of your files in your directory along with your other files. You might want to distinguish the backup files by using 'bkp' as the first or last three letters of the file name. Many people who undertake a major work on a computer have a set of backup files on another computer. For example, you might use a communications program (see Chapter 7) to transfer files from a mainframe to a microcomputer or vice versa.

The following section may be hard to follow if you are a new computer user. Don't worry about the details. Just read the section quickly to get a general idea of possible problems and solutions. You may need to refer back to it later when you have a problem.

Deleting files accidentally

Sometimes you will delete a file by mistake. If this happens, try the following:

1. Find someone to help you who knows the computer system you are working on. DON'T LOG OFF or switch off the machine.

2. On a time-sharing computer there may be a command that will undelete the file.

3. On a microcomputer you may have to depend on backup files that you have made or that the word processor makes automatically. For example, WordStar stores an older version of a file such as 'paper.txt' as 'paper.bak.' (On WordStar, you will have to rename the backup file before you can open it.)

4. The files on mainframes are backed up on magnetic tape every few days, so you may be able to ask the system operator to restore an earlier version of your file from the tape.

5. When you delete a file from a floppy disk, the file remains on the disk until the space it occupies is needed. You can't see that the file is there. You have to use a utility program such as Norton Utilities for the IBM PC and Copy II for the Macintosh to reconstruct your file. Ask a consultant about doing this.

Bad disks

Diskettes sometimes become unreadable. However, this does not necessarily mean that your data has been destroyed. You can use a disk utility to try to retrieve your files. See (5) above.

System crashes

From time to time a computer will crash (stop working). It may save the file you were working on; or, it may not. The only thing you can do to minimize the effects of system crashes is save your work regularly.

Loss of connection

The electronic connection between your terminal and the main computer may be broken. If this happens, you may still be logged on to the computer, in which case you can try to make a new connection, perhaps from another terminal, and 'attach' to your job. Ask someone to help you.

Problems arising from 'search and replace' commands

After issuing a global search and replace command, you may notice that your text has been changed in unwanted and irreversible ways. Probably the best thing to do in this case is quit (exit) the file without saving it, and then load in an older version of the file from the disk. This procedure works particularly well if you remember to save your file just before giving a search and replace command.

Deleting material by mistake

When you are working on a file, you may accidentally delete a block of text. If you are lucky, the word processor you are using will allow you to *undelete* the material. The important thing in this case is to undelete the material as soon as possible after deleting it.

   If you are writing a paper and you decide that there is a page or so that needs to be deleted, it is a good idea to save the page of text in a separate file before you delete it from your main file. You may decide later that you want all or some of the deleted material in your paper after all. In general, it is better to keep blocks of text somewhere accessible rather than to eliminate them completely. Once you have completed your work, you can always get rid of the extra text.

   What do you do if you delete a piece of your text and it is not possible to undelete it? It may be that the deleted material is in the version of the file that is stored on the disk. If there is no saved version of the file containing this material, then what you deleted cannot be recovered from the computer. If you printed an earlier version of your document that has the deleted material in it, you can just retype it. If not, you must reconstruct it from memory.

If you decide to exchange the version of the file appearing on the screen for the version last saved on the disk, then you can simply exit the editor without saving and call up the file on the disk. The disadvantage of doing this is that you will lose the changes you made since your last save. If you don't want to lose these recent changes, then try to get some help.

Questions

1. What operating system does your computer use?

2. What does an operating system do?

3. When do you have to format a disk?

4. How do you copy a file?

5. How do you delete a file?

6. What are the two most important ways of protecting your work?

7. Enter the important commands for your operating system in Appendix C.

6

More on editing

In Chapter 4 you learned how to move the cursor, scroll the screen, insert text, and delete text. Having mastered the basics of word processing, you are now ready to make use of more powerful features. In this chapter we will cover such functions as:

1. moving around a file

2. searching

3. search and replace

4. working with blocks of text

5. changing the appearance of your text

6. printing

Once again, you should experiment and practice on your computer after reading each section.

6.1 Moving around a file

Before you can insert or remove text, you must get to the appropriate part of your file. You can do this by moving the cursor in one of four directions (p. 62). Moving the cursor character by character or line by line is only appropriate, however, when the changes to be made are close together in the file. For greater distances, there are other commands you should use. For example, you may be able to move the cursor word by word, sentence by sentence, or paragraph by paragraph. (You can enter the commands used in your word processor for these functions in Appendix C.)

Cursor keys (if your computer has them) are convenient, but can easily be overused. It is important that you move on to more powerful cursor-positioning commands. You will often need to move the cursor over large distances in your file, and the short-distance movement commands you have learned so far are simply too time-consuming and inefficient for such tasks. Some word processors will allow cursor keys to be used in combination with other keys (shift and CTRL, for example) to execute more powerful movement commands.

Of course, if you are using a menu and pointer computer, then the problem of overuse of cursor keys will probably not arise because you can simply move the cursor around the screen by positioning the mouse, rather than using keys on the keyboard.

> ***** Don't repeat the same commands over and over; instead, choose a more powerful command. Don't type any text twice; it is quicker to copy what you have.

You may find that when using some of the more powerful movement commands, you will occasionally get lost. If this happens you should move the cursor to some familiar point, either the beginning of the file or the end. The fact that you are at the beginning or end will be indicated either in the status line or by means of a special character that acts as a *flag* or marker. On menu and pointer computers, your position in a file is indicated by the position of a rectangle in a *scroll bar* on the side of the window containing the file. If the rectangle is at the top of the scroll bar, then you are at the top of the file. (In MacWrite, the page number is indicated on the rectangle.) In fact, you can move through the file by using the mouse to move the rectangle along the scroll bar.

If you want to do some editing in the middle of a long paper, then scrolling through the file until you get to the part that you want will take some time. Here are some more efficient ways to quickly move through the file:

1. using the *goto* command

2. setting markers in the text

3. using search commands

Goto

Some word processors have a 'goto' command (pronounced like the English words 'go to') which allows you to jump to a particular page number. For instance, **goto 5** brings page 5 onto the screen. This method is only appropriate if you know the approximate page on which the text you are searching for is located.

Setting markers

Other word processors (such as WordStar) have commands that allow you to set place markers in the text. These markers might be entered as *ctrl 1, ctrl 2,* etc. Once these markers are set, another command will allow you to jump to the marker you specify. This is useful sometimes, but it does require that you set the markers and know where they are before you issue the search command.

The third and most powerful method of moving through your file is to use *search* commands. Since searching is an important computer technique, we will discuss it in some detail.

6.2   Searching

Searching is a word-processing feature that most clearly highlights the computer's processing power. Searching for a particular string of characters, often a word, is the sort of mechanical, repetitive task that is difficult for humans, but simple for computers. The computer, since it is not distracted by word meanings, noise, or other interruptions, can carry out a search quickly and accurately.

Performing a search consists of two parts. First, you give the command to execute a search. Second, you specify the target, i.e., the word or letters you want to search for. The search command itself is usually straightforward, though there may be a number of different options that you can choose which will be discussed below. Once the search command is given, the computer checks through the file, starting at the cursor, until the target is found.

Searching for a unique string of characters

One of the most convenient uses of the search command is to quickly get to a particular place in the file where you would like to start work. To do this, you might search for some uniquely identifiable string of characters, such as 'Chapter 2.'

If there are no unusual words or phrases in the section you are trying to locate, it may be useful to pick out a selection of letters and punctuation. For example, you may have the following lines of text:

```
The talks show the serious commitment of the leadership
(of both countries) to arms control.
```

Searching for the string **ship** or **ries)** will most likely move the cursor to the right place. If you have a printout of your file, you will easily be able to pick out a unique string to search for.

> **!**   You have to be careful of the computer's literal approach to searching. To a text editor, there is just as much distinction between **the pan** and **the   pan** as there is between **the pan** and **the span**, since a space is a character just like any other.

Searching using special markers

One way to arrange things so that you can always move to particular places in your file is to plant your own special markers in the file. For example, you may want to mark the beginning of each section with rarely used symbols such as # or $. Then, when you want to begin work at a particular section, you can immediately move the cursor there by searching for the symbol you used. With this method, you need to remember to delete the marks before you print the final copy of your paper.

Searching for information

A common use for searching is to retrieve a piece of information buried somewhere within a file. This basic use of a search as a sort of dynamic index is often needed when you are using an editor to look at a file that you didn't write, for example, a mail file containing all mail sent to you. For instance, you might want to find a friend's telephone number which you know is in one of the messages sent to you. So you search through the file looking either for the friend's name or for the word 'phone.'

Searching as a way to check for errors

Imagine that you are writing a paper on 'Heisenberg's Uncertainty Principle' and you notice that you have misspelled the physicist's name as **Hiesenberg**. You wonder whether you have made the same mistake elsewhere in your paper and so you search for the misspelled word to make sure that there are no more occurrences of it in your paper. In effect, you are searching for errors.

Peculiarities of search commands

Word processors vary in the way in which the search operates. You can get a feel for how your word processor treats certain cases by experimenting with the search command. If you search for **Heisenberg**, with capital H, will the computer find **heisenberg**? Perhaps. It depends on whether the search is 'case-sensitive,' that is, whether the search command distinguishes between upper and lower case letters. Test out the editor you are using. Perhaps your word processor lets you choose whether the computer search is sensitive to case.

If you perform a search for **heisenberg**, will the computer find **heisenbergian** or **heisenberg's**? The answer depends on how the computer program defines a word and whether the search command distinguishes whole words from parts of words. Some word processors allow you to specify whether the search is to be for a whole word or for just a part. Again, check the program you are using.

How far does a search go? Typically, the computer will start the search wherever the cursor is and check through to the end of the file. So you may have to position the cursor at the beginning of the file in order to search all the way through it. It is also possible to use a reverse search, which starts at the cursor and moves backwards towards the beginning of the file.

Searching using wildcard characters

'Wildcard' characters can often be used in a search command. Wildcard or dummy characters match any character or characters; they are called wildcard characters because they act like a playing card that can represent any value, like the joker. For example, in some word processors, the character **?** may be used in a search command to stand for any single character. A search for the string **Ann?** will find any sequence of four characters in which the first three are **A n n** and the fourth is any character. Thus the search would locate **Anna**, **Anne**, and **Anny**, for example.

When would you want to use this type of search? Well, the dummy or wildcard option allows additional flexibility in the search, enabling you to perform a search based on incomplete or uncertain information. For example, you might search for **Ann?** if you didn't know whether the name in a text was Anne or Anna—or if both were used. Obviously, if you know exactly what you are searching for, then there is no need to use a dummy character.

Another use of dummy characters is to search for a class of related words. For example, if you want to look for any one of **exhibit-1**, **exhibit-2**, and **exhibit-3**, you do not need to perform separate searches. You can simply search for **exhibit-?**.

The above discussion covers the basic use of wildcard characters. Further refinements are possible. For example, there may be different kinds of wildcard characters available in your text editor. A common one is * which will match any string of characters rather than just a single character. In addition, you may be able to select wildcard characters that match only certain types of characters, for instance, one for letters, one for numbers and one for punctuation symbols.

Failure of a search

What do you do if a search fails unexpectedly? You can check for the following problems:

- A spelling mistake in the search string.

- A spelling mistake in the target. This type of error is much harder to deal with. This is one area where a partially specified search string or a search string containing wildcards may be appropriate.

- Wrong case. Upper or lower case is wrongly specified.

- The presence of punctuation (or a carriage return) in the target rather than the expected space. This is tricky. If you search for **phenomenon** followed by a space, you will not find **phenomenon.** or **phenomenon,.** In addition, you may not find the word **phenomenon** when it occurs at the end of a line, since there it is followed not by a space but by a special (end-of-line) character.

- Wrong direction. The search probably starts at the cursor position and goes to the end of the file. Perhaps the target is in the part of the file preceding the cursor. Try a reverse search or make sure that you are at the beginning of the file when you issue the search command.

6.3   Search and replace

The mechanics of the *search and replace* (sometimes called 'find and replace') command are very similar to the search command. All the issues that were discussed concerning the different possibilities and pitfalls of search commands apply to search and replace commands as well. The crucial difference is that with the search and replace command, the text is actually changed, not just located.

There may be several useful options available with a search and replace command. First, you may be able to choose how extensive you want the change to be. Perhaps you want to change only the first instance of the target you are looking for. At other times, you might want to change *all* instances of the target in your file. This second option, replacing all instances of a target, is known as a 'global change.'

Another possible option is to use a modified search and replace command so that you are prompted before each change. In this case, the cursor will jump to an instance of the target text, and ask whether that instance should be replaced or not. The computer will act on your response, then jump to the next instance, and so on through your file. This gives you a slower but safer method of carrying out a global change.

The search and replace command is useful but somewhat dangerous. It has been found to be most dangerous late at night. At around midnight you realize that you have repeatedly made the same mistake in your file. The depression associated with this knowledge is quickly superseded by the realization that you can, with a few keystrokes, put your paper to rights. Without thinking too much (you know what to search for), you enter the global search and replace command. Seconds later your file has undergone drastic changes because the scope of the command turns out to have been greater than you had anticipated.

What happened? One problem may have come from homonyms, that is, words with the same form but different meanings, for example, the word 'set,' which may be a noun or a verb. The mistake of replacing the wrong instances of a homonym is often not obvious at first, but at some later time, you will notice a strange pair of words and realize what must have occurred. For example, imagine that you decide to modify some technical term that you have been using. You might be talking about verb tenses in English and realize that you have been using the term **present** when you should have used **present perfect**. In order to correct this, you decide on a global search and replace, changing **present** to **present perfect**. Unfortunately, the target is too widely defined because of the existence of different uses of the word 'present.' Consequently, unexpected changes occur. The text:

```
The present tense in English often causes some
difficulties ...
```

changes to:

```
The present perfect tense in English often causes
some difficulties ...
```

But in addition, the text:

```
I will present some results ...
```

changes to:

```
I will present perfect some results...
```

One way to avoid mistakes like this is to include more context. For example, you may limit the target of the command by changing `present tense` to `present perfect tense`. Here the danger is that the search will be too narrowly defined and you will not change all the instances of `present` that need to be changed.

Another possibility mentioned above is to choose a search and replace command with a *prompt* or *query* option. Then the program will search through the text and when the target word is found, it will be highlighted, and a prompt will appear allowing you to either change the word or leave it unchanged.

This section contains a considerable amount of detail. Don't worry if you don't understand everything that has been covered. You will discover for yourself many of the issues that have been raised. Just be aware that the changes you desire may not always be achieved on your first try.

The main way to avoid major disasters is to think through the change that you wish to make. Try to take the computer's perspective on the command you are giving. How could it be interpreted? How can you make it more specific?

The best thing to do is to try out the search and replace command on a test file. Check for:

- case sensitivity: upper versus lower case (Will a search for `bill` find `Bill`?)

- whole versus partial words (Will a search for `bill` find `billy`?)

- the treatment of punctuation (Will a search for `Bill` find `Bill,` and `Bill's`?)

> ***** Save your file before you carry out a global search and replace operation. If you get unexpected results, you can exit the file without saving and then call up the version you saved before executing the replace command.

The best way to check on the results of commands that modify your text is to read carefully through a printed copy of your file.

6.4 Working with blocks of text

One efficient way to modify your text involves selecting or marking a piece of text. The text you mark may be anything from a single letter to the whole file. Once this block of text (called a region or block) is marked, you can issue a command to change the marked text in some way. Common operations on blocks include the following:

- delete

- move

- copy

- change type style or fonts

- save as a new file

These operations are found in most word processors.

Marking a block

To mark a block of text, you put down a marker at the beginning of a block, then move the cursor and mark the end of the block. (In some word processors, the cursor may itself mark the end of a block.) The marked block has to be continuous, but otherwise there are no restrictions on what constitutes a block. Once a block is marked, it may appear highlighted on the screen in some way. See, for example, Figure 1.

What if you make a mistake in marking a block or decide to mark a new block? In either case you simply go ahead and mark a new block. By marking a new block, the old block automatically becomes unmarked.

An editor that can take advantage of a mouse makes it easy to mark blocks. Manipulating the mouse is a fast and natural way (after a little practice) to mark the beginning and end of a block. Editing using a mouse is a series of actions in which you first select a block and then give a command.

Deleting text

Your word processor will probably have commands for deleting characters, words, lines, sentences, and paragraphs. In addition, there is probably a command for deleting a block of text. Try deleting a block of text on a test file. Can you retrieve the deleted block?

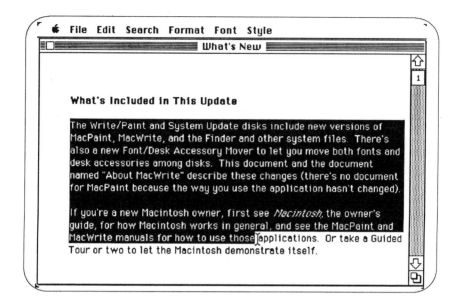

Figure 1. A marked block of text

Moving text

Moving text usually involves marking a block of text and then indicating by means of the cursor where it is to be moved to. There are two basic methods of moving text, and word processors differ as to which of these they utilize.

1. **Cut and paste** sounds innocent enough, but it does require a little faith in the machine. In this method of transferring text, you must first delete (or 'cut') the text, causing it to disappear. Next, you move the cursor to the place in the file where you want the text to reappear, and then retrieve ('undelete' or 'paste') the deleted text. After you have done this successfully a few hundred times, you become more confident of the fact that the text is really being stored in a 'buffer,' or temporary storage space, after deletion and is not lost forever. You should carry out the 'undelete' or 'paste' command as soon as possible after the delete or 'cut' command. Don't get distracted and start to do some other operation.

2. **Mark and move** is an alternative way to transfer text. You mark a block of text, which becomes highlighted on the screen, then move the cursor to the point at which you want to insert the text. You then give the command to move the block (called *move block* or *transfer region*) causing it to disappear from its old location and reappear at the cursor position.

> ***** It may be possible to move blocks containing diagrams rather than text. For example, it is possible to move a diagram or picture from MacPaint to MacWrite using the cut and paste approach.

Copying text

Copying blocks of text is useful in that it can save you from retyping material that you have already entered into the computer. It is often quicker to copy a block of text and make changes to it than to type in a new piece of text.

Changing type style or fonts

On certain computers, like the Macintosh, it is possible to change the appearance of a block of text by changing:

1. type style

2. type size

3. font

You may be able to change the type style in your text, using italics and boldface type, for example.

> ***** Try **NOT** to *mix* font styles and types in YOUR document, since the *result* is confusing and *HARD* to **READ**.

Changing the type size is useful for writing titles and other headings. Finally, you may be able to change fonts. If so, you might write your text in a roman font, but switch to a sans serif font for headings or titles. Compare the roman font in 'roman' with the sans serif font in 'sans serif.'

Saving text to a file

One operation that you will find useful from time to time is to save a marked block of text as a separate file. You need to do this, for example, when a file has grown too large to manage. By writing a block of text to another file (and then deleting the block in the original file) you can split a large file into two more manageable files.

It is a good idea when deleting a paragraph or more of text to save it in a file. Then if you change your mind later and decide to incorporate the material in your paper, you will still have the material available. If you are working on a file called 'biology-paper' and decide to delete a section of the file, you can mark the unwanted text and save it as a file called 'biology-extra1' before deleting the block in 'biology-paper.'

Many editors allow you to save a block or region as a separate file without leaving the main file you are editing. (Note that the block may equal the whole file.) You must check how to do this in your word processing program. If you are using WordStar, MacWrite or EMACS, you can look in Appendix A.

6.5 Changing the appearance of your text

When you first start using a computer you may be quite happy to stick with the settings of tabs and margins that are fixed by the computer program. These are known as *default* settings. As you become more familiar with the computer, you are more likely to want to change these settings to suit your own needs and preferences. Changing these settings alters the way the text appears on the screen and often the way it is printed too.

Changing the margin settings is usually fairly straightforward. When you change these settings, the text may dynamically change to conform with the new settings (as in programs such as MacWrite). Alternatively, the text may stay the same until you issue a specific command to reform the text (as in WordStar and EMACS).

In addition to changing the margin settings, you will need to find out how to do the following on your text editor:

- change the spacing (your papers will probably be double-spaced)
- turn justification on or off
- center text
- indent text

Most text is left-justified, that is, the text at the beginning of each line starts at the same column. The text in this book is also right-justified. This means that the right margin is straight rather than ragged. Many text editors allow you to switch *justification* on or off. Justification looks professional, but it is often harder to read than text that is not justified.

Centering text is useful for titles. Many beginners try to center text by putting a series of spaces before the title. This is the hard way to do it. Find the command for centering text on your editor and experiment.

> * If you use a command to center your text but it does not look centered, then you probably have some spaces (or tabs) before or after the text. Delete these and use the centering command again.

Producing an indented block of text, such as a long quotation, will take a little experimentation before you get it right. There are several ways to do it. How easy it is depends on the editor you are using. Here we will simply list some possibilities.

- use a tab before each line of the text to be indented

- temporarily reset the left and right margins, and set them back again after the indented block to continue the main text

- center the text to be indented (this will produce a ragged left margin, however)

- use a special quote environment if your editor or formatter has one.

6.6   Printing

Since there are different conventions for producing different types of documents, you will need to control the appearance of the printed copy of your file to conform with the appropriate conventions. Changing the appearance of the printout is very similar to making changes in the format of a paper as discussed in the preceding section. The major settings with respect to printing are:

- margins

- spacing

- justification

• font type and size

Once you have become proficient in the use of an editor you will probably want to make use of the formatting capabilities of the editor or of special programs like Scribe, TEX, and TROFF (see Chapter 14).

Often, what is printed is very similar to what appears on the screen; however, the printing process potentially changes the settings discussed in the previous section. You cannot guarantee that a printer will not change the format of your document to some extent. When you are first starting to adjust the placing of text, you will probably try adjustments such as padding the text with blank lines or physically adjusting the position of the paper in the printer. However, in order to get real control over the appearance of the printout, you need to become familiar with print commands. You can more closely control what the printout looks like by embedding print commands in your document. Print commands give instructions to the printer about margin size, spacing, underlining, and other things.

Margins

The margin settings (top, bottom, left and right) determine the placement of the text on the printed page. Remember, the margins on the printout may be different from the margins on the screen. An alternative to specifying both the top and bottom margin is to set the top margin and the text height. The bottom margin will then be determined by how much space remains on the page after the text is placed according to these two settings.

Spacing

Line spacing

Line spacing simply refers to the amount of space left between two lines of text. Some word processors do not allow you to set the line spacing at all. This is the case with EMACS. Double spacing is obtained by modifying the print command. Other word processors allow you to set the line spacing as on a typewriter. In this type of program, if you select double spacing, your text will be double-spaced on the screen and also as printed copy. Even if your word processor does have the ability to make text double-spaced on the screen, however, you should work with single spacing until you are ready to print the document.

Character spacing

There are various adjustments that can be made to the space that characters take up. The relative space taken up by printed characters is called *pitch*. For example, you may be able to change from a pitch of 10 characters per inch to one of 12 characters per inch, thereby squashing the letters together more. The notion of pitch does not apply when the printer performs *proportional spacing*. With proportional spacing, narrow characters such as 'i' take up less space than wide characters like 'w.' (Look at the 'w' and 'i' in 'wide.') In non-proportional spacing, each character takes up the same space: an 'i' is as wide as a 'w.' (Look at the 'w' and 'i' in 'wide.')

Justification

It was noted above that justified text is often harder to read than non-justified text. One problem that frequently occurs in justification is that in order to justify the text, the computer places irregular spaces between the words. Sometimes these spaces are quite long, making the text look somewhat strange.

The following text is not justified:

> As inspector general of the Moravian Missions, Oldendorp went to the Virgin Islands in 1772, just forty years after the first mission had been established. From there he produced a model report, and he talked with slave and slave owner alike, reported on pirates and adventurers of every kind, and commented on trade and commerce.

This text is justified:

> As inspector general of the Moravian Missions, Oldendorp went to the Virgin Islands in 1772, just forty years after the first mission had been established. From there he produced a model report, and he talked with slave and slave owner alike, reported on pirates and adventurers of every kind, and commented on trade and commerce.

Fonts

Your choice of different fonts or type styles depends in part on the printer that you are using. For example, an ImageWriter printer is a fairly good quality dot-matrix printer that will print whatever appears on the Macintosh screen. However, if you use a laser printer with the Macintosh, then what fonts will be printed depends in part on the particular selection of fonts that are loaded into the laser printer itself. Similarly, on a letter-quality printer, the form of the printed output depends on the element in the printer (the daisy-wheel) that contains the images of the characters. If you use a letter-quality printer, then the output will be good, like a typewriter's, but you will be limited in your choice of fonts. If you want to change fonts within a file, you may have to physically change the 'daisy-wheel' element that produces the printed characters.

Questions

1. On the editor you are using, how do you move the cursor:

   (a) one word forward
   (b) one word back
   (c) to the beginning of a line
   (d) to the end of a line
   (e) to the previous line
   (f) to the next line
   (g) to the beginning of a sentence
   (h) to the end of a sentence
   (i) to the beginning of a paragraph
   (j) to the end of a paragraph
   (k) to the beginning of the file
   (l) to the end of the file?

2. Does the search command on your computer distinguish between

   (a) whole versus partial words
   (b) upper versus lower case?

3. What is a wildcard character? Why is it useful in a search?

4. What would happen if you executed a 'search and replace' command to replace 'on' by 'in' in the following text?

   ```
   All electronic mail systems on computers
   share some common characteristics.  To send
   a message, an email user logs onto a
   terminal, writes the message, and gives a
   command to send the message to another
   user.
   ```

5. How do you mark a block of text on the word processor you are using?

6. Try

   (a) moving a block of text

   (b) saving a block of text as a separate file.

7. Is the following text justified?

Once you get used to using print commands, there are many things that you can do to alter the appearance of your text. You can change the position of the text on the page, the size of the margins, and the points at which the page breaks occur. Unfortunately, making these changes in one part of your file often has effects in other parts.

7

Communications

Adding a communications facility to a computer gives you access to a greater range of services than you can get on your own computer. For instance, you can read bulletin boards, get the latest Dow-Jones share information or send electronic mail to a colleague overseas.

There is no standard set of hardware and software specifications that covers all computers; each computer manufacturer follows its own design specifications. This is fine as long as you are using a computer by itself. But when you want one computer to connect up with another computer, problems arise because the two computers may not be compatible. It is as though they speak different languages.

If the mainframes on your campus are connected together in a *network*, then you will find that communicating with the other computers on the network is fairly straightforward. If you have a microcomputer and you want to communicate with other computers, then you will first have to acquire the necessary hardware and software.

7.1 Communications hardware and software

If you are working on a time-sharing computer, then you don't have to worry about the hardware and software aspects of communications. You can skip to the next section. If you are using a microcomputer, then to communicate with another computer you will need at least the following:

- some communications software

- a *modem*

- a telephone

Communications software

The communications software allows you to change a few basic settings so that your microcomputer will be able to communicate with different kinds of computers. For example, Figure 1 shows some settings chosen using MacTerminal, a communications program for the Macintosh. Don't worry about all these choices; most of the time you won't have to specify anything at all. If you need advice on the settings, you can ask the system operators of the computer you want to link up with. Or you can just experiment a little.

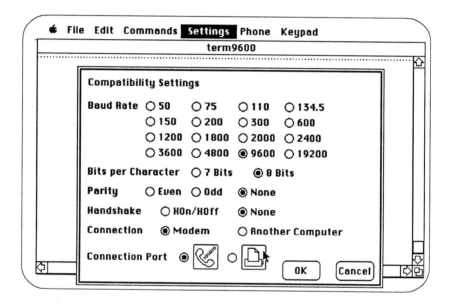

Figure 1. Settings for a communications program

Modem

The modem converts digital computer signals into an analogue form suitable for transmission over telephone lines. Another modem at the receiving end converts the signal back into digital form so that it can be read by the host computer, i.e., the computer you wish to connect to.

Most modems work at a speed of 1200 *baud* (bits per second), although older modems transmit data at 300 baud, which is a little slow for serious work. The delays caused by a 300 baud connection soon become frustrating and perhaps expensive since the longer you are connected, the greater the telephone and connect-time charges will be. Modems that operate at 2400 and 4800 baud are available, but they are more expensive.

Telephone

If you are connecting to another computer from your home, you will link the modem to your telephone. Unfortunately, the speed of transmission of data over telephone wires is limited, but it is acceptable.

An alternative to modem/telephone connections which is often used on campus is a direct wire connection. A direct wire connection is much faster than a modem/phone line connection, but the potential distance of transmission is more limited. Direct wire connections are commonly used to link computers together locally in a network, as described below.

A communications session

A typical session in which a microcomputer is used to link up with a mainframe computer consists of the following steps:

1. load the communications software

2. switch on the modem

3. dial the host computer

4. press return when the connection is made

5. log on to the host computer

6. work on the host computer

7. log off the host computer

8. switch off the modem

9. quit the communications program

You will have to check the manual for your communications software to find out in detail how to accomplish these steps.

7.2   On-campus communications

On college campuses, it is often the case that many of the computers are linked to one another in some way. For example, a group of microcomputers may be linked together to form a network. The advantage of linking microcomputers is that the microcomputer users can then share both hardware resources, such as printers, and software such as word processors and data base files. The mainframe computers may also be linked together in a network in a similar way.

Communicating with other computers on campus allows you to work at one computer while at the same time having access to a range of services available on other computers. You might want to communicate with other computers to perform the following tasks:

1. access software on other computers

2. send (and receive) electronic mail

3. read bulletin boards

4. transfer files between computers

5. use a variety of printers

6. search online library catalogues

Access software

Linking up with larger computers gives you access to a greater range of programs, including the following:

- spelling checkers
- formatting programs
- large data bases
- programming languages
- statistical packages

Electronic mail

Sending electronic mail (often called *email*) is a common activity on multi-user computer systems. A mail system allows you to send messages to other people who use the same computer system or network. If the person you want to communicate with is logged on, he or she will get a message on the screen indicating that your message has been received. If the recipient is not logged on, the message is kept in an electronic 'mailbox' until he or she logs on and reads it.

Mechanics of sending electronic mail

There are two approaches to sending mail on the computer. Perhaps the most common method is to call up the mail program by typing **mail** or something similar. You will have to provide the name (usually the account name) of the person you are writing to. If the recipient has an account on a different computer from the one you are working on, you will have to supply an *address*. Computer addresses are often prefixed by an 'at-sign', @. Thus in order to send mail to Daniel who works on a computer called Turing, the command given would be:

mail daniel@turing

Next, you may be prompted for a subject heading for the message. Enter a word or two that describes the topic of your message and press the return key. You may then get a prompt like this:

cc:☐

If you would like other people to receive copies of your message, you can type their account names in response to this prompt. Some people prefer to send copies of their messages to their own account name, so that they have a record of their correspondence. If you don't want to send any copies of your message, simply press the return key.

Finally, you are ready to type in your message. Unfortunately, you may not be able to edit your message in the same way as you edit a file; in fact, you may only be able to use the delete key for correcting errors that you catch immediately. You may even have to hit the return key at the end of each line because there is no word wrap capability.

When you have finished your note, you have to give a command to send it. Once your message is sent, there is no way to retrieve it. This may be embarrassing if you send off a message to the wrong person or if you send off a note by mistake before it is finished. This happens to everyone occasionally.

The other approach to sending mail, which may be the only possibility on some systems, is to write your message in an ordinary file using a text editor, and then send the entire file as a message. The advantage of this method is that you are able to edit your message to your satisfaction before sending it. Some systems allow you to choose whether you want to send mail by using just the mail system without editing capabilities, or whether you want to use an editor to compose your message first.

Mail may be sent to a single individual or to a group of people. Your teacher may have a class list made up so that he or she can send mail to all the students in the class without having to send it to each student individually.

Electronic mail is a new medium, with its own style. Often, conventions are relaxed with respect to normal English grammar and style, such as capitalization. It is better if you do not adopt these looser conventions. Try to send mail without spelling mistakes and grammatical errors.

Here are three examples of messages you might send.

```
Hi Dan,

Are you ready for a study break?

Mike
```

```
Professor Anderson,
I'd like your permission to take your course
on Compiler design.  I haven't taken the
prerequisite courses on Assembly language and
Advanced Computer Architecture, but I have
worked at Systems Software International on
the implementation of cross compilers.
Bill Chen
```

```
Professor Jenkins,

I am a student in your Econ 223 class.  I'm
writing my term paper on the extraction of oil
from the Athabascan tar sands and I'd like to
talk to you about the economic aspects of the
project.
Could I set up a meeting with you sometime
next week?
Maria Lopez
```

Receiving electronic mail

You will know when someone has sent you mail because a message will flash onto your screen. It will say something like:

`You have mail from Daniel`

To read your message, you will have to enter a mail program. After reading each message, you must decide what action to take. Appropriate actions include one or more of the following:

- reply to the message

- delete the message

- remail the message to someone else

- print a copy of the message

- save the message

- save the message as an ordinary file

- mark the message so that you can easily find it again

You will have to check how to do these things in the mail system you are using.

Messages to a terminal

On some systems, there is an additional mode of communication used for short messages. This involves sending messages directly to the screen of another user who is logged on to the same system. Since sending a message in this fashion may be viewed by the recipient as an intrusion, you should only use it in emergencies or with friends. The command may be **send** or **to**. You type:

to b.billie How's it going?

Then the message `How's it going?` will appear on the screen of b.billie's terminal.

Bulletin boards

If you do not have any mail to read, you can always read the messages that have been posted on an electronic bulletin board by other users. You have probably seen bulletin boards around campus, perhaps in your department or at the student union. These are boards on which messages and announcements are posted. Computer bulletin boards, which are called *bboards* (pronounced 'bee-boards'), fulfill several functions. They may be a general forum for announcements or discussions, where faculty and students advertise items for sale or rooms for rent, or even argue about political events.

Other bboards cover a variety of specialized interests, which may range from science fiction to UNIX. Figure 2 shows part of the bboard of the Stanford Macintosh Users Group (SMUG).

```
MM>bboard smug
Reading BBoard file <BBOARD>SMUG.TXT.1
N 1) 1-Mar Lance Nakata Menusort and Jclock (588
chars)
N 2) 1-Mar Lance Nakata CrashSaver (380 chars)
N 3) 1-Mar Joseph Mitchell 128K Mac for trade (497
chars)
N 4) 1-Mar Gustavo Fernand Next SMUG general meeting
- Krist (851 chars)
N 5) 1-Mar Michael Wang Student representative to
Apple (836 chars)
N 6) 2-Mar Lance Nakata Re:  "Scientist's Helper"
(?)  quer (666 chars)
N 7) 2-Mar Peter Gale TurboPascal for Mac?  (596
chars)
```

Figure 2. Part of a bboard

In order to read the messages on a bboard, you simply call up the bboard either at the exec level or from within the mail program. In the example in Figure 2, the user first entered the mail program. Then, at the mail program prompt, MM>, the command **bboard smug** was entered.

The response is a list of bboard items that haven't yet been read (hence the N on the left-hand side for 'not read'). For each message you can see a message number, the date of the message, the sender's name, and the subject of the message. The number in parentheses indicates the length (the number of characters) of the message.

You can look at any one of these messages by giving a read command followed by the message number of the item you want to read.

```
MM>read 7
Message 7 (596 characters):
Received:  from LOTS-B by LOTS-A with Pup; Sun 2 Mar
86 12:25:20-PST
Date:  Sun 2 Mar 86 12:25:15-PST
From:  Peter Gale <W.WIND@LOTS-B>
Subject:  TurboPascal for Mac?
To:  Smug@LOTS-A
Message-ID:  <12187559755.27.W.WIND@LOTS-B>

Has anyone heard a release date for Borland's Turbo
Pascal for the Mac, or a description of its
features? (According to InfoWorld, Phillipe Kahn
announced it at the Mac show in S.F. in Jan.)
————
R>□
```

Figure 3. Reading a message

On this system, in order to look at message 7 concerning TurboPascal, you type **read 7**, as shown in Figure 3.

Messages sent to you by electronic mail will look very much like this one. Don't worry about all the information given in the top half; all you are really interested in is the message in the bottom half.

Sending a message to a bboard is similar to sending mail, except that the address is a bboard rather than a person. You can check the details of sending messages to a bboard on the computer you are using.

File transfer

Transferring files between computers is a common activity on campus. The name 'file transfer' is a bit misleading, however, since what is transferred from one computer to another is not the original file, but a copy. What you end up with after a file transfer operation is two files on two computers.

Unfortunately, file transfer can sometimes be unreliable. Basically, you would like a file transfer program that is fast and error-free. In other words, you want the file to be transferred quickly without loss, addition or modification of data. It is difficult, however, to achieve both speed and accuracy. For example, if your file transfer program has an error-checking capability, then the transfer will be slowed down to some extent.

One file transfer program for large computers is *ftp*. To transfer a file, you go through the following steps:

1. call up the ftp program (by typing **ftp**)

2. specify the name of the host computer (the one you want to get access to)

3. log on to the host computer

4. send a file to (or get a file from) the host computer

5. exit from the ftp program

This process is illustrated in the following example, in which a file is sent to a computer called Russell.

```
@ftp
Stanford TOPS-20 FTP 3.0, type HELP if you need it.
FTP>open russell
< Vax/Unix Pup FTP - version 3.0 Server Russell
FTP>login barlow
Password:
FTP>send wwc4.tex
PS:<BARLOW>WWC4.TEX.60 (to remote file) filetrans.tex

PS:<BARLOW>WWC4.TEX.60 => filetrans.tex !!!  [OK]
FTP>quit
@□
```

As you can see, the process is quite straightforward. After calling up the ftp program, we access the host computer (Russell) and log on. Then we send the file WWC4.TEX to Russell, giving it the name filetrans.tex. Finally we quit the ftp program and return to the exec level. All the words typed by the user are shown in boldface. The only thing that was typed that isn't shown is the password, which as usual does not appear on the screen.

File transfer between a microcomputer and a mainframe over a telephone line will take longer and will be slightly more difficult to set up than the ftp session shown above. Also, the chance of error is greater. Still, transfer over telephone lines is often worth doing, since it is much better to transfer data from one computer to another and correct a few errors than to retype the whole file.

Why would you want to transfer files from one computer to another? There are several reasons for doing this. For example, you might transfer or *download* a file from a mainframe to a microcomputer disk so that you can work on the file at home on your microcomputer. Conversely, you might want to transfer or *upload* a file from a microcomputer to a mainframe in order to use the higher quality printers available on the mainframe. Finally, it is often a good idea to transfer copies of your important files to another computer for safekeeping.

Printers

As mentioned above, one reason to transfer a file from a microcomputer to a larger computer is to take advantage of the fancier printers that are available. A large computer is likely to have better printers than your microcomputer; for example, laser printers are commonly available with large computers, but are quite expensive for microcomputer owners to buy. Thus you might write a paper using your microcomputer, printing out the rough drafts on a dot-matrix printer; you can then transfer the final version to the mainframe so that you can print the paper on a good quality printer. (An alternative is to take the diskette containing your finished paper to a store or campus facility where you can pay to print it out on a laser printer.)

Library catalogues

Another use of communications is in searching library catalogues from your computer, as described in Chapter 11. One advantage of using a computer to search the library catalogue is that it increases your access to the library; you don't have to physically go there in order to get the reference information you require. In addition, you may be able to capture references or other information directly in your files and so reduce the amount of typing that you have to do.

7.3   Off-campus communications

Most of your computer communications will be on campus, but there are off-campus services that you might use occasionally, such as:

1. electronic mail

2. bboards

3. commercial services, such as news and business information

4. commercial data base services, such as DIALOG

The mainframe that you use may be set up to communicate with other computers off campus. Off-campus links are likely to be through one of the following computer networks:

- Darpanet

- Tymnet

- Telenet

- Bitnet

- Csnet

The first one, Darpanet (formerly Arpanet) is maintained by the United States Department of Defense. The others are provided by commercial organizations, so if you make use of them you will be charged. To find out more about communicating off campus from your mainframe, you should talk to your system administrators. There are restrictions on the use of some of these networks. For example, you cannot use Darpanet for advertising purposes, nor for any commercial or personal gain.

Electronic mail

Mainframe computers are connected world-wide; hence, it is possible to send computer messages virtually anywhere as long as the computer you are using is connected to the appropriate network. To get your message to the person you want to communicate with, you need to know his or her computer address.

There are various ways in which you can send mail off campus. Commercial services such as CompuServe provide a variety of services including electronic mail facilities. However, for academic purposes it is more useful to use a network service (such as Darpanet or the others listed above) that provides world-wide links among colleges and research institutions.

Bboards

Off-campus bboards offer a much greater range of expertise and knowledge for the discussion of particular topics than bboards on campus. And in fact there are a great number of bboards set up to cater to groups interested in specific topics. Bboards concerned with topics of interest to computer users are very common; for example, there are bboards for Macintosh users and for UNIX users. In addition, bboards are also used for non-computer interest groups. For example, there is a bboard in Los Angeles that provides contact between actors and film directors.

Some bboards require you to pay a subscription fee to use them. For others, all you have to pay is your telephone bill if you are using your microcomputer at home.

Commercial services

More and more information services are becoming available on computers. These services allow you to carry out banking transactions from your home, buy and sell shares of stock or find out what the Dow-Jones index is. These services are provided by commercial networks such as CompuServe.

Since these 'information utilities' are mainly set up for business, rather than for the academic community, they will not be discussed further here.

Commercial data bases

There are some international companies that offer a service that may be useful to you in your academic work. Companies of this type, such as DIALOG, maintain several data bases of bibliographic information.

These services are usually used by large organizations rather than individuals, and so you should approach a librarian to get advice about searching one of the data bases available. The steps involved in setting up a DIALOG search are discussed in Chapter 11.

DIALOG has set up an organization that allows individuals to search certain data bases in off-peak times, in other words, at night or on weekends. This organization is called Knowledge Index. Individual subscribers who have a modem and a computer are able to search the data bases made available by Knowledge Index. You should seek advice from a librarian before paying a subscription fee for these services.

Questions

1. What do you need in order to link a microcomputer to a mainframe?

2. Give three reasons why you might want to communicate with other computers.

3. What are the steps involved in sending mail on your computer?

4. How do you read a message on your computer system?

5. What are some bboards that you have access to?

6. Discuss the consequences of the fact that if you have a micro-computer and the appropriate hardware and software, you can dial up computers all over the world.

8

Data bases and spreadsheets

In this chapter we will concentrate on two uses of computers: data base managers and spreadsheet programs. Data bases provide a convenient way to store information. (If you want to see straightaway how to set up a data base, you can turn to Section 8.2.) Spreadsheets are also used to store information, but their main role is in performing numerical calculations on data, as will be discussed in the second half of the chapter.

8.1 Working with data bases

A *data base* (sometimes written database) is simply a store of information in a structured form. Everyday examples of personal data bases include appointment books, address books, and bank statements. These information stores contain data in a well-known and standardized format for easy reference.

Since a college or university is in many ways a repository of stored information, it is not surprising to find that a variety of computer data bases are used in the academic environment. For instance, you might create a data base to store research data (such as the results of an experiment) or the speeches of John F. Kennedy. Alternatively, you might make use of ready-made data bases such as census reports, land-use data, or a library catalogue.

For your academic work, perhaps you keep track of information by putting notes on index cards. For example, you might write down a bibliographic reference on a card, as shown in Figure 1. In this example, the top line contains the name of the author on the left-hand side of the card; title and publication information are given in subsequent lines. Following this is the book's call number, or library identification number, to make it easy for you to find the book in the library. (Note: Chapter 12 discusses the use of index cards and data bases for keeping track of research and bibliographic material.)

```
Sharples, Mike


        Cognition, Computers and Writing.

Ellis Horwood:   Chichester, England 1985

PE 1404 S46
```

Figure 1. An index card used to record a reference

A single index card by itself, however, is not of great use. What makes index cards really useful for storing information is that each one forms a small part of a larger system in which the same type of information is organized in the same way. Normally, one works with a whole stack of index cards, ordered in some logical fashion. This makes it easy to find the information you need on a particular card.

Computer data bases contain the same sort of information as a stack of index cards. However, the power of the computer makes it potentially far more useful as a research tool. A computer not only can store a vast amount of information in a small amount of space, but also allows that data to be retrieved in ways that would be very difficult and time-consuming using index cards.

There are three main reasons for adding data bases to your academic toolkit. One is convenience. Once a data base is set up, information can be stored in a way that allows rapid retrieval and easy modification.

The second reason applies to data base management programs, which are special applications designed to help you get more information out of your data base. Data base management programs (also called data base managers) are able to sort or find information based on characteristics that you choose yourself. The use of these programs to sort information will be discussed in Section 8.2.

A third reason for using a data base manager, which is quite subtle, is to search for patterns in your data. Once you have a data base in the computer, the retrieval of information may itself be a kind of manipulation of data, which can reveal patterns in the data that would otherwise be difficult to perceive.

Unfortunately, learning how to use a data base manager and entering the data may take a considerable amount of time. Because of the investment of time involved in setting up data bases, you will probably want to make use of them selectively. For example, you may find it worthwhile to set up a computer data base to deal with the research results that you will use in your thesis or dissertation, but not for notes you make for a term paper.

Using an editor to construct a data base

Many students keep bibliographic references on index cards. If you wanted to store this information on a computer, then probably the first thing that comes to mind is to use a text editor. You can open a file and simply list your references in alphabetical order by author, as shown below.

```
Anderson, S. 1982.  Where's Morphology?  Linguistic
Inquiry 13.571-612.


Corbett, G. G. 1979.  The agreement hierarchy.  Journal
of Linguistics 15.203-224.


Fassi Fehri, A. 1981.  Theorie lexicale-fonctionelle,
controle et accorde en arabe moderne.  Arabica 28.29-32.
```

Is this any better than having a set of index cards? It is, in a number of ways. First of all, once you have a computer file of references, the information is accessible and you will be able to transfer it directly into papers that you are writing on the computer. (How to do this is discussed in Section 9.2.)

What if you want to add another reference? Well, you can just move the cursor to the appropriate point in the file and add the new entry. Thus, adding information (called *data entry*) is straightforward. What do you do when you want to 'retrieve' a bibliographic reference? Here again you can use the editor to find the information you want by using a special *search* command (see Section 6.2). Thus, the editor allows you to construct a simple data base in which information can be conveniently stored, easily modified, and quickly retrieved.

Text editors, while they may be useful for information arranged in a very simple structure like a bibliography, are not designed to take full advantage of the computer's data processing abilities. As long as you are going to take the trouble to enter a large amount of data into the computer, it is worth considering the advantages of programs that are specifically designed for record-keeping. Such an applications program, called a *data base manager* or DBMS (data base management system), allows you to create and manipulate your own data bases with great flexibility.

> **!** If you plan to transfer data from a data base management program directly into an ordinary text file produced by an editor, then you must check whether this is possible *before* you start to enter data in the data base.

8.2   Using a data base manager

The main steps in setting up a data base using a data base manager are the following:

1. loading the data base manager

2. designing the data base format

3. entering data

4. retrieving data

5. modifying data

> ***** Don't forget to save your work often and make backup copies of your data base files.

As an example, let us imagine that you want to construct a data base to keep track of the addresses of your colleagues. First, you have to decide what information you are going to include. In this example, we will include name, street address, city, state, and zip (postal) code.

Loading the data base manager

To get started, you need to load the data base software and open a new data base file.

Designing the form

When using index cards, you work within an implicit framework or design. That is, you select a particular place on the card where you write the name, address, and other desired information in a particular sequence. The framework is implicit because you probably won't write explicit labels like <u>Name</u> preceding each piece of information.

The equivalent of an index card in the data base is a single entry or *record*. Each record contains information under a number of categories, which are explicitly labelled to indicate the type of information the category contains. Thus, each record in our example has five categories of information: name, street address, city, state, and zip code.

The necessity for making explicit the structure of the information in a data base means that you must first design a kind of electronic form before you can begin to enter data into a new data base file. To construct this form, you must decide on the number of categories of information that you want to store. In a data base, these categories are called *fields*. Since each record in our example contains five such categories, it is necessary to construct a form that is divided into five fields.

For each field, you must provide a heading or label that describes the contents of the field (Name, Address, etc.). In addition, you may have to specify the type of data that each field can hold, either text or numerical data. You can choose text as the type of data even if you want to enter figures such as dates or zip codes. You only need to specify numerical data for a field when you want to perform numerical operations.

Figure 2 shows a data base form in a program called Microsoft File. The bottom half of the screen shows the form, in which the five category labels for our address file have been added. These labels also appear as headings in the data base itself, which is shown in the top half of the screen. (Once the form is completed, it will be hidden from view so that you only see the actual data base.)

Entering data

Once you have designed the form, you can enter your data. Data entry is very much like filling in the blanks on an ordinary paper form. To enter information into the data base, you must do the following:

- move to a field in a particular record

- enter the data

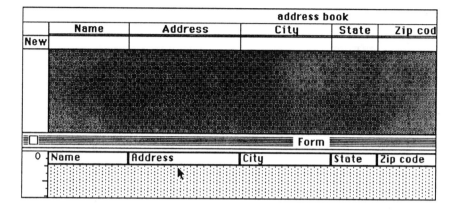

Figure 2. A data base form

- press return and move to the next field

You will be able to move both forwards and backwards through the data base to get to specific points at which you wish to enter data. Once the cursor is positioned in the appropriate place, you can simply type in the corresponding data. Don't worry if you make a mistake; you can always use the delete key to remove the error.

After entering some information, the data base looks like the screen shown in Figure 3. In this example, there are just six entries (or records) in the data base. Each of these records contains the five fields of information we chose in our form. The information contained in the fields may be only partially visible, but the size of a field can easily be changed when necessary so that all the data can be seen.

Retrieving data

There are two main ways of retrieving data using a data base manager. One way is by means of a *search*. Performing a search in a data base is similar to searching using a word processor. To carry out a search, you give a search command and then provide the string of characters you want the computer to search for. It checks through the file and stops at the record containing the target string.

	Name	Address	City	State	Zip code
1	Bold, John	47 Crabtree Ct.	Boston	MA	02134
2	Everdene, Danie	89 Allington Way	Barchester	CT	14618
3	Oak, Gabriel	336 Madding Lane	Denver	CO	77277
4	Bennett, Elizab	37 Sand Hill Rd	Menlo Park	CA	94025
5	Gresham, Franc	2327 22nd St.	San Francisco	CA	94114
6	Roberts, Lucy	3909 Valley St.	San Francisco	CA	94163
New					

Figure 3. The completed data base

You can also carry out a search that will retrieve a range of records rather than just one. For example, you might search for all zip codes greater than 94024 and less than 94115. The result will be a list of records whose zip codes fit the search. Another example is a search for all the books by a particular author in a computerized library catalogue. (In Chapter 11, we will discuss how to search an online library data base.)

The other retrieval method used by data base managers is *sorting*. Sorting refers to rearranging all the entries in a data base according to a specified type of information. For example, suppose you wanted to arrange the data base shown in Figure 3 so that the records appear in alphabetical order by name. To do this, you must use the sort command and instruct the computer to list the records in alphabetical order of the first field (the Name field). See Figure 4.

The computer then sorts the records and redisplays them as shown in Figure 5. As you can see, the names in the records are now in alphabetical order.

However, perhaps you decide you would rather order the entries with respect to the numerical order of their zip codes. This is very easy to do. Again you give a sort command. This time the sort command acts on the zip code field. The computer re-sorts the records and presents the results, as shown in Figure 6.

address book				
	Name	Address	City	State	Zip cod
1	Everdene, Danie	89 Allington Way	Barchester	CT	14618
2	Bold, John	47 Crabtree Ct.	Boston	MA	02134
3	Oak, Gabriel	336 Madding Lane	Denver	CO	77277
4	Bennett, Elizab	37 Sand Hill Rd	Menlo Park	CA	94025
5	Gresham		Sort		14
6	Roberts,				63

Sort   Clear

	Name	Address	City
1	A->Z		

Figure 4. The sort command

address book				
	Name	Address	City	State	Zip code
1	Bennett, Elizab	37 Sand Hill Rd	Menlo Park	CA	94025
2	Bold, John	47 Crabtree Ct.	Boston	MA	02134
3	Everdene, Danie	89 Allington Way	Barchester	CT	14618
4	Gresham, Franc	2327 22nd St.	San Francisco	CA	94114
5	Oak, Gabriel	336 Madding Lane	Denver	CO	77277
6	Roberts, Lucy	3909 Valley St.	San Francisco	CA	94163
New					

Figure 5. Data base entries displayed in alphabetical order

	Name	Address	City	State	Zip code
1	Bold, John	47 Crabtree Ct.	Boston	MA	02134
2	Everdene, Danie	89 Allington Way	Barchester	CT	14618
3	Oak, Gabriel	336 Madding Lane	Denver	CO	77277
4	Bennett, Elizabε	37 Sand Hill Rd	Menlo Park	CA	94025
5	Gresham, Franc	2327 22nd St.	San Francisco	CA	94114
6	Roberts, Lucy	3909 Valley St.	San Francisco	CA	94163
New					

Figure 6. Data base entries displayed in zip code order

This sorting capability can be extremely useful, particularly for more complex data bases. Most data base management programs have the ability to sort data along several dimensions at once, which is quite difficult to do by hand. For example, you can sort the data in our example first by city and then, within each city, by zip code. Look at Figure 7 to see the result of this sorting operation. The records are sorted by city in alphabetical order; if the city entry for two or more records is the same (e.g., San Francisco), then the records are sorted by numerical order of the zip code.

Modifying the data base

There are two types of modification that can be made using a data base manager. One involves modifying the form, and the other, modifying the data.

Most data base managers are flexible enough to allow you to modify the electronic form you used to create the data base. For example, you may decide that you want to add a new field or remove an old field. Alternatively, you may want to make other changes such as altering the name or title of a field. You will have to check your manual to see how to accomplish these changes.

If you want to alter the information within particular records, you can position the cursor at the point you wish to make a change,

	Name	street	city	state	zip code	
1	Everdene, Dan	89 Allington Wa	Barchester	CT	14618	
2	Bold, John	47 Crabtree Ct.	Boston	MA	02134	
3	Oak, Gabriel	336 Madding La	Denver	CO	77277	
4	Bennett, Eliza	37 Sand Hill Rd.	Menlo Park	CA	94025	
5	Gresham, Fran	2327 22nd St.	San Francisco	CA	94114	
6	Roberts, Lucy	3909 Valley St.	San Francisco	CA	94163	
New						

Figure 7. Data base entries arranged by city and zip code

and then use simple editing commands. New records are added by typing information into the record marked 'New' at the end of the data base. Records can also be deleted or copied to a new data base file.

8.3   Working with spreadsheets

Spreadsheets are applications programs that allow you to store and manipulate numerical, often financial, data. Because spreadsheets are such an improvement over the 'paper and pencil' ledger systems used by businesses until just a few years ago, their development gave an important boost to the spread of early microcomputers.

All spreadsheets, such as Lotus 1-2-3, Multiplan or Excel, follow a standard format. The layout, as you can see in the Multiplan spreadsheet in Figure 8, consists of a large page divided into numbered rows and columns. Spreadsheets are quite large. What you see on the screen is simply a window revealing a small part of a giant page containing perhaps hundreds of rows and columns.

Thus the whole spreadsheet is made up of boxes or *cells*, which are identified according to their position in rows and columns. In the spreadsheet shown in Figure 8, the cells are identified by means of numbers prefixed by R (for row) and C (for column). As you

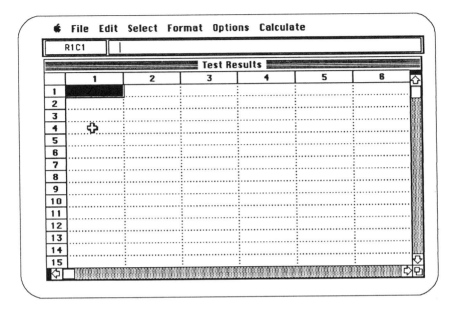

Figure 8. A spreadsheet—Multiplan

can see, the cell located at the intersection of the first row and the first column is highlighted in black. This cell, since it is in Row 1, Column 1, is identified as R1C1. Similarly, R5C7 designates the cell in the fifth row, 7th column, and so on. (Other spreadsheet programs use identifiers consisting of letters and numbers, for example, A1, D6, H90; but in either case the organizing principle is the same.)

In this spreadsheet, the plus sign (+) serves as a pointer. The pointer is used to select a cell. Using the mouse, you move the pointer to a cell and click the mouse button. (On prompt and cursor computers, you use cursor-movement keys to move around the spreadsheet.) The selected cell is highlighted in black. At the top of the spreadsheet, information about the selected cell is indicated in a *status line*. On the left side of the status line, the identifying label of the selected cell appears. In addition, whenever a cell is selected its contents appear on the right side of the status line. In Figure 8, since cell R1C1 is empty, this portion of the status line is blank.

Each box or cell in the spreadsheet can hold one piece of data, which might be a numerical value or a label (e.g., a heading like 'Expenses'). In each cell, you can enter one of the following:

- a number or a date

- a word (e.g., a heading)

- a formula

We will discuss each of these in the example below.

8.4   An example of a spreadsheet

At the simplest level, you can think of a spreadsheet as a means of storing numerical or other data in lists or tables. To enter data in a spreadsheet, you go through the following steps:

1. call up (load) the spreadsheet program

2. select a cell by moving the cursor or pointer

3. enter data (e.g., a heading or a number)

4. repeat (2) and (3) as necessary, saving the spreadsheet from time to time

5. save and exit

For example, let us suppose that you are a teaching assistant for a course and need to keep records of students' test scores. A spreadsheet is a good way to store such records. After loading the spreadsheet, you open a new file and go through the process outlined above. You select a cell, for example, R4C2 (row 4, column 2), enter the name of the first student and press the return key. Then you move one cell to the right, to cell R4C3, and enter the student's test score. If you make a mistake, you can use the delete key to remove the error and then enter the correct material. You continue until you have entered all the students' names and their test scores, as illustrated in Figure 9.

By adding a title and appropriate headings for the columns, you can make the organization of the spreadsheet clear. Since spreadsheets can become very complex, a clear layout with well-labelled cells is important. When you have a final version of the file, you might want to print out a copy of the spreadsheet.

On menu and pointer computers, spreadsheet commands such as *print* are chosen from menus, as discussed on page 44. On prompt and cursor computers, spreadsheet commands are often prefixed by a slash (/); the command to print, for example, might be /p.

R16C6							
Test Results							
	1	2	3	4	5	6	
1							
2			Test 10/1				
3							
4		Abboud	75				
5		Akimoto	80				
6		Chen	66				
7		Gonzales	72				
8		Ishikawa	73				
9		Piñón	76				
10							
11							
12							
13							
14							
15							

Figure 9. A spreadsheet containing test scores

Before quitting the spreadsheet, make sure that you have saved the final version and given it a suitable name. The next time you want to work on the file, you might be able to open the spreadsheet file directly, or you may have to enter the spreadsheet program first and then load the spreadsheet file.

Values, labels and formulas

In the test score example, the spreadsheet is being used to simply store data in the form of numerical values (75, 80, ...) and labels (Abboud, Akimoto, ...) in a table format. One advantage of using a spreadsheet for this type of data is that the spreadsheet provides a pre-set table format so that data entry and formatting are quite easy. As we have seen, however, simply storing data is the least demanding use of a computer.

The computer really works for you when it is processing information. Processing information in spreadsheets means performing numerical calculations, or 'number crunching,' on the values stored in the cells.

You can think of a spreadsheet program as having a calculator contained within it. This calculator is linked to all the cells, enabling you to perform arithmetic operations (addition, multiplication, etc.) on the numerical values of the cells. For example, you can instruct the spreadsheet to add up the values contained in a series of cells and enter the result in a new cell.

To perform these arithmetical operations, you have to specify the following:

- a cell to store the result of the calculation

- an arithmetic function

- the cells whose values are involved in the calculation

An example showing how this process works will be discussed below.

Calculations in a spreadsheet are not just limited to simple arithmetic operations. Most spreadsheet programs include functions such as average, square, log, and numerous others.

The processing power of a spreadsheet is harnessed by the use of formulae, or more often formulas, which are associated with particular cells. We will discuss formulas next.

Use of a formula

To give a very simple illustration of the use of a formula in a spreadsheet, let us continue working with the test score example. Suppose that you would like to calculate the average score for the class on this test, and wish to enter the result at the bottom of the test score column, in cell R11C3. (See Figure 9.)

To do this, you enter a formula (rather than a numerical value) in cell R11C3. The formula tells the spreadsheet how to calculate the value that you want to enter in the cell. The formula in this case is quite straightforward; it will simply represent the average of all the test scores. Since these test scores are already entered in the spreadsheet, all you need to do is indicate the function 'average' and use the pointer to pick out the cells containing the test scores.

Step by step, you do the following:

1. select cell R11C3

2. enter the symbol = to indicate that you are going to enter a formula, rather than a word or number

3. choose *average* from the list of numerical functions

4. move the pointer to cell R4C3 and press the mouse button

5. move the pointer to cell R5C3 and press the mouse button

6. continue down the column until you have selected all the cells up to R9C3

7. press return

R11C3	⊗	=AVERAGE(R[-7]C:R[-2]C)				

Test Results

	1	2	3	4	5	6
1						
2			Test 10/1			
3						
4		Abboud	75			
5		Akimoto	80			
6		Chen	66			
7		Gonzales	72			
8		Ishikawa	73			
9		Piñón	76			
10						
11			=AVERAGE(R			
12						
13						
14						
15						

Figure 10. Using a formula in a spreadsheet

Figure 10 shows the spreadsheet after executing step 6 above. As steps 1 to 6 are executed, the status line shows not only the cell selected to hold the average (R11C3) but also the formula associated with that cell. In the formula shown in the status line, the range of cells you chose for averaging is also indicated. R[-7] refers to the cell seven rows above the selected cell; R[-2] is the cell two rows above the selected cell. Thus the values for these cells and all those between them will be included in the averaging function.

Pressing the return key causes the spreadsheet to calculate the average of the test scores and enter the result in cell R11C3, as shown in Figure 11.

More complex spreadsheets can be built up in a similar manner. The formulas can take information from cells anywhere on the spreadsheet and incorporate it in complex calculations.

Modifying spreadsheets

There are many ways to modify spreadsheets. For example, you may want to change individual numbers or words on the spreadsheet, the

File Edit Select Format Options Calculate

R19C6	

Test Results

	1	2	3	4	5	6
1						
2			Test 10/1			
3						
4		Abboud	75			
5		Akimoto	80			
6		Chen	66			
7		Gonzales	72			
8		Ishikawa	73			
9		Piñón	76			
10						
11			73.67			
12						
13						
14						
15						

Figure 11. The result of a formula is calculated

position of the data on the spreadsheet, or you may want to edit the
formula associated with a particular cell. As you might expect, you
will easily be able to do all these things on your spreadsheet. For
instance, if you found that you had entered one of the test scores
in Figure 11 incorrectly, a simple way to make the change would
be to highlight the appropriate cell, delete the old value, and enter
the new correct value. You will have to check in the manual to see
how to perform more complex editing operations on your spreadsheet
program.

What happens to all the calculations already carried out by the
spreadsheet when you edit the numbers and formulas in your cells?
The wonderful thing about the spreadsheets is that they will automatically carry out all the necessary recalculations. Simply changing
a single value makes the spreadsheet recalculate all the figures that
depend upon that value.

The use of data bases and spreadsheets

Data base managers and spreadsheets are sometimes combined with
other applications programs, such as word processors and communications programs, into what is called an *integrated program*. In
addition, data bases may allow you to modify the form of the data

so that it is suitable for inclusion in reports. Spreadsheets often have a component which enables you to display graphs based on the data entered in the spreadsheet.

In this chapter, only the most basic uses of data bases and spreadsheets have been introduced. Nevertheless, you can probably see the potential power of these programs. Once you have had some practice in designing data bases and spreadsheets, you will be able to use them to produce complex models of business or other systems.

Questions

1. Give an example of a computer data base in everyday life.

2. What are records and fields in a data base?

3. Discuss the advantages and disadvantages of using a word processor rather than a data base manager to store information.

4. In the data base program you are using, how do you move forwards through the data base? Backwards?

5. What is the difference between a search and a sort?

6. Discuss the differences between data bases and spreadsheets.

7. What does a spreadsheet consist of?

8. What is the first and the last:

    (a) row

    (b) column

    in the spreadsheet you are using?

9. How do you distinguish labels, data and formulas in your spreadsheet program?

9
Advanced editing techniques

After using an editor for a year or so, you will have a good understanding of the way in which it works, and will not experience many 'surprises.' At this stage, when you have mastered most of the editor's commands and can predict what the likely outcome of any instructions will be, then you are ready to explore some advanced editing techniques. If you are a relative novice, you might want to read this chapter just so that you get an idea of what the possibilities are.

What advanced editing techniques will be available to you depends to some extent on the editor that you are using. Editors tend to have the same elementary features, but they vary with regard to the more advanced features they offer.

In this chapter, we will cover the following topics:

1. using macros

2. moving text from one file to another

3. using a word processor in conjunction with other programs such as formatting programs, spelling checkers, and online dictionaries

4. customizing your editor

If you find yourself using a particular command several times in a row, then you are not using your editor to its fullest potential. There are two ways of correcting this problem: you can use a more powerful command that is supplied by your editor, or you can define your own command. This latter option is called defining a *macro*.

How do you find out what powerful commands are available? One method is to read or reread the manual for your editor. Alternatively, you may be able to use an online help system. Both these methods will help you learn new commands or discover new options for commands you already know.

9.1   Using macros

If you need a command that is not supplied by your editor, you may be able to construct the command yourself by stringing together simpler commands. The resulting 'super command,' defined by the user, is called a macro. Because macros are so useful, they are found in many applications programs besides editors, for example, spreadsheets and data base managers.

There are three steps involved in using a macro:

1. defining the macro

2. naming and saving the macro

3. executing the macro

Look in the index of your manual to see if there is any mention of macros. If there is no facility for defining macros, you may be able to find a separate applications program that will let you define macros to use in your editor. For example, one program for the IBM PC that gives you the ability to create macros is ProKey; there is also a program for the Apple Macintosh called MouseTracks.

Defining a macro

You will have to find out how to define a macro on your word processor. MacWrite and WordStar (Version 3.3) do not have a macro capability at present, but EMACS does. In EMACS you can define a macro by entering a special mode in which everything you type at the keyboard is recorded in the computer's memory. Later, when you give a command to execute the macro, this stored recording of your keystrokes will be 'played back.'

Perhaps you are not yet quite sure what sort of thing a macro would do. Well, let us look at a simple example. Assuming that your word processor has a command to delete a word, we might create a command to delete three words at once. The new command, or macro, can be constructed on the basis of the simpler word-deletion command.

To define such a macro in EMACS, you enter the macro definition mode by typing the following command:

ctrl x (

(That is, the command *ctrl x* followed by a left parenthesis.) Once you do this, then whatever you type at the keyboard, whether commands or text, is recorded. For this example, you simply repeat the command to delete a word three times. Even though you are defining a macro, the commands you give as part of the definition still affect your file and so three words will be deleted. You then end the macro definition by typing the following command:

ctrl x)

Saving and naming a macro

Once you have defined your macro, the next step is to give it a name and save it in a file, which can also contain other macros. For example, the macro just defined could be given a name like '3d' and saved in a special macro file.

Executing a macro

Now that you have defined and named your macro, you can execute the command any time you wish. In EMACS, you would give the command:

ESC x **3d**

The computer will respond to this command by deleting the first three words following the cursor.

This is a simple example, but it may suggest to you the power of the macro capability. You can build up a whole set of macros, some quite complex, based on the basic commands found in your word processing program. For example, you might define a 'letterhead' macro that automatically enters your address at the top of the page in letters that you write on the computer.

If a macro works, it is very gratifying; your text changes in front of your eyes, as if somebody were typing commands very quickly at the keyboard. You get the satisfying feeling of saving yourself a lot of work. Naturally, there are potential dangers. You may give a macro and then look on helplessly as your text is efficiently transformed into garbage. Make a copy of your file before trying the macro, or at least save the file before executing the macro. In case something goes wrong, be prepared to quit without saving after executing the macro. You could also experiment with a new macro using a test file.

9.2   Moving text from one file to another

In Chapter 6, you learned how to move a block of text from the file you are working on into a new file. What do you do if you have some text in two separate files and you want to transfer text from one of the files to the other? There are several possibilities; which one is best depends both on what you want to do and on what features your word processor has available.

Here are three ways of transferring text between files:

1. adding one file to the end of another file

2. inserting one file into the middle of another one

3. transferring part of a file to another file

There are probably several ways to accomplish each of these operations. Below we will describe some basic methods that are useful and efficient.

Append

Adding one file to the end of another file can often be accomplished with the operating system command **append**. If you want to add a file called 'references' to a file called 'biology-paper,' you can give a command similar to the following:

append references biology-paper

After execution of the command, the file 'references' is the same as it was, but the file 'biology-paper' has grown due to the addition of a copy of the file 'references.'

The append option is not available on some menu and pointer computers; if this is the case with your computer, you will have to use one of the other methods of transfer such as 'cut and paste,' described below.

Inserting a file into your text

Suppose you wish to put the contents of a file called 'section2' in the middle of another file. Most word processors allow you to do this. In EMACS, for instance, you position the cursor in the place where you want to insert the file, then you give the command:

ESC x **insert file section2**

Check to see if there is a command for inserting a file on the word processor you use. Try it out.

If you use a word processor like MacWrite, you can 'cut and paste' from one file to another. To insert a file in this way, you open the file that you want to insert, and then select the whole document. Next, you select the command *copy*. You close the file and open the second file, the one you want to insert the file into. Finally, you position the cursor in the appropriate place and choose *paste*. The contents of the first file will then appear inside the second.

Split screens and multiple windows

When starting to work on a document, you are presented with a text area—the computer equivalent of a blank page—which shows a portion of your file. Generally, it is better to work with as much text as possible displayed on the screen. If you can only view a few lines of text at a time, it is more difficult to produce a coherent structure when you are writing. This is one disadvantage of menus: they take up valuable space on the screen. (Some menu-based word processors like WordStar allow you to hide the menu once you have become familiar with the commands, so that the whole screen can be used to display your text.)

It is very useful sometimes to split the text area of the screen into two parts so that you can work on two separate files at the same time. Having this ability makes it easier to move text (or graphics) from one page to another or from one file to another. Similarly, a window editor may allow you to open more than one window at once so that you can view two separate files simultaneously.

Suppose, for instance, you have used the results of an online bibliographic search to create a file containing references. One way to add the references to the end of your paper is to use **append** to attach the whole file of references to the end of the file containing your paper. However, if you wanted to add only a selection of the references, you could use a split screen (with a screen editor). In this case you would use the following procedure:

1. Open the file containing your paper.

2. Split the screen into two.

3. Make sure the cursor is in the lower half of the split screen and open the file containing your references. The top half of the screen will then contain the paper and the bottom half will contain the references.

4. Mark (or delete and immediately undelete) a block of text containing the reference(s) you want to transfer.

5. Move the cursor to the top half of the screen.

6. Position the cursor at the appropriate place in the file containing your paper.

7. Transfer (or undelete) the block of text.

8. If there are more references you wish to insert, move the cursor to the lower half of the screen and repeat steps 4 - 6 until you have transferred all the required references.

9. Return to a full screen.

This is a fairly complicated procedure, but it is very useful. It is similar to transferring text from one part of a file to another; what you have to know in addition is how to split the screen and how to move from one half of the screen to the other. (Simply moving the cursor will probably not work.) After you have successfully performed this operation several times, it will become quite easy. It is just like physically cutting text from one paper and pasting it into another.

An essentially equivalent procedure is used for transferring text in a window editor. Instead of splitting the screen, you simply open a second window. (Not all window editors have this capability, however.)

In some cases, it may be useful to look at two parts of a long file at the same time. If you have a split screen, or two windows, you can look at the beginning and the end of the same file. For example, you may want to check what you wrote in the introduction to a paper, while you are writing the conclusion. Another use of split screens is to look at what you wrote in your original outline while you are writing the actual paper.

9.3   Word processing and ancillary programs

In this section, we will look briefly at two programs that you can use in conjunction with your word processor. These are:

1. formatting programs

2. online dictionaries and spelling checkers

Formatting programs

Editors always allow some control over the format of texts. For example, you can change the margin settings and perhaps the font. But for other formatting tasks, you may need to use a special formatting program such as Scribe, TROFF, or StarIndex. The newer editors are incorporating more and more of the formatting features found in formatting programs, so you may not have to use a separate program.

If your editor has some formatting capability, you may be able to see directly on the screen how the page will appear when it is printed out. This property of editors is known as *wysiwyg*, which stands for 'what you see is what you get.' This means simply that what you can see on the screen is what your document will look like when it is printed out. You can see, for example, the margins, the line spacing and the page boundaries or *page breaks*.

The fact that you can see the placement of text and page breaks means that you can detect formatting problems on the screen, and can make corrections without having to get a printout.

However, if your editor does not have these capabilities, you may want to use formatting programs to do the following:

1. add footnotes

2. add a bibliography

3. add section headings

4. add an index

Using a formatting program is a two-step process. First, you work in the editor, entering appropriate formatting commands in the text and saving the file. Next, you must run the file through the formatting program. This program interprets your formatting commands and produces a new file (containing footnotes, a bibliography, etc.), which you can then print.

Adding footnotes

As an example, let us look at how a footnote program works. Before discussing special footnoting programs, we will consider how you might insert footnotes using an ordinary editor.

The following text shows an example of a footnote created by an editor. The small raised number or superscript is termed the 'footnote call'; the actual footnote below the text is called the footnote body.

This is an example of a footnote call in the
text using a superscripted number.[1] The
footnote body appears either at the bottom of
the page or at the end of the document.

---

1. This is the body of the footnote.

In an editor, you can make the footnotes yourself by putting a superscripted number in the text and adding the body of the footnote to the end of the paper. This method works quite well for most purposes. The only disadvantages are that you have to keep track of the numbers of the footnotes and if you want to add or delete a footnote, you will have to renumber all the subsequent footnotes.

If you want footnotes to appear at the bottom of the page, then you will have to do quite a bit more work. You will have to adjust the amount of ordinary text on each page in order to leave the appropriate amount of room for the body of the footnote. If changes are made to a page containing a footnote, the footnote body may be sent to the top of the next page and you will have to reformat each page. This method of producing footnotes is probably not worth doing, given how much trouble it is.

A footnote program has two main advantages. First, it frees you from the difficult task of arranging the text to leave room for the footnotes. The program is able to automatically arrange the text on the page and place the footnotes at the bottom of the page (or at the end of the paper, if you prefer). Secondly, it automatically numbers the footnote calls and the footnote bodies for you. The only thing you have to do is make sure that the order of footnote calls matches the order of the corresponding footnote bodies.

To put a footnote call in your text, you must mark it in a way determined by the particular program you are using. For example, some programs use the symbol # as a marker of the place where the superscript number will appear in the printed version of the paper.

Next, at some convenient point following the footnote call (for example, at the end of a paragraph), you can enter the footnote body, separated from the regular text by some special symbols.

Here is an example in which the footnote call is marked by # and the footnote body is enclosed in curly braces and marked by ##.

```
This is an example of a footnote call # in a
text that will be run through a footnote
program.  Here is another footnote call.# The
footnote body can appear anywhere in the text
as long as it is in the correct sequence.  {##
This is the body of the first footnote, which
follows the second footnote call in this
example.} {## This is the body of the second
footnote.} You can continue with the rest of
the text without worrying about the format of
the page.
```

Once the text is written and saved, it must be run through the footnote program. The program takes the file and replaces the markers indicating footnote calls (# in the above example) by superscripted numbers. The program also places the footnote bodies, preceded by ## and enclosed in curly braces, at the bottom of the page or at the end of the file, depending on what you specify.

The result of running the above text through a footnote program is shown below.

```
This is an example of a footnote call¹ in a
text that will be run through a footnote
program.  Here is another footnote call.² The
footnote body can appear anywhere in the text
as long as it is in the correct sequence.  You
can continue with the rest of the text without
worrying about the format of the page.
_____
1.  This is the body of the first footnote,
which follows the second footnote call in this
example.
2.  This is the body of the second footnote.
```

When you use such a footnote program, you can make changes quite easily. If you want to add a new footnote in the middle of your text, you simply insert the footnote call and the footnote body. You then run the document through the footnote program once more. The computer will add the new footnote, renumber accordingly and arrange the text on each page for you. Furthermore, you can always run the program with different options to produce footnotes formatted in a different way. The great advantage of using such a program is that the computer is doing the difficult work of formatting and footnote numbering for you.

Other formatting functions, such as adding a bibliography or adding section headings, often work in just the same way. You must first insert some special commands in the text, then save the file and call up the formatting program. The formatting program takes your text file and produces a new file, probably with a different extension. You can then print out this new file as your finished document.

Online dictionaries and spelling checkers

Computer aids, such as spelling checkers and online dictionaries, are a supplement, not a replacement for checking by humans. You will always have to read carefully through what you have written. A computer will find only some of the mistakes that you make.

If you have an online dictionary, you will be able to check the meaning of any English word. The computer dictionary shown in Figure 1 is run by typing the command **webster** to the @ prompt. In response to this, the computer prompts you for a word. You enter the word to be checked (in this case, **occasion**). The computer then gives the dictionary entry for the word. If a word is not found (for example, if it is spelled wrong), then the program may offer some alternatives.

A spelling checker is a very useful aid in producing error-free papers. Running a paper through a spelling checker program will usually reveal at least one typing mistake (e.g., `teh` for 'the') in addition to actual spelling errors. However, the spelling checker will probably not find all the mistakes that you have made, for reasons that are discussed below.

A spelling program will take a file and search through it word by word, checking each word against the entries in its dictionary. If it finds a word in your file that it does not recognize (because it isn't in its dictionary), then it will *flag* the word and prompt you for some action. The spelling checker may also provide one or more 'guesses'; that is, it may give a list of words from its dictionary that are similar to the word in your file. For each word that the spelling checker picks out, you must make a choice. You can 'accept' the word, that is, keep the original word, or you can 'correct' the word

```
@webster
Word:  occasion

1 oc.ca.sion n [ME, fr.  MF or L; MF, fr.  L
occasion-, occasio, fr.  occasus, pp.  of occidere
to fall, fall down, fr.  ob- toward + cadere to fall
-- more at OB-, CHANCE] 1 :  a favorable opportunity
or circumstance 2 :  a state of affairs that
provides a ground or reason 3 :   an occurrence or
condition that brings something about 4 a :
HAPPENING, INCIDENT b :  a time at which something
happens 5 a :  a need arising from a particular
circumstance :  EXIGENCY b archaic :  a personal
want or need -- usu. used in pl. 6 pl :  AFFAIRS,
BUSINESS 7 :  a special event or ceremony :
CELEBRATION -- SYN see CAUSE

2 occasion vt oc.ca.sion.ing :  to give occasion to
:  CAUSE

Cross-references:
1.  cause
```

Figure 1. An online dictionary

by replacing it with the word suggested by the spelling checker. In addition, there may be some other alternatives: you may be able to type in a correction, or you may add the word to a subdictionary (perhaps a dictionary of technical terms).

How can a spelling checker miss errors that you make? We noted above that the spelling checker goes through your document word by word. It can only check the form of the words; it cannot judge the content. Since a spelling checker has no information about the connection between words, it cannot check style, development of ideas, consistency or grammar. In other words, a spelling checker will find no fault with a 'sentence' such as:

```
The with purple crawls mammoth.
```

Nor will it catch mistakes in agreement, such as:

```
a sentences
The children sings.
```

More subtle mistakes that the spelling checker won't be able to catch include phrases such as:

```
the tow singers.
```

Here, you might expect the checker to catch **tow** as a misspelling of 'two.' However, since **tow** is a perfectly respectable English word in its own right, the spelling checker won't flag this word as a misspelling.

How about the following phrase:

```
she gave a a good performance.
```

The repetition of the word 'a' is likely to slip through, unless the spelling checker has a special capability to check for repeated words.

Some programs sold under the name 'grammar checkers' do try to use structural information as a clue to good style. They may check the average length of sentences or the number of prepositions or passive verbs in a paper and use the results as indicators of possible stylistic problems. However, since good writing is closely tied to clear thinking, these structural indicators are not likely to reveal much to you about how well-written a text is.

9.4   Customizing your environment

As you get to know a particular computer environment, you will be able to change it to comply with your preferences. For example, you may find that you always change the default margin settings when you start to work on a file. To avoid this, you can change the actual default. The result is that the default will be a setting that you have chosen, not one that the program designer happened to set.

We will not discuss the customization of programs in detail, since it is by nature a very program-specific operation. We will simply outline three ways in which you can personalize the programs that you use.

1. using init files

2. renaming or redefining commands

3. using abbreviation programs

Initialization files

Some editors, such as EMACS, allow you to construct an *initialization file* (called 'emacs.init') which modifies the editing environment to suit your preferences. Each time you call up the editor, it looks in your directory to see if there is an 'init' file. If there is, then the commands in the init file are read by the editor, just as if you had entered them directly from the keyboard. These commands may set the margins, turn on autosave (a capability to automatically save your file every 10 minutes or so), turn on word wrap, load your macro file, etc.

Init files are not only used in editors; they exist for mail and other programs as well. In fact, you can probably set up an init file containing commands that are read by the computer every time you log on. In this case, your whole working environment can be set up exactly how you want it.

Renaming and redefining commands

It is possible to use init files to redefine the commands that you use. Here you can do two things. First, you can change the form of a command. If you don't like to use the command **kill** to log off, you can define a new command, for instance, **bye**, to mean the same thing as **kill**. Once you do this, you can use **bye** and the computer will 'translate' this into **kill**. Or, you could define a command to save yourself from typing a long command that you use often. For example, you could define **ben** to mean 'mail bennett@csli.stanford.edu.'

Secondly, you may be able to change the way that a command operates. For example, in UNIX you can use a command called **alias** to define commands. For instance, in one of the init files that is read by the computer when you log in, you might insert the following command:

alias rm rm -i

The command **rm** deletes files. The command **rm -i** also deletes files, but it asks for confirmation from the user first, making it less likely that you will delete a file by mistake. The 'alias' command given above defines **rm** as **rm -i**. What this means is that when you give the command **rm paper.tex**, the computer checks through the alias commands, where it finds **rm** defined as **rm -i**. The result is that every time you give the command to delete a file, the computer prompts you to check whether you really want to delete the file.

Abbreviation programs

Some programs allow you to use abbreviations while you enter text. EMACS, for example, has an abbreviation mode for this purpose. In abbreviation mode, you can either define your own abbreviations or read in a file containing predefined abbreviations. For instance, you might abbreviate 'computer' as **comp**. Once you have defined this abbreviation, you don't have to enter the word 'computer' in full; you can simply type **comp**. When you follow this with a space or a punctuation symbol, EMACS will expand **comp** into computer. (Abbreviation programs are sometimes called 'glossary programs.')

You can also use an abbreviation program to help correct your typing errors. For example, if you find that you often type the word 'the' as **teh**, then you can define **teh** as an abbreviation for 'the.' Then, whenever you make this typing error, the computer will automatically correct it for you.

Questions

1. Does your word processor allow you to define macros?

2. What is the difference between a footnote call and a footnote body?

3. If you are using a formatting program, there are two stages that you must go through before you print out a file. What are these two stages?

4. Adding formatting commands to your text means that you have to enter fairly complex commands. How could you reduce this extra work load?

5. Test your spelling checker. What mistakes does it find? What mistakes does it miss?

6. How many mistakes do you think a spelling checker will find in the following sentence?

```
        Their was an old man who livid inn a sheo.
```

7. Why would it be a bad idea to use the abbreviation **a** for 'autonomous'?

Part II

Computers and Academic Work

10

Library research

As a student at an American or British institution, you are responsible for learning the subject matter of the courses you are taking. In most cases, you will have to work with library sources, both books and journals, to supplement the material contained in lectures and course textbooks.

In this chapter, you will learn how library materials are classified and shelved, and how to use the *card catalogues* to find them. In the next chapter you will find out how to search for library materials using a computer. You need to know how to perform both manual and computer searches because each one may be used in different circumstances. For example, older books may be catalogued on cards, but not on the computer, while newer books may be in the computer data base but not in the card catalogue.

10.1   Library classification systems

How are your books arranged at home? Perhaps they are shelved randomly, or perhaps they are stacked wherever they will fit. If you have ever considered how to organize them, then you have come across the problem that libraries face on a large scale. Should you arrange books by title, by author or by subject?

How do librarians arrange library books so that users can most readily find them? They could conceivably arrange the books on the shelves in alphabetical order according to the title or according to the author's last name; but in fact, books are mainly shelved by subject area. This means that all the books in the same part of the library deal with the same general subject area, and books on the same shelf are on the same subject. Having the books arranged by subject makes things much easier for you; for one thing, you don't

```
151                      QT165
12                       I56R
A236

(Dewey                  (Library of
Decimal)                Congress)
```

Figure 1. Two call numbers

have to go all over the library looking for books for a single term paper topic.

Placing books according to topic or subject area makes it easier for library users to 'browse.' Browsing means looking at a particular section of the library to see what you can find. You are not sure exactly what you are looking for, but you hope that by looking in the right section you will find some books that will be useful to you.

Library of Congress and Dewey Decimal classifications

Two systems of classifying books by topic are in common use in American libraries: the Library of Congress classification and the Dewey Decimal classification. Many British libraries use the Dewey Decimal system. Which of these classifications your library uses does not matter very much; the important thing is that each library uses a consistent system that makes it easier for users to find books.

A	General Works	N	Fine Arts
B	Philosophy	P	Language & Literature
C—E	History	Q	Science
G	Geography	R	Medicine
H	Social Sciences	S	Agriculture
J	Political Science	T	Technology
K	Law	U	Military Science
L	Education	V	Naval Science
M	Music	Z	Bibliography & Library Science

Figure 2. Library of Congress general subject areas

The Library of Congress and Dewey Decimal systems are different in form, but are based on similar principles. The main idea in each is to classify books according to their subject matter. On the basis of this classification, each book is assigned a *call number*, or identifying label consisting of a series of numbers and/or letters. (See Figure 1.) The first line of the call number indicates the general subject area. Subsequent lines break the topic down into smaller and smaller sub-topics.

T		Technology
	T	Technology (General)
	TA	Engineering (General). Civil Engineering (General)
	TJ	Mechanical engineering and machinery
	TK	Electrical engineering. Nuclear engineering
	TP	Chemical technology
	TS	Manufactures
	TX	Home economics

Figure 3. Library of Congress subclasses for the subject Technology

In the Library of Congress classification, the general subject areas are coded as letters of the alphabet. The major subject areas are shown in Figure 2. Subclassifications of these general subjects are indicated by adding a second letter, as shown in Figure 3.

In the Dewey Decimal system, the general subject areas are coded as numbers. The major subject divisions are shown in Figure 4; an example of subdivisions is shown in Figure 5.

You do not have to know these numbers; most people don't. They are included here to give you an idea of the system involved in assigning a call number to a book. The main thing to remember

000	Generalities	500	Pure Sciences
100	Philosophy	600	Technology
200	Religion	700	The Arts
300	Social Sciences	800	Literature
400	Language	900	Geography & History

Figure 4. Dewey Decimal subject areas

```
600          Technology
      610    Medical sciences
      620    Engineering and allied operations
      630    Agriculture
      640    Home economics
      650    Management
      660    Chemical technology
      670    Manufactures
      680    Manufactures for specific uses
      690    Buildings
```

Figure 5. A Dewey Decimal subclassification—Technology

is that whatever classification system your library uses, each book is uniquely identified by its call number. The call number, which is printed on the spine of the book, identifies the book and associates it with a particular topic.

10.2   Finding books in the library

When you are looking for a book, you will most likely go through the following three steps:

1. Look in the *card catalogue* for a card for the book.

2. When you have found the card, write down the call number given on the card.

3. Use the call number to locate the book on the library shelves.

Using the card catalogue

The most efficient way of searching for a book is by first looking in a card catalogue (or in a computerized catalogue as discussed in the following chapter). All books in the library are documented; in other words, for every book in the library there is an information card (or other type of record) ordered in a catalogue.

The card catalogues, which are stored in long wooden structures with numerous small drawers holding the cards, are generally located in some central area of the library. There are three types of information cards: subject, author, and title cards. Find out where the three types of cards are kept in your library; in some libraries they are all filed together in one catalogue, while in others they may be placed in separate catalogues.

Sources of information

The main sources of information in the library are as follows:

Books Perhaps the prime source of academic knowledge. Books provide general, though perhaps slightly out-of-date information; they supply good information for essays and background reading.

Serials These include annuals, journals, and conference proceedings. Journals are the main source of specialized up-to-date information.

Bibliographies Books listing the literature on a particular topic. Bibliographies are usually intended to be as complete as possible; the listings are collected by a researcher specializing in the topic. Therefore, bibliographies can be very useful if you want to carry out extensive research on a topic.

Indexes and Abstracts Important for up-to-date, specialized research. Indexes, which contain lists of journals, articles, books and/or dissertations pertinent to different disciplines, can save you a considerable amount of time in searching for information relevant to a topic. Abstracts, as the name suggests, contain a summary of the contents of a bibliographic source, which is often a journal article. Ask a librarian for advice on which indexes or abstracts are relevant to your field.

Government Documents Publications of state, national or foreign governments or government agencies.

Theses and Dissertations An important source when you are doing advanced research. If the library does not have the thesis or dissertation you require, a librarian can probably order it for you through the inter-library loan service.

Finding books by author

Since citations for books found on class reading lists and in bibliographies frequently begin with the author's name, you will often be able to locate a book by looking up the author's name in the catalogue. The cards are arranged in alphabetical order, with the author's last name first. (So William Shakespeare is filed under Shakespeare, William.) If you have any problems finding the author's name in the catalogue, ask a librarian—there may be some slight peculiarities of ordering the names that is causing the problem.

Doty, Charles Stewart

HC255   The industrial revolution. Edited by C. Stewart
.D64   Doty. New York, Holt, Rinehart, and Winston [1969]
          135 p. illus. 24 cm. Bibliography: p. 131-135.
          (European problem studies)

1. Great Britain–Economic conditions–1760-1860–Addresses, essays, lectures. 2. Great Britain–Industries–History–Addresses, essays, lectures. 3. Europe–Industries–History–Addresses, essays, lectures.

Figure 6. An author card

The author card gives quite a lot of information, as you can see from Figure 6. The most important information, if you simply want to locate the book on the shelves, is the call number, which appears on the left side of the card under the author's name.

* Remember: if you are looking for a specific book, first search the catalogues, not the shelves.

Finding books by title

Another way to find a particular book in the card catalogues is to look up its title. It may be that you are only able to remember the title and not the author's name. Or, you may know the author's last name only, for example, Smith, and you don't want to look through all the hundreds of books written by people named Smith.

Determining alphabetical order

There are a few peculiarities involved in ordering titles alphabetically. For example, minor grammatical words like 'the' or 'a' are not taken into account when sorting books in alphabetical order. Hence a book called *The Teaching of English* will be filed under the title *Teaching of English*.

Another small problem is what to do when comparing two similar titles like *Teach Yourself English* and *Teaching of English*. In many libraries the former precedes the latter. Such libraries use the 'word-by-word' system of alphabetizing. The two titles are the same up until the 'h' of *Teach...*; then one word ends and the other has *-ing*. The shorter word is ordered first in the word-by-word system.

However, there is an alternative system of alphabetizing in which *Teaching of English* precedes *Teach Yourself English*. In this system, called the 'letter-by-letter' system, the spaces between the words are ignored for purposes of ordering. In fact, the two titles are compared as though they were *TeachYourselfEnglish* and *TeachingofEnglish*. Thus the 'i' of 'teaching' is compared with the 'y' of 'yourself,' which means that *Teaching of English* comes first.

Again, ask a librarian if you encounter any problems.

A title card contains the same information as an author card; the main difference is that title cards are alphabetized by title, and so the book's title is usually placed at the top of the card above the author's name. On a title card, as on an author card, the call number appears near the top left of the card for easy reference (see Figure 7).

The industrial revolution.

HC255 .D64	Doty, Charles Stewart. The industrial revolution. Edited by C. Stewart Doty. New York, Holt, Rinehart, and Winston [1969] 135 p. illus. 24 cm. Bibliography: p. 131-135. (European problem studies)

1. Great Britain–Economic conditions–1760-1860–Addresses, essays, lectures. 2. Great Britain–Industries–History–Addresses, essays, lectures. 3. Europe–Industries–History–Addresses, essays, lectures.

Figure 7. A title card

GT. BRIT. – ECONOMIC CONDITIONS – 1760-1860 – ADDRESSES, ESSAYS, LECTURES

HC255 .D64	Doty, Charles Stewart, The industrial revolution. Edited by C. Stewart Doty. New York, Holt, Rinehart, and Winston [1969] 135 p. illus. 24 cm. Bibliography: p. 131-135. (European problem studies)

1. Great Britain–Economic conditions–1760-1860–Addresses, essays, lectures. 2. Great Britain–Industries–History–Addresses, essays, lectures. 3. Europe–Industries–History–Addresses, essays, lectures.

Figure 8. A subject card

Finding books by subject area

Under what circumstances do you need to find books by subject area? Most often, you will search by subject when you are doing some research for a paper on a particular topic. In this case you will have to look at the subject cards in the card catalogue. The subject cards are distinguished from the author and title cards by having, at the top of the card, the subject in upper case letters or red ink. (See Figure 8.) The call number occupies the same position as it does on the author and title cards.

Naturally, there may be more than one book on a particular topic; in fact, there may be numerous books for each separate topic or subtopic. For books filed under the same topic, the cards are ordered alphabetically either by their titles or by their authors. In addition, a single book may be classified under a number of different subtopics. In this case, the book will have a separate card for each topic and subtopic under which it is catalogued.

Let us consider an example of how you might go about using the subject catalogue to find out what books are available on a given topic. Suppose you are going to write a paper about the disposal of radioactive waste. Assuming you don't yet have any references to books on this topic, your first task will be to find some books which will allow you to start your research.

The first difficulty that arises is this: You know that the subject catalogue will group books together which deal with the same subject; but how do you know what words the cataloguing system will use to classify your topic? For example, should you look up 'waste,' 'pollution,' 'nuclear waste,' 'radioactive waste,' or 'waste, radioactive'?

One way to get started is simply to go to the card catalogue and try some of these possibilities. The catalogue heading 'Pollution,' you find, reveals at least a hundred cards. You may or may not be patient enough to look through them to see if there is a subheading on radioactive pollution. Trying a few more possible subject names that seem reasonable or logical to you will probably result in a few references to check. Once you have a couple of call numbers, you can go to the shelves and browse in that area to see if there is anything that looks promising.

This trial-and-error method of searching the card catalogue is usually sufficient for the beginning stages of a research project. However, it can be rather time-consuming because you are not sure whether the reasonable-sounding heading you chose actually exists somewhere within the group of subject cards through which you are searching.

A librarian approaching this type of task would carry out a more efficient search by first checking the list of subject names used by the library's cataloguing system. For example, a library using the Library of Congress system will have a book available near the card catalogue which lists all the subject headings and subheadings used in that system. (If you cannot locate the book of subject headings for your library's system, ask a librarian to help you.)

Narrowing the topic

Whichever method you use to search for material on the disposal of radioactive waste, you may find that there is an extremely large number of books on the subject. What this suggests is that the topic is probably too broad to make into an interesting paper. It is clear that you will have to narrow your focus considerably, perhaps by picking some specific aspect of the subject.

The process of refinement of a topic on the basis of initial research is quite normal in academic work. You pick a topic to write about and then discover through a preliminary search of sources that it is a topic big enough for a life's work. The next step is to refine your topic by taking a more narrowly-defined aspect and continuing the search for appropriate material. This step may have to be repeated several times.

Breadth of search

Note, however, that even when your topic is sufficiently limited, you still have to decide how broad your search will be. For example, if your topic is marine disposal of radioactive waste, you must decide whether or not to check books on the more general topic of radioactive waste. Such books probably will contain a certain amount of information on the 'marine disposal of radioactive waste,' although a great part of their contents may be irrelevant as far as your particular topic is concerned.

The advantage of including some materials of this type in a broad search is that it may be useful for you to have an overview of a more general topic before you begin to research the more specific one. Books on radioactive waste, for example, may help you find out about the general principles of radioactive waste disposal. You can then apply these principles to the more specific problem of the marine disposal of radioactive waste.

An alternative strategy is to perform a narrow search on a highly specific topic. One disadvantage of this is that you may not find anything at all. If you do find a reference, however, you will be able to gather very specific information on the topic.

Locating books on the shelves

Let us assume that you have now collected a few call numbers of books with which to start your research. The next step is to find out where the books are shelved in the library. The areas of the library containing books for general circulation are called the *stacks*. To find out where the books you want are located, look for directory maps or signs displayed on the walls of the library. There will probably be two types of maps or notices. One, which looks something like Figure 9, will tell you which floor or which part of the building to go to.

Call numbers	Location
A — B	Lower Level
C — F	1st Floor
G — Z	2nd Floor
10 — 300	East Annex
... — ...	...

Figure 9. Finding call numbers in the library

In addition, on each floor there will be a more detailed plan that lists the ranges of call numbers found in different areas. To find a book, look at the first line of its call number and then check the library plan. The plan will direct you to the area where books with that general call number are shelved. Once you are in the appropriate area, finding the library shelves that correspond to the first line of your call number should be straightforward. Ask a librarian if you are confused. Books marked T are placed before TK and books marked 600 are placed before books marked 610. Next, look for the second line of the call number. Narrow down your search until you find the book.

If the book is not present in the place it should be, look around a little since it may have been shelved incorrectly. If you still can't find it, the library staff will be able to help you. They will check to see if someone else has checked out the book. In any case, they will help you get a copy of the book.

10.3   Finding journal articles in the library

For more detailed research, and for the most up-to-date academic information, it is necessary to consult journal articles in your field. The most recent issues of journals are usually displayed on open shelves in an area called 'current periodicals' or something similar. Past issues of the same journals, however, may be stored in a different place.

If you know which journal you are looking for, then you can look in the title catalogue to find its call number. If you are trying to find useful references on a specific topic, then you will probably check for journal references to your topic in indexes and abstracts for the field that you are working in. There are many abstracts and indexes covering various fields, for example, *Engineering Index, Psychological Abstracts*, and *Biological Abstracts*. Ask a reference librarian for advice about which indexes and abstracts would be useful for your search.

To get information about journal articles you have the following choices:

- check abstracts

- search indexes

- check the bibliographies of articles on your topic that you have already found

- read one or two prime journals regularly as they come out

Library reserves

If your professor has recommended or assigned some books or journal articles for class readings, it is possible that these materials will be kept 'on reserve' at the library. This means that the books have been taken off the shelves and placed in a special area called 'library reserves' or 'reserve section.' To use reserve materials, you must go to this special area and request them from the library staff. You will probably need to identify the class they are reserved for, either by giving a course name or number or by giving the professor's name. You can then check out the book for a limited period of time, usually a few hours or perhaps overnight. If you are late in returning the book, you will have to pay a fine.

10.4   Where to get help

If you would like to find out more about the facilities available at your library, there are generally four main sources of information:

1. classes offered by the library

2. library leaflets

3. guided library tours

4. librarians

Some libraries have available typewriters, copy machines, private study rooms, lockers, materials on audio or video cassettes, perhaps even computers. Be sure to find out what your library has to offer.

Questions

1. What system of classification does your library use?

2. What is the general call number of your field of study?

3. What information is contained in:
   (a) bibliographies
   (b) indexes
   (c) abstracts

4. What are the steps involved in finding a book, once you have a reference to the book?

5. What are the steps for finding a journal article when you have the reference?

6. What are the steps for finding out what library materials are available on a particular topic?

7. Find out whether your library uses the 'word-by-word' system of alphabetizing, or the 'letter-by-letter' system.

11

Library searching using a computer

Using a computer to search for library material is quite easy and can save you a considerable amount of time and effort. The computer equivalent of a library card catalogue is a database (called an *online* catalogue) containing *records* of books in the library. Searching a library data base, like searching a card catalogue, involves looking for references based on a book's author, title or subject heading. (In addition, you may be able to search using other information such as call numbers.) The result of a computer search is typically not a single card corresponding to a book in the library, but rather a list of *citations* or references.

In this chapter, we will look at a step-by-step example of a computer search of a library catalogue. Next, we will discuss methods of searching for library materials by author, title, and subject on an online catalogue. In the final section, some advanced online searching techniques are described, and the advantages of using a commercial data base (DIALOG) are considered.

There are several reasons why you might use a computer-based library search (at least some of the time), rather than the traditional card catalogue:

access Some systems allow you to search the data base without going to the library. This means that you can check references from wherever you have access to a terminal, at any time of day.

speed Computer searches are much faster than manual searches.

flexibility With a computer, you can search the catalogue using different kinds of information simultaneously. For example, you may be able to narrow a search by using both an author's name and a subject area.

partial information It is not necessary to know all the details of a reference to perform a computer search; you can search using whatever information you have.

exploration Because computer searching is fast and flexible, you are much more likely to look to see what books are available on a given topic than if you had to thumb through a card catalogue. The computer makes it easy to explore what is in the library. A computer search involves many choices; it is much more of an interactive dialogue between you and the data base than the more straightforward card catalogue search.

These advantages notwithstanding, you should not put all your faith in the results of a computer search. If you cannot find a citation in the data base, it does not necessarily mean that the book is not in the library. Older material, for example, may not yet have been entered into the computer. Or you may have misspelled a name or command while performing a search. It is prudent to use the online data base in conjunction with the help offered by more traditional library services such as the card catalogue.

The basic steps in searching an online catalogue are as follows:

1. Find a terminal and (if necessary) access the library data base.

2. Read the instructions on how to perform a search.

3. Search for the library material using the information you have (title, author, subject area, or some combination).

4. Refine the search if necessary.

5. Display the results.

6. Save, print, or simply note down the references or call numbers you want.

You should be able to carry out your own searches of an online catalogue with little difficulty. Reading the instructions provided by the library will probably help you be more efficient in your search. Ask the library reference staff for more advice, if necessary.

The following section takes you through the steps of a sample search to give you a clearer idea of what is involved.

11.1   An example of a computer search

Library data bases vary just as much as word processors do, but there are some basic techniques that should be applicable to whatever system you are using. In this section, we will introduce computer searching techniques using Stanford University's online catalogue as an example.

You can search the catalog if you have any of the following information:

Type of Search:
     A AUTHOR'S name
     O ORGANIZATION as author
     TP TITLE PHRASE, phrase beginning the title
     T TITLE, any words
     S SUBJECT words
     SN SUBJECT, person's name

TYPE OF SEARCH: ☐

Figure 1. An example of a menu

There may be terminals in the library that are ready for you to use, or you may first have to log on to the computer that contains the library catalogue. Once you are connected to the online data base, you can begin your search. The first screen that you see may contain a menu of choices as shown in Figure 1. The alternatives are displayed (A, O, TP, ...) and the computer prompts you with the phrase TYPE OF SEARCH. Notice the cursor following this prompt. (See p. 9 for information on prompts and cursors.)

By responding with one of the letters that are displayed in the menu, you can tell the computer what kind of search you want to perform: **a** for author, **o** for organizations, etc. Let us suppose that you want to find a certain book on computers. You cannot remember the name of the book, but you know that the author is Feigenbaum. Thus you need to look for all the books (and other library materials) by authors named Feigenbaum. To do this, respond to the prompt TYPE OF SEARCH: by typing **author feigenbaum** (or **a feigenbaum**, for short) and pressing the return key to enter your

TYPE OF SEARCH: **author feigenbaum**
Catalog Headings / Search: Find AUTHOR FEIGENBAUM
Result filed under 8 headings:

1) Author: Feigenbaum, Harvey B, 1949- (Citations: 1 Book)
2) Author: Feigenbaum, Irwin (Citations: 1 Book)
3) Author: Feigenbaum, Dorian, 1887- (Citations: 1 Serial)
4) Author: Feigenbaum, Rita (Citations: 1 Book)
5) Author: Feigenbaum, Harvey (Citations: 3 Books)
6) Author: Feigenbaum, Gail (Citations: 1 Book)
7) Author: Feigenbaum, Edward A (Citations: 10 Books)
8) Author: Feigenbaum, A V (Citations: 2 Books)

To see a heading: type DISPLAY followed by a heading number.
To see a full citation: type DISPLAY FULL followed by a number.
To begin a new search: type FIND or BROWSE.
To select a different file:type SELECT.
For more information: type HELP or OPTIONS.

YOUR RESPONSE: ☐

Figure 2. Searching for books by Feigenbaum

command into the computer. This command instructs the computer
to find all the library materials in the data base that are authored
by Feigenbaum. (As usual, commands typed by the user are shown
in boldface type.)

The result of starting this search is shown in Figure 2. As you
can see, there is a considerable amount of information on the screen.
This screenful of information may seem confusing at first; but since
the information is presented in a consistent way on the screen for
each search, you will soon learn where to look for the information
you need. Once you get used to the program, you will be able to
take in the information that you want at a glance.

Let us look at the screen in Figure 2 in more detail. The first line
shows the command that was entered to start the search (**author
feigenbaum**). In the second line, the computer tells you what search
is being carried out, and the third line shows you how many headings
have been found. In this search, eight headings were located. (The

YOUR RESPONSE: display 7
Catalog Headings / Search: Find AUTHOR FEIGENBAUM
Heading 7 has 10 citations.

7) Author: Feigenbaum, Edward A
7.1) Feigenbaum, Edward A. THE FIFTH GENERATION :
   Rev. and updated. (New York : c1984.)
      LOCATION: HD9696.C63J3 1984: Math & Comp Sci; Meyer
7.2) Feigenbaum, Edward A. THE FIFTH GENERATION
   (Reading, Mass. : 1983.)
      LOCATION: HD9696.C63J315 1983: Engineering
7.3) Feigenbaum, Edward A. THE FIFTH GENERATION
   (Reading, Mass. : 1983.)
      LOCATION: AL AFD KGf: Law
7.4) Feigenbaum, Edward A. THE FIFTH GENERATION
   (Reading, Mass. : c1983.)
      LOCATION: HD9696.C63J315 1983: Meyer
7.5) Feigenbaum, Edward A. THE FIFTH GENERATION
   (Reading, Mass. : 1983.)
      LOCATION: HD9696.C63J315 1983: Jackson Business

To see the next page: press RETURN.
To scan headings: type SCAN followed by a number.
To see a full citation: type DISPLAY FULL followed by a number.
To begin a new search: type FIND or BROWSE.
For more information: type HELP or OPTIONS.
YOUR RESPONSE: ☐

Figure 3. Displaying books by Edward Feigenbaum

headings here correspond to different authors named Feigenbaum.)
Looking at the list, you recognize Edward Feigenbaum as the author
that you are looking for.

What do you do to continue the search? The last line on the
screen is another prompt from the computer: YOUR RESPONSE. Above
that is a list of the choices that are available as responses to this
prompt (DISPLAY, FIND, etc.). In this case, you want to see the
citations under heading 7, and so you give the command display 7.

This command and the computer's response are shown in Figure 3. The important information here is the list of ten citations (or
references) for Edward Feigenbaum. (Only five of these citations are

shown on the screen.) You recognize the book, *The Fifth Generation,* as the one you are looking for.

YOUR RESPONSE: **display full 7.1**
Catalog Headings / Search: Find AUTHOR FEIGENBAUM
Heading 7 has 10 citations.
7) Author: Feigenbaum, Edward A
Citation 7.1

AUTHOR: Feigenbaum, Edward A.
TITLE: The fifth generation : artificial intelligence and Japan's
             computer challenge to the world / Edward
             A. Feigenbaum and Pamela McCorduck.
IMPRINT: New York : New American Library, c1984.
             xviii, 334 p. ; 18 cm.
LOCATION: HD9696.C63J3 1984: Math & Comp Sci; Meyer
OTHER: McCorduck, Pamela, 1940-
TOPICS: Computer industry–Japan.

        This heading continues on the next page

To see the next page: press RETURN.
   ...   ...
To get more information: type HELP or OPTIONS.

YOUR RESPONSE: ☐

Figure 4. Displaying one book in full detail

In fact, what appears on this screen is a list of citations corresponding to different copies of the book, located in different libraries. For each copy, the citation gives both the call number (e.g., HD9696.C63J3) and the name of the library where the book is located (Math & Computer Science, Meyer, Engineering, etc.). All the citations here look very similar; however, if you examine the list carefully you see that the first (citation 7.1) is a more recent version than the others and so has a different call number.

You have several possibilities at this point. You could write down the call number, end the computer search here and go to the stacks to look for the book. Alternatively, you can get even more information about citation 7.1. To do this on the Stanford system, you type the command **display full** followed by the citation number, as shown in Figure 4.

This full display, of which you can see only one screenful here, gives more complete information about the book, including the full title, the authors (note that there is a second author: Pamela Mc-Corduck), the date of publication, and the publisher. As you become more proficient at using the online catalogue, you will be able to take advantage of the extra information in this display.

Notice that this display (like catalogue cards) gives the topic that the book is classified under (i.e. **Computer industry -- Japan**). This information is useful if you want to look for more books on the same subject area. You could carry out a subject search using this information (see p. 172).

This example of a search illustrates an important property of the online catalogue: you can find a book fairly easily even if you don't know the full reference. The more information you have about a book, the quicker you will be able to find it. For example, if you know both the author and the title, or even part of the title, you can perform a combined author and title search. We will look at an example of an author/title search below.

Menu-driven and command-driven searches

The search illustrated above was based on menus, and so is called a *menu-driven* search. In this type of search, as in all menu-driven programs, the computer presents a list of command options in the form of a menu. You choose one of these options and press the return key. The computer responds to your command, perhaps by giving a list of citations, and then presents you with another menu listing the next possible set of responses.

A second type of search can be characterized as *command-driven*. In this latter type of search, there is no menu present; there is only a prompt. You must type in the command that you want to use (such as **find, display**, etc.), rather than enter a response chosen from a menu. For example, in a command-driven search, we would have carried out our search by entering the command **find a feigenbaum**. The find command starts a new search. You must also specify what kind of search you want to perform. Here, the command **a** is used because you want to perform a search based on the author. Finally, you supply the name of the author that you want the computer to search for.

The advantage of a menu-driven search is that all the information you need is displayed on the screen in front of you. However, using a menu is a little slow. The command-driven search is harder because you have to know what commands are appropriate. However, when you know the commands, you are better off using a command-driven search since it is quicker and gives you more control over your search.

A command-driven search

The Stanford online catalogue allows you to use either a menu-based mode or a command mode for searching. From now on, we will use the command mode. Let us return to the Feigenbaum example discussed above to see how we could carry out another type of search in command mode.

If you know the author and part of a title, you can find a book very quickly with the command **at**. For example, you enter the command **find**, followed by **at** (which stands for 'author and title'), followed by **feigenbaum/fifth**, as illustrated in Figure 5. The slash distinguishes the author from the title in this two-pronged search. (Remember, this command is used on the Stanford system; the command on your own library's online data base may be different.)

YOUR RESPONSE: **find at feigenbaum/fifth**
Catalog Headings / Search: Find AT FEIGENBAUM/FIFTH
Result filed under 3 headings:

1) Feigenbaum, Edward A / Fifth Generation Artificial Intelligences and Japan's Computer Challenge to the World (Citations: 1 Book)
2) Feigenbaum, Edward A / Fifth Generation Japan's Computer Challenge to the World (Citations: 1 Book)
3) Feigenbaum, Edward A / Fifth Generation Artificial Intelligence and Japan's Computer Challenge to the World (Citations: 4 Books)

YOUR RESPONSE: ☐

Figure 5. A combined author and title search

The computer responds as usual by stating what the current search is and how many headings were found. What is interesting in Figure 5 is that heading 1 has a typing mistake in it: the title contains the word 'Intelligences' rather than 'Intelligence.' Since the search was based on the word 'fifth' (by chance), all three headings were found. But if the words 'intelligence' or 'artificial intelligence' had been used in the search command, only two of the headings would have shown up in the result. As it happens, this error in the data base did not affect the search, but it serves to illustrate the fact that computer data bases may have errors, just as in card catalogues, cards may be misfiled.

If your library has an online catalogue, why don't you try out a simple search before reading further?

11.2   Basic searching

In this section, we will cover the basic techniques of searching by author, title, and subject, to parallel the discussion of using a card catalogue in the previous chapter.

Searching by author

When performing a computer search, it is simplest to use lower case (small) letters for all names and subjects. For example, Margaret Mead would be entered as **margaret mead**. In fact, when searching for an author, the author's name may be entered in several forms. To search for books by Margaret Mead, for instance, all the following forms of the anthropologist's name can be used on the Stanford system:

- mead

- margaret mead

- m mead

- mead, m

- mead, margaret

How much of the name you specify depends on how much of it you know. For example, if you know that an author's first name is Alexander, then it is better to enter the full name, rather than the abbreviation **a**. Specifying the author by giving a first name as well as a last name will probably result in a search that is small enough for you to be able to look through the headings. Giving the extra information will be an important time saver in cases in which the last name is a common one.

To get an idea of the difference that specifying first names makes, look at the three searches in Figure 6. (Only the number of citations found for each search is shown here.) The first search, for a last name

YOUR RESPONSE: **find author mead**
Books Citations / Search: Find AUTHOR MEAD
Result: 190 citations

YOUR RESPONSE: **find author m mead**
Books Citations / Search: Find AUTHOR M MEAD
Result: 81 citations

YOUR RESPONSE: **find author margaret mead**
Books Citations / Search: Find AUTHOR MARGARET MEAD
Result: 67 citations

Figure 6. Searching for an author

only, yields 190 references. Adding a first name initial halves this number; and adding a full first name reduces the list still further.

Searching by title

In searching for titles, you don't have to give the exact title. The command **title** (or **t**) allows you to specify whatever words in your title you happen to know. If you specify a single word like **economic**, for instance, then the result will be a list of all the titles in the catalogue containing the word 'economic.' If you search for a title by giving the words **economic** and **theory**, the result will be a list of all the books that contain the words 'economic' and 'theory' in their titles.

The order in which you enter words in the title is not important in a search of this type. The computer looks through the data base for titles in which all of these words appear. This means that the search result will be larger than you might expect. For example, our search would find not just titles containing the phrase 'economic theory,' but also titles like *Classical* **theory** *of* **economic** *growth*. In such a search, the computer will find all the titles that contain, somewhere within them, the words that you have typed. This can add up to quite a large number of titles, as Figure 7 shows.

Suppose, however, that you are looking for a book and you know that the first two words of the title are *Economic Theory*. In this case, what you need is some way of using this extra information to specify a search that is more restricted than the title search discussed

YOUR RESPONSE: **find title economic theory**
Books Citations / Search: Find TITLE ECONOMIC
THEORY
Result: 484 citations

Figure 7. Searching for a title

YOUR RESPONSE: **find tp economic theory**
Books Citations / Search: Find TP ECONOMIC THEORY
Result: 152 citations

Figure 8. Searching using title phrase

above. You don't want all the books that have these two words in
the title; you just want those books whose title begins with *Economic Theory ....* On the Stanford computer you can use the search
command **tp**, or **title phrase**, which searches the catalogue for a
match between the words you type and the beginnings of titles. The
difference in results for the two types of searches (**title** and **title
phrase**) can be seen by comparing Figures 7 and 8.

YOUR RESPONSE: **find tp economic theory.**
Books Citations / Search: Find TP ECONOMIC THEORY.
Result: 5 citations

Figure 9. Searching for the exact title phrase

You can further limit your title search by requiring that the title
contain *only* the words that you type. To do this on the Stanford
system, you type the title followed by a period. Figure 9 illustrates
the use of this type of search. The results show that the computer
found five books in the library with the title *Economic Theory.*

In summary, if you use the command **find t** (for title), then a search using the words **economic** and **theory** will find all the books with those two words somewhere in their title. The command **find tp** (for title phrase) finds only those books that start with the words 'Economic Theory ...'. Using the command **find tp** and adding a period after the two keywords will limit the search to only those books named *Economic Theory*. This means that books with the title *Economic Theory and Practice* will be found in the first two types of search, but not in the third.

---

* If you are performing a title search, you should choose words from the title that distinguish the book you are looking for. You should not specify function words like *the* and *of*. It is recommended that you omit common words such as the following from your title search:

American	economic	international
analysis	education	Japan
art	English	modern
century	Europe	new
church	foreign	research
committee	France	science
conditions	Germany	study
criticism	government	theory
development	history	world

Searching by subject

In searching by subject on the computer, we face the same basic problems as when searching for subject cards in the card catalogue: namely, how do we know what the appropriate subject headings are? However, because computer searches can be performed very quickly, it is easy to try a search using a reasonable subject term. The command used in the Stanford online catalogue for searching for a subject is **subject** or **s**.

Not surprisingly, searching for a general subject such as **economics** or **history** will give a large list of citations. Since a computer can find a vast amount of material with just one search, it makes sense to narrow the subject you are searching for by choosing terms that are as specific as possible. You can always extend the search later, if necessary. One way of finding appropriate subject headings for a topic you are researching is to start by searching for a book that you know on this topic. When you display the citation for this book in full, you can look under the heading marked topics for appropriate subject headings. In Figure 4, for example, the Feigenbaum citation was listed with the subject heading Computer industry -- Japan.

```
COMMAND: browse subject phrase economics - history
Catalog Headings / Search: Browse SUBJECT ECONOMICS -
HISTORY
Result filed under the following headings:

-3) Topic:    Economics–Greece–History (Citations: 2 Books)
-2) Topic:    Economics–Hist–France (Citations: 1 Book)
-1) Topic:    Economics–Hist–Italy (Citations: 1 Book)
 0) Topic:    Economics–History
              (Citations: 205 Books, 2 Serials)
 1) Topic:    Economics–History–Addresses Essays Lectures
              (Citations: 19 Books)
 2) Topic:    Economics–History–Argentine Republic
              (Citations: 2 Books)
 3) Topic:    Economics–History–Australia (Citations: 1 Book)
 4) Topic:    Economics–History–Bibliography
              (Citations: 4 Books)
 5) Topic:    Economics–History–Brazil (Citations: 1 Book)
 6) Topic:    Economics–History–Collected Works
              (Citations: 1 Serial)
 7) Topic:    Economics–History–Congresses
              (Citations: 6 Books)
 8) Topic:    Economics–History–Europe (Citations: 2 Books)
```

Figure 10. Searching for subject heading Economics - History

In addition, your system may provide a way to look at subject headings. (This is the computer equivalent of looking in the book of Library of Congress subject headings.) For example, Figure 10 gives a list of headings related to Economics -- History. If you are interested in performing this kind of search, you might ask a reference librarian for help.

Multiple search terms

One advantage of using the computer is that you can give more than one search term at a time. Giving two search terms for a subject narrows the search, since the items in the result must be classified under both of the subjects you specify. (You might have to think about this for a minute to see why.)

COMMAND: **find subject economics history**
-Result: 237 headings to SCAN
COMMAND: **scan**
Catalog Headings / Search: Find SUBJECT ECONOMICS HISTORY
Result filed under 237 headings:

1) TITLE: Carnegie Endowment for International Peace
             Division of Economics and History Economic
             and Social History of the World War
             (Citations: 1 Book)
2) Topic: Economics Laboratory Inc–History–
             Addresses Essays Lectures (Citations: 1 Book)
3) TITLE: Simbabwe Geschichte Politik Wirtschaft Gesellschaft
             Auswahlbibliographie Zimbabwe History
             Politics Economics Society (Citations: 1 Book)
4) Topic: Urban Economics–History (Citations: 2 Books)

Figure 11. Searching for the subject 'Economics and History'

Figure 11 shows the result of looking for the subjects **economics** and **history**. Performing this search was quite taxing for the computer, because it had to search through all the items under 'history' and all the items under 'economics' to produce the items in both subjects. Unfortunately, the result produced from this narrowed search contains 237 citations, which is still too many to look through.

Another problem arises when you begin to scan, or look over, the books that were found. The first few titles of the result are given in Figure 11. From these you can see that the citations are not arranged by subtopics, thus making it difficult for you to pick out books of interest.

There are various techniques for further refining or narrowing a search result, as we will see in the next section.

Pros and Cons of Online Searching

Advantages

- you don't have to go to the library to see what materials are available

- you can search quickly

- searching is more flexible; you are not limited to looking for subject, author or title cards

- you can combine search categories, using AND and similar commands

- the computer is more likely to have recent library acquisitions

- recent topics that haven't yet been classified as subject headings are more likely to be found with a general title or subject search, e.g. cd-rom, laser disk, strategic defense initiative

- you can combine distinct concepts, e.g., milk AND radiation, saccharine AND rats, etc.

Disadvantages

- using the computer is expensive, though it may be free for you

- online catalogues are in general not as complete as card catalogues; some have only more recent citations

11.3   Advanced search techniques

In this section, we will briefly cover some powerful searching techniques.

Using AND, OR *and* NOT *in searches*

The command terms AND, OR and NOT can be used very effectively to control the extent of a search. The efficient use of these terms is a skill that takes some time to acquire, but you can start to use them in simple search commands.

Searching with AND

Basically, AND is used to restrict the scope of your search. The fact that AND reduces a search, rather than extends it, may seem a little counter-intuitive at first. But if you think about it, you can see why a search with AND is more restrictive. A search for A AND B places two conditions on the result: it must satisfy A and it must satisfy B. Since it is harder to satisfy two conditions than it is to satisfy one, you can limit your search using AND.

The use of AND can be illustrated by looking at a search for a book with two authors. For example, you could search for books that are authored by both Strunk and White by giving a search command as illustrated in Figure 12. This means that the result will be limited to just those books that are by both authors. It will not give the books written by White alone, nor those written by Strunk alone. In order to show that AND restricts a search, you can perform a search for just the author Strunk and compare the results with those for Strunk and White. Figure 13 shows that a search for the books of Strunk alone results in 17 citations, as compared with the 10 citations found in Figure 12.

COMMAND: **find author strunk and white**
-Result: 10 citations in Books
1) Strunk, William, THE ELEMENTS OF STYLE / 3rd ed. (New York : c1979.)
LOCATION: PE1408.S772 1979: Lane Medical Reference
2) . . .

Figure 12. A search using AND

Searching with OR

Using OR has the opposite effect of AND: it extends the scope of a search. This is because in an OR search, only one criterion (out of

COMMAND: **find author strunk**
-Result: 17 citations in Books

Figure 13. A search for a single author

two) needs to be satisfied in order for a citation to be included. For instance, a search for **strunk** OR **white** would give all the books written by either Strunk or White. The result is a kind of double search—OR allows you to collapse two separate searches into one operation.

It is unlikely that you will use OR when searching for authors; however, you may find it useful when there are two terms (or synonyms) for the subject that you are interested in. Using OR is one way of getting around the problem of not knowing what terms are used as subject headings. Here are some cases in which OR is frequently used:

- synonyms, e.g., optical disk OR laser disk

- variant spellings, e.g., harbor OR harbour, disk OR disc

- irregular plurals, e.g., mouse OR mice

- abbreviations, e.g., ATP OR Adenosine Triphosphate, EMR OR electromagnetic resonance

The extension of a search by using OR is illustrated in Figure 14. The first search for the subject Adenosine Triphosphate gives three citations. A search for Adenosine Triphosphate OR ATP produces 12 citations.

Searching with NOT

The operator NOT is like AND in that it allows you to limit or restrict your search. Asking for the books written by **strunk** NOT **white** would give a result slightly smaller than the one given for **strunk**, since it would include all of Strunk's books except those he wrote with White.

You would rarely use NOT with searches based on the author's name, but may use it frequently in title and subject searches. If, for example, you wanted to find out about the history of the town

COMMAND: find s adenosine triphosphate
-Result: 3 headings to SCAN
COMMAND: find s adenosine triphosphate or atp
-Result: 12 headings to SCAN

Figure 14. A search using OR to include abbreviations

of York in England, you might carry out a search on the subject
york. Unfortunately, you would pick up the large additional subject
of New York. To avoid this, you can search for **york** NOT **new**. To
see the difference in results of these two searches, look at Figure 15.

YOUR RESPONSE: **find subject york**
Books Citations / Search: Find SUBJECT YORK
Result: 10698 citations

YOUR RESPONSE: **find subject york not new**
Books Citations / Search: Find SUBJECT YORK NOT NEW
Result: 375 citations

Figure 15. Searching using NOT

Searching on part of a word

Under some circumstances, choosing a particular search term can
narrow your search more than you want it to. For example, if you
carry out a title search on **microcomputer**, then you will miss potentially useful references containing microcomputers or microcomp-
uting. If you are unsure of a particular spelling or want to extend
the scope of your search, you can use *truncation* or *stem searches*.
Truncation is indicated by the sharp sign (#) on the Stanford catalogue. Truncation is particularly useful for catching both the singular
and plural forms of a word. For example, **weapon#** will catch both
weapon and weapons.

An iterative search using AND, OR *and* NOT

1. YOUR RESPONSE: **find subject radiation or radioactiv#**
   Books Citations / Search: Find SUBJECT RADIATION OR RA-
   DIOACTIV#
   Result: 1430 citations
   1) TECHNIQUES FOR SITE INVESTIGATIONS FOR UN-
   DERGROUND DISPOSAL OF RADIOACTIVE WASTES. (Vi-
   enna : 1985.)

2. YOUR RESPONSE: **and s disposal**
   Books Citations / Search: Find SUBJECT RADIATION OR RA-
   DIOACTIV# AND SUBJECT DISPOSAL
   Result: 198 citations
   1) TECHNIQUES FOR SITE INVESTIGATIONS FOR UN-
   DERGROUND DISPOSAL OF RADIOACTIVE WASTES. (Vi-
   enna : 1985.)

3. YOUR RESPONSE: **and subject marine**
   Books Citations / Search: Find SUBJECT RADIATION OR
   RADIOACTIV# AND SUBJECT DISPOSAL AND SUBJECT
   MARINE
   Result: 4 citations
   1) CONTROL OF RADIOACTIVE WASTE DISPOSAL INTO
   THE MARINE ENVIRONMENT. (Vienna : 1983.) LOCA-
   TION: TK9152.I5 no.61: Engineering

Figure 16. An iterative search

An efficient use of searching techniques using AND, OR and NOT
is illustrated in a search for books on the disposal of radioactive
waste (continuing the example from the last chapter). The search
proceeds as shown in Figure 16, with the steps numbered to show
the sequence. The first command, which starts the search, is for the
subject **radiation** OR **radioactiv#**. The truncation here is meant
to catch **radioactive** and **radioactivity**. The result is nearly 1500
citations. In (2) the search is restricted by starting the command
with the operator AND. The subject **disposal** is specified, with the
result that the number of citations is reduced to about 200. The
third command restricts the result still further by adding the subject
marine. The result is now four citations, the first of which appears
to be a useful source.

This iterative search indicates the power of computer searching.

By using the repeated application of AND, OR and NOT, you can exert a fine degree of control over your search. There is no equivalent of such a search using a traditional card catalogue.

Summary of online searching

Extending a search

If you want to widen a search, the following techniques are appropriate:

- using the operator OR (p. 176)

- using truncation (p. 178)

- searching on a more general subject

Limiting a search

If you want to limit or focus your search, you can try one of the following:

- using the operator AND (p. 176)

- using the operator NOT (p. 177)

- searching on combined categories, such as author and title (p. 168)

- using a title phrase command (see p. 170) rather than title

---

11.4   An extensive on-line search of DIALOG

Searching an online library catalogue is extremely useful for finding references to books that might be of use to you. Unfortunately, the references you find will not have a great deal of information about the contents of the books they refer to. Furthermore, the catalogue cannot help you find references to journal articles on your topic, nor tell you the contents of articles whose references you already have. To find this additional information, you need the computer equivalent of abstracts and indexes.

Fortunately, the in-depth research information contained in these library sources is actually available online through commercial data base companies such as DIALOG. Companies like DIALOG have assembled a number of databases which can be accessed by computer over a telephone line.

The advantage of performing a DIALOG search is that you can get access to a large number of index and abstract sources. In fact, DIALOG consists of numerous smaller databases, covering a wide range of subjects. Using DIALOG allows you to find a considerable amount of material relevant to a topic, whether it is in journal articles, dissertations, or books. The material you come up with will depend on the set of data bases that you search.

A selection of DIALOG data bases

- Aerospace Database

- Biosis Previews

- Congressional Record Abstracts

- Economics Abstracts International

- Inspec

- Mathsci

- Medline

- Moody's Corporate News-International

- Sociological Abstracts

To take advantage of the service offered, you will have to make inquiries at your university library. It is hard for you to use commercial data base services by yourself for two reasons. One is the fact that these companies are set up to work with large institutions, with which they have continuing accounts.

Another reason why you should consult the library is that it takes some skill to search these data bases. You would have to know not only how to run *iterative searches* (see p. 179), but also how to adjust your search to the specific characteristics of different data bases—what subject headings are used, for instance. Since you have to pay for the time that you are connected to the data base, the more inefficient you are, the more it will cost you to perform a search.

To perform a search of DIALOG, you would probably go through the following procedure:

1. Ask about DIALOG at the college library.

2. Fill out a form detailing your search objectives.

3. Discuss your search with a librarian.

4. Perform the search. This will probably be done by the librarian, but if possible you should be present.

5. Wait for the results to be sent to you.

6. Pay for the search.

During the search, you select abstracts or citations that look interesting, and DIALOG will send them to you at an additional cost. (You may also be able to capture the search session directly onto a disk.)

Knowledge Index

It was mentioned above that DIALOG is set up to provide access to data bases by research and business organizations. However, since the corporations only use the data bases during office hours and since a growing number of people have microcomputers with modems, DIALOG now makes some of its data bases available to individual subscribers. This DIALOG service for individuals is called Knowledge Index.

If you decide to make use of Knowledge Index, you should check that the data base you are interested in searching is available before applying for an account. Knowledge Index only offers access to approximately 25 data bases, compared with the hundreds available on DIALOG. It is probably a good idea to ask a librarian for advice concerning the suitability of services such as Knowledge Index for your reference needs.

Once you have an account, a typical Knowledge Index session might proceed as follows:

- use the modem to connect over a telephone line to the DIALOG computer (see Chapter 7)

- log on (or sign on) by giving your account name and password

- select the data base you want to search

- perform your search

- make a record of the items you are interested in

- log off or select another data base to search

If you are using a microcomputer to make the connection, you should be able to transfer all the output from the search that shows on your screen directly to a file on your disk. You should try out this technique of capturing a session on disk by logging on for a short session. If you perform a long search and fail to write the results to the disk, you will have wasted your money. Also, before you log on, make sure you have enough space left on your disk to record the results of your search.

Once you have logged on, you will be charged on the basis of how long your session lasts, i.e., for your *connect time*. Connect time costs are between $20 and $30 an hour. You will also have to pay a one-time fee of about $30 to $40 to open your account. You should also check to see if you will be billed a minimum amount every month, whether or not you use the service. An average search is likely to cost about $15. Careful advance planning of your search strategy (before logging on) will help to keep the cost down.

Using the results of a commercial data base search

The result of your computer search may be either a file containing a record of the whole search, or else a printed list of citations and abstracts sent to you by the database company. If you captured the search in a file, then you should make an *archive copy*, that is, a copy for storage purposes, before you start to manipulate the information in the file. In your archive copy, keep everything that was in the original file, including the search commands that you used. This will help to avoid duplication if you decide to carry out another search sometime in the future.

Searching the college library

One result of your data base search is a list of citations. Some of these will not be relevant to your work. For the ones that are, you can look for the material in your college library. If you are looking for books, you will be able to use an online library catalogue, if available, to help you find what you need.

Setting up a database

You might also use the results of a search to set up your own data base of information. For example, you can put the abstracts of particular articles into a data base directly. (The use of data bases for organizing such information is discussed in the following chapter.) Alternatively, you can use the results of the search to set up a list of references using a word processing program.

Questions

1. If your library has both a card catalogue and an online catalogue, what are the differences in coverage? In other words, do both systems have information about the same set of library materials? If not, how do they differ?

2. Is the online catalogue used by your library command-driven or menu-driven? Is there a choice of modes?

3. What are the commands used on your library's system for finding books:

   (a) by author
   (b) by title
   (c) by title phrase?

4. Which of the following searches is likely to produce more citations:

   (a) **find subject economics** OR **subject Cambridge**
   (b) **find subject economics** AND **subject Cambridge**

5. If you are comfortable with your library's online catalogue, try to perform a simple iterative search

6. What indexes and abstracts in your field are available in a commercial data base service?

12

Taking notes and organizing information

Every student finds it necessary at some time or other to take notes from class lectures or readings. Notes are useful aids for review and for writing; and in addition, the note-taking process itself seems to aid the learner in retaining more information. The value of taking notes, however, crucially depends not only on how the notes are taken, but also on what is done with them afterwards. In this chapter we will discuss techniques for taking good notes and organizing the information they contain so that it will be easily accessible when you need it.

The first part of this chapter covers taking notes from books and lectures. The second part discusses organizing notes for a paper, using either index cards or a computer.

12.1 Taking notes from books and lectures

A key thing to remember about taking notes is to be systematic. Students who have a system for organizing both their lecture notes and their notes from readings tend to do well at college. You need to take notes, organize what you have written, then reorganize the information as you learn more. This means that a considerable amount of time will be spent going over your notes and reorganizing them.

Taking notes from books

The main problem in taking notes from books or other written sources is in being able to extract information relevant to your task in a short time. You can spend a huge amount of time reading books and making notes without preparing yourself particularly well for an exam or for writing a paper on a particular topic. Therefore, it is crucial that you learn to recognize what information is pertinent to a topic or argument and what is irrelevant. To do this, it is best to develop a strategy for quickly becoming familiar with the content of an article or book.

Before actually reading any of the text, you should glance at the abstract (if any), introduction, section headings, and conclusion. This is called getting an overview. Once you find the part that is relevant to your topic, you can scan through the appropriate section, perhaps by looking at the first sentence of each paragraph to find out the general content of the material. Then, if you need to read the section in more detail, you will find it much easier than if you did not have a general overview. In addition, having an overview will make it easier for you to take coherent notes on the specific material of interest to you.

> ***** Scanning is very important for extracting key information from books and articles. Scanning means quickly looking through the text, checking headings, titles or pieces of selected paragraphs to find the information you want.

The principles behind taking and organizing notes from books and articles are similar to the principles for taking and organizing notes from lectures. Rather than repeat the information twice, we will discuss how to take notes and organize information in the next section.

Taking notes from lectures

Taking notes in a lecture is more difficult in some ways than note-taking from books. You have to understand what the professor is saying and at the same time select the important points and write them down in understandable English. Moreover, in most cases lectures are less structured than books. The professor may digress in unplanned ways, or may begin talking about a new topic before the last one is quite finished and then return to the original topic later. And, unlike taking notes from a book, in a lecture you don't have the advantage of being able to slow down whenever the material becomes difficult, or go over parts of it you haven't understood.

There are two ways to approach note-taking in lectures. The first is to construct a conceptual framework or outline as you listen to the lecture, fitting in information wherever it belongs logically.

Some professors will structure their lectures so that it is very easy for you to produce structured notes of this kind. In such lectures, the framework is explicit; the relation of each part to the whole is clearly indicated. (The framework is often quite explicit in books, making it easier for you to take structured notes.)

An alternative note-taking strategy is to simply write down in brief form what the professor is saying so that you capture a lot of material without fully processing what is said. If you use this method, then it is essential that you go through the notes a few hours after the lecture and rewrite them into a framework.

Even if you adopt the first style of note-taking, it will be very useful for you to work through your notes shortly after you have taken them. Working through your notes might include rewriting them, adding extra notes and comments or entering the notes into a computer. Re-doing your notes is, of course, time-consuming and it is unlikely that you will be able to do it for all your classes. However, such a procedure will give you a deeper understanding of the material.

> ***** It is important that you review lecture notes a short time after you have taken them; within 24 hours is best. After that, you will forget a lot of the material and won't be able to reconstruct it from your notes.

It is important to remember that what you write down has to be meaningful when you read it at a later date. Be consistent in your abbreviations and leave enough signals and headings so that you will be able to reconstruct the basic flow of information or argument.

The main elements involved in taking and assimilating notes from lectures (and books) can be summarized as follows:

- constructing a framework

- fitting in new ideas with what you already know

- distinguishing and sorting information

- refining and reorganizing

- following up on areas about which you are unsure; testing yourself

Constructing a framework

Learning is always easier once you have a framework for the material to be learned. It is hard to construct a framework while a professor is presenting information. It is harder with some professors than others. But in any case you should try to fit the information into some basic pattern, even if you adopt the first note-taking strategy mentioned above. This basic pattern will help you a lot when you go back over your notes and construct a more developed framework later on.

> *   Try different approaches to taking and organizing notes. Find out which method is most successful for you.

One thing that will help you construct a good framework is doing the assigned reading before each lecture. Lectures will be twice as valuable if you have built up a proper background of knowledge into which you can fit the new information presented in the lecture.

> *   Readings may be recommended as part of the course. You should regard these readings as more or less obligatory. Read as much as you can, and skim the rest. Unless you are spending time doing laboratory or programming work for the course, it is essential that you read background material; the lecture notes by themselves are usually not enough.

Fitting in new ideas

Once you have constructed a preliminary framework on paper, then you should try to fit new knowledge into the framework by comparing and contrasting, i.e., making note of similarities or differences with areas you know already. New knowledge may be an extension of what you know, or it may simply be examples and illustrations. Or, it may be a new awareness of distinctions that you did not perceive before. Naturally, you will be continually modifying your mental framework to accommodate this new knowledge; you may even have to construct a new written framework which is only loosely linked with the original.

Distinguishing and sorting information

A lecture consists of a number of different kinds of information. The professor will spend a certain amount of time on background information, and a certain amount on main ideas. Some material may be repeated from earlier lectures, and some will be new. Some ideas will be central points, while others are of less importance. In this way a lecture is no different from a textbook. Part of your task is to recognize what kind of information you are being given and to mark it in your notes appropriately. You may want to choose some note-taking conventions such as indenting supporting arguments and examples, or using different colors of ink to underline particular kinds of information such as definitions. You may find it useful to add some of this extra 'signalling' when you are reworking your notes after the lecture.

Of course, the content of the information you are presented with varies, depending on the field that you are studying. However, there are some basic kinds of information that can be distinguished. These include the following:

Key ideas Key ideas form the basis of the framework that you want to set down on paper and eventually fix in your mind. When you can determine what the key ideas are, you will be able to fit the whole lecture (or chapter) into a coherent scheme. Since key ideas are so important, you should emphasize them on the page, perhaps by marking them with an asterisk, or by using boldface type if you are using a computer.

There may be one key idea for the entire lecture which you can specially mark by enclosing it in a box. Alternatively, the lecture may be a progression of points without any apparent hierarchical structure. In this case you can mark each of the points by number.

If you prefer to enter your notes into a computer, you may want to use a special 'notecards' applications program that allows you to organize key facts using a representation of index cards linked together in a hierarchy.

Examples Books and lectures invariably contain examples which illustrate the main point under discussion. You should take clear notes on the example. It will help in fixing the main point in your mind. In your notes, you should label the information as an example; if there is more than one example for a particular point, number them. It is also a good idea to make clear the relations between main points and examples using indentation or colors.

Lists Some of the material presented in lectures will be essentially a list of facts, such as the properties of different chemical substances or the geological formations found in a certain area. Try to impose some structure on these facts so that you remember them more easily. Visual associations or associations based on the form of the words in the list are often helpful.

Definitions Definitions are always important, since they are constructed in order to make ideas precise. It is often hard to reconstruct a definition from memory, even if you feel you know what a term means. Make the definitions in your notes stand out from the surrounding notes in some way, so that you can easily review all the definitions given in class.

Quotations The professor may use a quotation from a particular author in a lecture. Quotations are usually given to illustrate a point or to show how someone approached a particular issue. In most cases, you need only take down the essence of the quotation. When you are writing a paper, professors usually prefer that you find your own quotations from sources you consult yourself, rather than using quotations given in class.

Anecdotes Anecdotes, or short personal stories, are probably the easiest to remember and least useful of the types of information presented in lectures or books. While anecdotes may illustrate a point the professor is making, their main function is more likely to be to sustain students' interest or to mark a break in the discussion. Unfortunately, anecdotal information by itself will not be helpful to you in essays or exams; usually, therefore, it is not necessary to note down anecdotes.

Refining and reorganizing

As you read more and learn more, you will be able to refine your notes to make them a more effective studying aid. You will be able to add relevant points, clarify important issues, and restructure information in a more logical way. Some students find that entering their class notes into a computer each evening greatly enhances what they learned in class that day. Revision after a longer period of time is also extremely useful. For example, near the end of a term you might want to combine your notes from lectures and readings for a course into a single coherent framework. This active reorganization will help fix the material in your mind, since it will force you to think about how all the different topics fit together. And naturally, having such a well-structured body of information will make the task of studying for the final exam much easier.

Ultimately, you will have to make the decision of how much time you will put into reorganization and revision of your class notes. Just be aware that systematic revision of notes is an extremely effective way of deepening your knowledge of a subject.

Organizing information in order to write a paper is an even more complex task than restructuring class notes, since it requires synthesizing information from a number of different sources. This topic will be discussed in Section 12.2.

Following up on weak areas

In order to learn, you have to continually fill in gaps in your knowledge. Trying to construct a framework and fit what you know into a coherent pattern will help you realize exactly what things you are unsure about. You can then try to understand these things either by looking for explanations in your text or by asking the professor, a teaching assistant, or another student. A considerable amount of learning comes from fellow students; don't hesitate to talk to your colleagues and ask about things that you are unsure of.

12.2 Organizing notes for a paper

Suppose you are going to write a paper developing some aspect of a topic briefly covered in your class lectures. If you have several sheets of rather poor lecture notes and some odd scraps of paper containing notes from unspecified books and articles, then it is likely that the task of writing your paper will be daunting. You have nothing to work with or build on; it is like starting from scratch (i.e., starting from the very beginning). However, if you have been building up an organized set of notes on your topic as you have progressed through the course, then writing your paper will be a great deal easier, especially under time pressure.

There are two basic aspects to organizing information. One is rather mechanical; you must choose a way to physically store the notes you have collected. The better organized and more accessible this information is, the simpler your writing job will be.

The second aspect of organization is conceptual. You have to have some basic plan for organizing your material by type of information and by topic before you can actually carry out the mechanical task of getting your notes into some kind of storage system.

The most important characteristics of a good information storage system from your point of view are: 1) you must be able to easily add, delete, or modify information, and 2) when you want a particular piece of information you should be able to retrieve it easily, without having to look through a large amount of irrelevant information.

These two properties, of course, are characteristic of computers. However, it is possible to have an efficient non-computerized storage system which may be preferable to the computer for certain tasks. In the rest of this chapter, we discuss the two storage systems which have been found to be most efficient for academic work, namely, the index card system and the computer system.

Organizing notes on index cards

The traditional way of storing and organizing scholarly material is on index cards. Since many of the basic principles behind both computerized storage systems and index card systems are the same, we will consider the index card method in greater detail, limiting our discussion of computerized systems to the ways in which they differ from index card systems.

```
Lockwood, William B.


An informal history of the German language.


London  :   Deutsch, 1965.

PF3076.L6
```

Figure 1. An index card for a bibliographic reference

Two basic types of information which you will need to distinguish when constructing your paper are 1) content material, which may ultimately appear in some form in the body of your paper, and 2) bibliographic information. Bibliographic information is usually kept separate from content material since it has its own special form of organization. A common way of keeping track of bibliographical sources is to put each source (whether book or article) on its own special card, and arrange the cards alphabetically by author. So, for example, for a book you might have a card like the one in Figure 1. The call number is placed on the card to save time if you need to take the book out of the library again later.

Organizing content material is more complex. Since what is stored is mainly ideas rather than simple names and titles, there is much more room for variation in how the information may be arranged on a card and then ordered. The important thing is to choose a system and stick to it.

The most efficient way of using index cards to store notes for a paper is to have each card hold just a single piece of content information. In most cases, the card also indicates the bibliographic source from which the information was taken.

```
OLD HIGH GERMAN


     Background Info.


  Dates of 0. High Germ.  period
  8th century to approx.  1050 A.D.

               Lockwood 1965 p24
```

Figure 2. An index card for content information

Index cards are most useful for storing paragraph-size chunks of information. Often, they contain a point that fits somewhere into your general argument, or a basic fact, as in Figure 2. They may also contain individual definitions or quotations.

> * Put only one point on each index card.

With quotations, it is particularly important to provide an exact reference to the source from which you obtained the quote. All quoted material in your paper needs to be referenced. Be sure to note the exact source, including page number; this will save you a great deal of time later when you need to give the references in your paper or to check that the information is accurate.

Citing references is also important for other types of information, such as controversial claims or facts that are not well known by the potential readers of your paper. Numerical data such as statistics must also be referenced.

> ***** Write down the reference at the same time as you write down a quote, statistic, or controversial claim.

The actual ordering or sequencing of your cards presents the greatest problem in the index card system. As mentioned earlier, you need to be able to easily add or modify information, and you need to be able to find exactly what you want when you want it. Since ideas can be ordered in a large number of ways, it is best to use a system that closely corresponds to the order in which you intend the topics to appear in your paper. This means you must develop an outline of the material you propose to cover in the paper. Outlining is discussed in the following chapter. For now, we will assume that you already have a general idea of what material you will cover and the approximate order in which the topics will be presented. This order can always be changed as the topic develops in your mind; the index cards can then be reordered accordingly.

You can start your ordering system by putting the main topics and subtopics in your outline down on index cards which will serve as place-holders. Figure 3 shows a sample place-holder card for the subheading 'West Germanic' under the main heading 'Germanic Languages.' Put one set of headings on each card and order the cards in the same way as the outline is ordered: main heading, followed by subheadings and subsubheadings, another main heading, etc.

Next, as you start reading about each of the topics and subtopics in your outline, put whatever points you think you may be able to use in your paper down on additional index cards. These cards contain the headings, subheadings, etc. at the top of the card, followed by the actual content information. Figure 4 is an example of a content card corresponding to the place-holder card in Figure 3. Remember to use a separate card for each point, definition, or piece of data, and to indicate a reference wherever necessary.

```
┌────────────────────────────────────────────────────────┐
│                                                          │
│   GERMANIC LANGUAGES                                     │
│                                                          │
│   West Germanic                                          │
│                                                          │
│                                                          │
│                                                          │
└────────────────────────────────────────────────────────┘
```

Figure 3. An index card as a place-holder

As you accumulate content cards, you can order them by slotting them in between the appropriate place-holder cards. Ultimately, you will have a large stack of index cards consisting of smaller 'topic' units grouped between place-holder cards.

```
┌────────────────────────────────────────────────────────┐
│                                                          │
│    GERMANIC LANGUAGES                                    │
│                                                          │
│                                                          │
│       West Germanic                                      │
│                                                          │
│                                                          │
│    Languages in the West Germanic branch of              │
│    Germanic include English, Frisian, Dutch,             │
│    Afrikaans, Low German, and High German.               │
│                                                          │
└────────────────────────────────────────────────────────┘
```

Figure 4. A 'content' card with headings

For cases in which a single card is relevant to more than one subsection, you may find it useful to use some form of marking to indicate cross-referencing of topics. For example, it is possible to mark the edge of the cards with different colors so that the colors show on the side of the stack. Then, all the cards of the same color may be selected easily, even if they are widely separated from one another in the stack. Alternatively, you could punch out a mark in the side of the card in a position which indicates another topic to which the point is relevant.

As time goes on, you may find you want to change the basic order of your paper. For example, you might want to make the second section of your paper into the fourth. As long as you don't number the cards, simple reorganizations like this can easily be carried out. Changing the headings is more problematic; you may need to use adhesive labels on your cards to cover over old headings and write new ones. The larger the set of cards and the more fundamental the reorganization you want to carry out, the more complex the rearrangement of cards becomes.

For this reason, many people prefer to use a computer to store the information from which they will construct a paper. Computers are particularly valuable for very large writing tasks such as master's theses and long research reports.

Index cards versus computer data bases

Advantages of index cards:

- easily transportable (can be taken into the library)

- cheap

- simple

Advantages of computer data bases:

- efficient storage

- excellent for searching for particular items

- excellent for sorting information

- sometimes possible to transfer material (such as references) directly into your paper

Organizing notes using a computer

There are a number of different computer programs that will help you organize your notes. Some of these are specialized applications that are in essence computerized index cards. There may be a special computer laboratory at your university where you can try out these different programs to see if they are useful for you. Alternatively, you might use standard word processors and data base programs. The use of word processors and data base managers for organizing notes is discussed in the rest of this section.

Using an editor

The simplest way to store your notes on a computer is by using an ordinary word processing program. The advantage that this has over index cards is that you can quickly search through the file or files for material on a particular topic. For example, you can search for a word such as `Frisian`. (See p. 83 and p. 115 for information on searching.)

To make searching easier, you can put some special markers into the file that will help you retrieve information. For instance, you can put in key words, sometimes called 'descriptors,' which are labels for individual pieces of information. You can then find your notes on particular topics by searching for these descriptors. The more descriptors you use, the more possibilities you will have for cross-referencing your material. You will need to think carefully about the descriptors you use, just as you have to think carefully about the headings and subheadings you use in organizing index cards.

Using an editor also allows you to transfer material such as references directly into your paper. However, if you transfer content rather than reference material, make sure you process the raw information properly and, even more importantly, make sure you are not guilty of plagiarism. See Section 13.1.

Editors are probably most useful for storing bibliographic information, which has a very simple structure. You will probably build up your bibliography gradually, adding new entries at appropriate places in the alphabetic sequence. Some of the information in your bibliographic file, such as library call numbers and descriptors indicating the contents of each source, can be entered on what are called 'comment lines.' These are special non-printing lines that appear on your screen, but do not appear on a printout.

The advantage of using a word processing program to maintain your bibliography is that when you are finished with your research,you will have a finished bibliography ready to print out. The entries on index cards, in contrast, would have to be entered into the computer.

Using a data base manager

You can also use a data base management program (see Section 8.2) to store and manipulate the information you gather in the course of your research. A data base manager gives your stored information much more structure than a simple word processing program. Such a data base is, in fact, conceptually very similar to a stack of index cards.

In a data base, the equivalent of a single content index card is the *record*. Each record has a number of *fields* or places for storing specific types of information. These fields form the basic structure of the data base. This structure makes it very easy to search the data base or sort through it for particular kinds of information.

Again, you will have to spend a little time designing your data base and deciding on the categories (fields) you are going to use. The following is a general list of headings for a record that might help you organize your own data base.

date: the date the record was entered

source: a citation for the work from which you obtained the content information contained in the record

heading: a label for a general topic under which the information falls

descriptor: a more specific topic

text: your notes on a specific point described by the heading and descriptor

label: a label for where the information fits into your outline, e.g., '1a,' '2b'

type: a description of what type of information is contained in the text field, e.g. 'definition'

To find material, you can use a search command similar to a search command in a word processor. You can search for words you used in the heading or descriptor fields in order to look at particular sets of records. Or, for finding a particular piece of content information, you could search for a word or phrase in the text field.

Data bases are at their most useful when it comes to sorting or reordering the data they contain. Let us assume that the data base you use has the headings given above. In this case, you can sort (and re-sort) all the records in the following ways:

- chronologically, by using the date field

- by topic, using the heading and/or descriptor field

- by type of information, using the type field

- in outline order, using the label field

Another possibility is to retrieve a selection of records. For example, you might be able to retrieve all records with a date field greater than ($>$) 1/1/75 and less than ($<$) 6/1/76.

Suppose that you want to print out all the records in order of the outline that you have made. To do this, you first sort the records alphabetically based on the entry in the label field. If the labels contain numbers as well, these will also be ordered sequentially, e.g., A1.2, A1.3, B1.1, etc. Next, you print out just the text fields of the records , so that you have the factual skeleton on which to base your paper.

If you want to change the organization of the records to reflect an improved outline, you can simply edit the entries in the label fields and then re-sort the entries by label.

---

* If you use a data base to store your notes, make sure that you have back-up copies of all your data base files.

Questions

1. What is scanning? Why is it useful?

2. Give two advantages of using index cards to store academic information.

3. Give two advantages of using a data base manager to store academic information.

4. Would you rather use index cards or a computer data base manager to keep track of your lecture notes? Why?

13

Writing an academic paper using a computer

Writing papers is a key part of academic life. Unfortunately, it is quite difficult to write a good paper, particularly within the period of time usually allotted for the task at college or university.

As we have seen, using a computer can help you a great deal with the mechanics of writing: editing, formatting, and some checking of spelling. It can also help you organize your research results. However, what the computer cannot do is write your paper for you. You have to do the intellectual work; you have to think clearly, organize, and finally, put what you want to say in writing. In other words, even with a computer, most of the work involved in writing a paper is up to you.

Knowing how to use a word processor, then, is not the same as knowing how to write a paper. In Chapters 4, 6, and 9, you learned how to use word processing programs. In this chapter we will move from the mechanics of word processing to the mechanics of writing, concentrating mainly on writing skills, rather than on the functioning of the computer.

There are a number of different approaches to writing an academic paper. In the method described in this chapter, the process is divided into four stages: preparation (before you start writing), making an outline, writing a first draft, and revising your paper. In addition to learning what is involved in writing a paper using this method, you will see how the computer can help you during every stage of the writing process.

13.1   Before you start writing

Computers and writing

In the earlier chapters of this book, you learned about some of the advantages of using computers for academic work. In Section 5.3, we saw that using a computer also requires a little foresight; special precautions have to be taken to avoid disasters. In the first part of this chapter, we will briefly discuss some potential problems that may arise during the process of writing a paper on the computer.

Problems can be minimized if you keep the following in mind:

1. security

2. size of files

3. scheduling

4. fatigue

Security

Throughout this book, we have emphasized the importance of making sure your work is secure. Be systematic in making backup copies of your files. Save your work often, and save each printout you produce until you make a new one. Then, in case something happens to your files, you can always retype your paper from a printout.

Size of files

If your paper grows to more than 15-20 pages, divide it into two separate files. A file longer than 20 pages becomes too unwieldy to work with. It takes a long time to move through a large file and it is easy to lose your place. You can always combine the files again for the final copy (see Sections 6.4 and 9.2), or you can print out the files separately.

Scheduling

Give yourself plenty of time. Computers and printers tend not to work very well when there is a deadline approaching. Getting the paper out of the computer once it is written takes longer than you might expect. Furthermore, when deadlines are imminent, everyone will want to use the computers and printers, and so you will have to take your turn.

Fatigue

Spending a lot of time at the computer can be physically exhausting. The strain on the neck, back, and eyes due to peering at the screen for an extended period of time is considerable, and because you are concentrating, you may not notice it until you get up. Positioning your computer and chair in a comfortable manner will help somewhat, as well as looking away from the screen periodically to rest your eyes.

> ***** Physical exercises and regular breaks from the computer will allow you to work longer and more effectively.

Choosing a topic

The first step in writing a paper is to choose a topic. In finding a topic, you might follow these steps:

1. Pick a topic area that

   (a) you find interesting

   (b) is suitable for the course

   (c) can be researched in the library or libraries available to you.

2. When you have fulfilled the requirements in (1), check that the topic can be covered in the time that you have available to write the paper. Is it well-defined and restricted enough for you to give more than just a survey of the field?

3. Carry out a preliminary search for materials.

4. Refine your topic based on the results of the search.

You should start with the assumption that you will refine your initial topic after some preliminary investigation. Most topics selected by students for research papers turn out to be too broad for a term paper. Furthermore, the precise topic of your paper will be affected by what you choose as the thesis of your paper, as described below.

Developing a thesis

Before you start to write, you need to have some idea of what you are going to say in the paper. You first need to develop an 'angle,' or a particular approach to your topic. This will allow you to arrive at a basic claim or argument, called a thesis, which you would like to put forward as the main idea in your paper. Once you have a thesis, then if you were asked what your story was on this topic, you could answer in one or two sentences. For instance, you might summarize your thesis by saying that most people think that x is the true/only/best way to approach problem y, but that you have found that (1) there are difficulties with this approach (which you can describe) and that (2) another approach, x', is superior for the following reasons: a, b, c, etc.

If someone asked you what your paper was about and you said that on some particular issue, Friedman said x, Keynes said y and Galbraith said z, then you don't have a thesis and you will find it difficult to write an acceptable paper. What you have in such a case is background material for a paper. It may be that you need to go back and do more research before you become aware of a problem on which you can take a particular position. Alternatively, you may need to narrow down your topic to some extent before you can find a thesis that you can defend. (See Chapters 10 and 11.) Or you may need to do a bit of creative thinking. But ultimately, what you must do is decide on some idea, argument, or point of view to make into your thesis.

If you want to get an idea of what is appropriate as a thesis in an academic paper, you can look at the introductions of journal articles in your field. The thesis of a paper is generally stated somewhere in the introduction, in a paragraph (or sometimes a sentence) called the thesis statement. Looking at a few thesis statements should help you understand the kinds of issues that are discussed in academic papers.

Don't think that you have to make a major new discovery in your paper. In the beginning stages of research you are not expected to make a large contribution. One thing you might do is define a problem that has not been addressed before, and take one or two basic steps towards a solution. A paper along these lines typically states the background to the problem, lays out a partial solution, and ends with a statement about what research still needs to be done before the problem can be solved.

When you come to choose a topic and thesis, you should talk to your professor about your ideas. The professor will be able to judge whether or not the topic is appropriate, and perhaps will guide you toward a specific area that is suitable as a paper topic.

Once you have a thesis, it is much easier to see the form your paper will take. In order to demonstrate your thesis, you have to set out the background to the problem, then provide evidence and examples to support each of your arguments. The resulting conceptual outline forms the backbone of your paper. In addition, you will have to decide how to deal with possible objections that the reader might have.

> * Explaining the content of your paper to someone else may help you define your thesis in your own mind.

Research

Once you have a topic and a preliminary thesis, you are ready to start collecting information that you will use in presenting your analysis. (How to organize research information, using either index cards or a computer data base, was discussed in Chapter 12.)

This section presents a few guidelines to keep in mind when doing academic research at American and British universities. These guidelines, which form part of the academic conventions you will be expected to follow in your paper, include the following:

1. use multiple sources of information

2. use academic sources

3. process the information

4. don't plagiarize

Using multiple sources of information

It is important to use more than one bibliographic source for your paper; don't find just a single book or article on the subject that you are going to write about. Writing a paper is not like writing a summary of a book or an article. It is an individual contribution synthesized from several sources of information. Using material from several sources will help you to construct your own way of looking at a problem rather than adopt someone else's.

An important thing to remember is that your paper should cover a topic that is in some way distinct from the specific topics addressed in your source material. If one of the sources has already addressed exactly the same topic and put forward the same thesis, then you won't contribute much that is new; you will simply be going over old ground. You should aim to develop your own perspective on a topic rather than simply restating or reviewing other people's work. (Of course, different kinds of writing may be needed in your academic work, but usually you will be expected to take a point of view that is novel in some way.)

For various reasons, many foreign students construct a paper by taking the structure of one source and adding bits of information to it from other sources. This expansion or modification of a single source is not acceptable as a paper at universities in the English-speaking world.

Using academic sources of information

Most of your information should come from academic rather than general sources. In other words, refer to academic journals and books rather than popular journals (like *Time*) and newspapers. You might find it useful to check encyclopedias as part of your background reading, but don't rely on them as a main source of information for your paper. The problem with encyclopedias is that they are not specialized, not up-to-date, and usually don't indicate what primary sources they use. Furthermore, as a consequence of being general, they simplify their subject matter too much for work at the graduate level. If you are not sure what are appropriate sources of information in your field, you should ask your professor or a librarian. (See Chapters 10 and 11 for a discussion of locating sources on your topic.)

Processing the information

It is essential that you process the information that you gather. Processing means taking the facts that are relevant and fitting them into your own framework. If you go through this information-processing stage, then you will never be faced with the problem of trying to alter the language of a source document so that you can incorporate the idea or fact it contains into your own paper.

If you find that you are trying to restate the material from the original source more or less sentence by sentence, then you are approaching the task of writing a paper in the wrong way. The first thing you need to do in such a case is to go back and develop your own focus for the paper, one that is different from any one of the sources.

Another thing you can do to avoid the restatement problem is to note down the information you are using in brief form on index cards or put it into a data base, as discussed in the previous chapter. Then, in order to use a piece of information, you will have to clothe it with your own words so that it fits smoothly into your paper. Alternatively, try reading your notes for a section and then putting them away before writing; this will make what you write more consistent in style and more coherent in form. You will probably need to refer back to the notes for factual information, but you can check the facts later after you have written the section.

A final word on the topic of processing information: Remember that there is an enormous difference between undigested notes and an academic paper. Don't be tempted to use the computer to string your notes together to produce a 'paper.'

Plagiarism

Knowing what makes an acceptable paper is quite difficult for many foreign students studying at American or British universities. By now, you should be getting the message that it is important for you to find a unique focus for any paper that you write. Once you do this, it will be much easier for you to avoid falling into the trap of plagiarism. Much of the above discussion of sources and processing information was intended to help you avoid plagiarism.

Plagiarism simply means the representation of another person's ideas or language as your own. If you don't acknowledge in your paper that an idea came from another source, then the assumption is that the idea is yours. Similarly, if you don't put text in quotes, then it is assumed that you constructed the prose yourself, with no reliance on any other text.

> ! Plagiarism is taken very seriously at British and American universities. Make sure that you acknowledge other peoples' ideas. More importantly, you must not use someone else's language—even in a modified form.

One reason that plagiarism is considered to be a serious academic offense comes from a general philosophy underlying higher education, which holds that students are expected to make some individual contribution to their field of study. This view predominates over an alternative view of higher education as a transfer of knowledge from teachers to students. But whatever the reason for the serious view taken of plagiarism, the penalty for it is likely to be no credit for the course you are taking. More serious consequences follow if a student has plagiarized extensively.

It is hard for some foreign students (because of their different educational backgrounds) to get used to these ideas, but it is important to come to terms with them if you want to do well at university. Even if you avoid plagiarism to the extent that you are not punished, you will be penalized in terms of grades if you do not develop your own thesis. The more your paper is a restatement of information you were presented with, the less credit you will get. On the other hand, you will get credit for developing your own ideas in a paper—even if they are different from those of the professor.

As a foreign student, it may be tempting for you to use the words and phrases that you find in your sources. You must avoid this temptation. It is no better to simply substitute your own word or phrase here and there, while maintaining the same basic grammatical construction of the original. This is more or less the same as copying the material directly.

You should be aware that it is very easy for your professors to determine whether or not you wrote the text in your paper. Passages that are based on someone else's writing 'stick out like a sore thumb.' Everyone has a distinctive writing style; when you import parts of someone else's writing, it will simply not fit in with your own.

---

* There are several advantages of using your own words and constructions in your writing. Your written English will improve faster, your work will be more highly valued, and you will avoid trouble.

13.2   Making an outline

Once you have a basic thesis and have done some preliminary research on your topic, then you are ready to start writing. It is difficult to describe how to write, because there is no single approach to writing that suits everyone. It is assumed in this chapter that you will approach the writing task by first deciding on what areas you will cover and making an outline showing the basic structure of the paper.

When you are thinking of what to say in your paper, you will come up with a series of ideas which will be on different levels of organization, for example, major themes, supporting arguments, examples, and analogies. You can put down these ideas straightaway in a list; however, it helps to fit them into some kind of preliminary organization as you think of them. Doing this will force you to consider how you will present your main ideas and what the logical development of these ideas will be. Furthermore, a very basic organization will make the overall structure of your paper more apparent when you look over this plan at a later date. A mere list of ideas will make it hard for you to reconstruct what you were thinking of.

An example of a simple outline is given in Figure 1. The traditional way to write down an outline is to use a combination of numbers, letters and indentation to indicate sections and subsections. On the computer, it is probably better to use indentation and symbols such as '−,' '#,' and '+' in place of numbers. This allows you to make changes easily without having to worry about renumbering. You can note under each part what you intend to cover, pertinent examples, etc. There is no need to follow a linear order here; you can skip from section to section as you come up with ideas.

The notes contained in your outline are only for you, and so you can use any time-saving techniques, such as abbreviations and other symbols, that you use when writing for your own benefit. Whether you write in complete sentences or in phrases is up to you. Some ideas may be well worked out, making it easy for you to write them in prose. Other ideas may be just starting to form in your mind, and so you will jot down only a basic description of the point you want to make.

There are various general schemes that you can follow in writing an outline. For example, you may want your paper to develop according to one of the following patterns:

Historical perspective You start with early approaches or ideas on your subject and trace their development. The final part of the paper concentrates on your contribution and how it fits in with what has been done in the past.

Logical basis First you set out your premises or assumptions, then present a logical development or analysis, followed by your conclusion.

Problem to Solution You start with an interesting, unsolved problem, then discuss the merits and disadvantages of previous attempts at a solution. Finally, you present and defend your own solution.

Set pattern Some writing, such as lab reports, may follow a standard format, which includes sections such as Procedure, Results, Discussion, etc.

Rather than try to choose a particular abstract structure for your paper, what you should do is simply work out what you need to do to present and support your thesis. As long as you have a clear idea of what you want to say and have an awareness of the reader, you will be able to produce a reasonable structure for your paper. The

Editing

- **Introduction**
  ```
  Different styles of writing.
  Creativity versus execution
  ```
- **Calling up the editor**
  ```
  Getting a document or file = finding a
      blank page (creating a file) or finding
      pages that have already been written.
  ```
- **Writing text**
  ```
  Commands and text (importance of
      control keys)
  Word wrap — no need to press return
  End of paragraph — press return
  ```
- **Saving text**
  ```
  How important it is to save often.
  Everyone loses text — examples.
  Computer crashes, or someone
      bumps computer and plug falls out.
  Frequency of saving
  ```
- **Modifying text**
  ```
  The Basics
          Moving the cursor
          Inserting text
          Deleting text:  chars/words/lines
              sentences/blocks
      Formatting
  ```

Figure 1. A simple outline

task remaining is then to make choices about how to put across your ideas and what order to use in presenting your arguments.

> ***** In much, though not all, academic writing you should directly and forcefully present your thesis, rather than simply giving subtle hints here and there about what your position is.

Computers and the outlining process

It has to be said that in some ways computers and humans are not good matches. Computers operate in a fundamentally different way from humans. You have probably discovered this fact by now; you will have found that using a computer involves adapting your behavior to fit in with the computer, rather than the other way around. Learning to use a computer is in large part getting to know how computers work and adapting to that style.

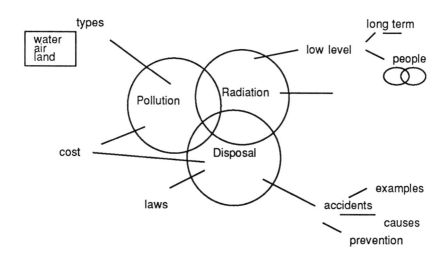

Figure 2. Developing your ideas

Working in this computer style suits some people quite well and others not at all. If your creative thinking is more organic than linear, or if you think in a graphical way, then you might be better off using paper and pencil to formulate your ideas initially. In the pre-writing stages you may want to draw diagrams or pictures to help you formulate your ideas. Perhaps you will come up with a diagram like Figure 2.

The more you become accustomed to using computers, the greater the proportion of work you will do on the computer. As a beginning computer user, you may find it much easier to work on an outline by jotting ideas down on paper. This is fine; there is no advantage to using a computer if it does not help you. Clear thinking is much more important at this stage than using a computer. But however you start, at some point you will have to formulate the paper in a linear form, that is, turn an organic or hierarchical structure into a form in which the points you make follow in a linear sequence. At that point you may want to start writing on the computer.

If you find you can write directly on the computer even when you are still formulating your basic ideas, then you can take advantage of its flexibility to move text around in your basic outline until you are satisfied that you have a reasonable structure. In fact, there are applications programs that are specially designed to help you make an outline. These programs, sometimes called *idea processors* or *outliners*, are designed to let you develop ideas as they come to you. With these programs, you construct an outline in the form of a list of headings that cover the main points of your paper; to elaborate the structure you add subheadings and subsubheadings until you cover the subject matter you intend to treat.

> *   Thinking carefully about what you want to say is the greatest help in creating a good structure for your paper.

The great advantage of such programs is that they allow you not only to list headings and subheadings, but also to rearrange them. When you move a heading into a different position, all of its subheadings are moved as well. Thus, a preliminary organization can easily be changed when you have worked on your topic extensively enough to see a more natural or logical way to present your arguments.

Some outliners, e.g., ThinkTank, allow you to enter text directly into your outline file, under the appropriate headings. This approach allows you to move back and forth between outlining and writing. With other programs, you must transfer the completed outline into a compatible word processor, and then enter your text into the newly-created outline file.

The final outcome of using these programs to expand on an outline will be a complete paper divided into sections and subsections, each of which contains a certain amount of text. At that point you can decide whether or not you want the section headings to be part of the final paper. For instance, you may want to keep only the major headings to help guide your reader through the text.

13.3   Writing a first draft

After producing a well thought-out outline, you can move on to the actual writing. It is important to remember that what you write can always be improved later. You do not have to get the words or sentences or paragraphs one hundred percent correct the first time. The main thing is to start to get your ideas down in some kind of sentence form.

If you do not have a good outline, however, then you will probably waste a lot of time by writing chunks of prose that will not be relevant to the final paper. When you start writing without having a good outline, what you are doing is exploring different possibilities in full-blown prose. It is much simpler to work with ideas first in outline form.

---

*   In writing a paper you can follow this famous advice:

- say what you're going to say

- say it

- say what you said.

Writing an introduction

With a reasonable outline, you should be able to write a draft introduction without too much difficulty. You know what the paper is going to cover, and most important of all, you have a thesis. You should state your thesis, that is, the central idea or argument that forms the basis of your paper, right away in the introduction. You don't need to develop it fully, of course, until later in the paper.

A good basic pattern for an introduction contains the following parts:

1. a basic problem or question

2. your approach; a statement of your thesis

3. overview of topics addressed in each section of the paper

Since the paper is bound to evolve to some degree as you write it, it makes sense to leave some of the more detailed writing until you have written the rest of the paper. Many people write their first draft with only a very sketchy introduction; it is much easier to write the complete introduction once the rest of the paper is finished.

Writing the body of the paper

With a well worked-out outline in hand and a draft of your introduction, you should be able to start writing the rest of your paper without too much difficulty. However, it is still likely that some sections will be easier to write than others. By having an outline in the form of headings and subheadings, you can break up the task of writing a paper into a series of smaller sub-tasks of writing sections and subsections.

Since you are using a computer, there is no need for you to start at the beginning and work through to the end. You can work first on the sections you feel most comfortable with. For other sections, you should make a start by including some notes about what you are going to cover. If you make some initial attempt to tackle the problem of what to write in these harder sections, then it is likely that some ideas will work around in your subconscious, making it easier to write those sections when you return to them later. Remember, you will be able to revise what you have written.

> *   It is much easier to revise what you have written than to start writing on a blank page (or screen).

One of the keys to good writing is writing good paragraphs. Each paragraph in a paper should convey one basic point or idea. The main idea is often expressed in the first sentence of the paragraph and the remaining sentences typically support or exemplify the main idea. If the 'one idea – one paragraph' structure is not present in your paper, then it will be difficult for your readers to follow the logical development of the paper. Your paragraphs are unlikely to be perfectly formed the first time you write them; you will have to revise them in subsequent drafts. We will discuss paragraph structure further in Section 13.4.

Writing the conclusion

Since the conclusion is the last thing your reader will see, and thus is likely to form the reader's final impression of your paper, it is important to get it right. You want a paper that finishes on a good note, not one that trails off at the end or simply stops after twenty pages.

Your conclusion does not have to be long, but it has to be a well-structured finale to your paper. The conclusion often contains a summing up of the main point or points of a paper. In addition, you might add some comments about the consequences or implications of what you have shown, or some questions or problems that remain for further research. You may find that some of the material that you originally wrote for your introduction, but didn't include there, will be appropriate for the conclusion.

Computers and the writing process

One advantage of using a computer to write your paper is that you can often enter text in your file that shows on the screen but does not print out. Using a special character such as % or two dots (..) on the left of a line of text will prevent that line from being printed. Lines marked in this way are called comment lines. Comment lines are very useful because they allow you to put comments, or reminders to yourself, at places in the text that you want to work on later. The comment is often a very rough form of a point that you want to make, but cannot yet formulate in prose.

Even if your word processor does not have this feature, you can choose a special symbol to make your own comment lines yourself. Then before printing out your text, you can search through the paper, deleting the comments as you find them.

Another use of this 'comment' feature is to hide blocks of text that you decide not to use in the paper. Earlier it was suggested that instead of deleting a paragraph of text that you no longer want, you should save it in a separate file in case you find that you need it after all. An alternative is simply to make the paragraph into a comment by prefixing each line with whatever comment symbol your word processor uses.

13.4   Revising your paper

The first draft of your paper can be viewed as an exercise in getting your ideas down in writing. It is usually only during the revision process that a paper evolves from a collection of ideas, meaningful only to you, into a coherent and clearly expressed piece of scholarship that can be presented to others.

For non-native speakers, the revision process is more difficult than for native speakers, in the sense that there are more language errors to revise. However, you probably have an idea of the mistakes that you generally make when writing English, and so can check for them systematically.

> ***** Keep your reader in mind as you check through the paper. Try to see your paper through the reader's eyes.

Below are some things to check when revising your paper. Each of these topics will be discussed in more detail in the following pages.

Overall organization Is the paper organized in a logical manner? Is there an introduction setting out a problem or situation, and containing a thesis statement? Does each of the main parts of the paper contribute toward developing the thesis? Is there a conclusion stating what you have demonstrated?

Paragraph structure Is there one clear idea per paragraph? Which sentence expresses the main idea? Does the rest of the paragraph either lead up to, expand or exemplify this main idea? If the answer is no, you must repair the paragraph.

Transitions Is the reader guided from one point to the next by markers in the text? Is there a smooth flow of ideas or argument between sections and between subsections?

Sentence structure Does each sentence contain a subject and a verb? Does the verb agree with the subject? In complex sentences, are the clauses making up the sentences joined together appropriately?

(Section 14.1 discusses some further ways to check your paper when making final revisions, concentrating mainly on style.)

Checking overall organization

Checking the overall organization of a paper is something that would be very hard for a computer to perform. Such checking requires understanding each part of the paper and judging whether the parts are joined together in a way that forms an acceptable whole. As yet, only humans are capable of making such judgements.

In examining the organization of your paper, you should consider the following points:

- Do you provide enough background? (To answer this, you must examine your assumptions about the level of knowledge of your reader.)

- Is the evidence provided in your paper adequate to support your case?

- Is each section of the paper well-structured? Is each section and subsection a coherent, self-contained unit?

- Do the parts of the paper fit together so that the development of an argument is clear? Are there any unstated assumptions that the reader needs to know in order to follow your logic? If so, state them.

- Do you deal adequately with objections that a reader might have?

Keeping your readers in mind will actually help you write your paper. The process of considering how you can explain your thesis to your readers will help you focus on what the main issues are and what you need to do to support your position.

Checking paragraph structure

The basic unit in an academic paper is the paragraph. Each paragraph conveys information about a single topic or idea; and every paragraph is structured in a particular way. For example, the first sentence in the paragraph often contains the main idea and the following sentences are a combination of examples, justifications or expansions of that main idea. Here are several common templates, or basic patterns, for paragraphs. Actual paragraphs are likely to be a mixture of these types.

- idea plus examples

- idea plus justification

- idea plus expansion

- concept plus definition

- statements leading up to a central idea or a conclusion based on them

- statements based on a temporal or procedural order (e.g., First the liquid is heated to boiling point. Then ...)

- statements based on causal order (e.g., When air and petrol are mixed in the correct proportions, a spark will cause a small explosion. The gas produced by this oxidation process increases the pressure in the chamber, causing the piston to move.)

Once again, don't worry about the particular type of structure a paragraph has; instead, you should concentrate on what the main point is that you want to convey in the paragraph. Once you have this idea, writing the paragraph simply becomes a matter of deciding what other information is directly relevant to the idea. Are you going to give examples, some justification, or some consequences? Once you have chosen the information to be contained in the paragraph, you can decide on the actual order of the main and supporting ideas. Do you want the supporting material to lead up to the main idea? Or do you want to present the idea first, and then expand on it? If you are having trouble with a paragraph, experiment with some of these possibilities until you are satisfied with the result.

> **!**   Paragraphs go wrong when they lack a single clear idea.

What is wrong with the following paragraph?

```
In a set of experiments, mice were given large
daily doses of alcohol for five weeks. Following
this, the experimenters found that withholding the
alcohol caused the mice to exhibit bizarre behavior.
The use of alcohol is growing in epidemic propor-
tions among the affluent young in the U.S.A.
```

This paragraph is badly formed because it does not have a clear topic. It seems to be about the effects of alcohol on mice, yet the final sentence is about the consumption of alcohol by young people. Repairing such paragraphs usually involves separating the two ideas and developing each one fully in its own paragraph.

It is possible for a paragraph to have a good topic statement but still be awkward to read because the sentences do not fit together well. A paragraph must have both a clear topic sentence *and* good connections between the central statement and the supporting material.

Checking transitions

When writing your paper, you should think about how you can make it easy for your reader to follow your ideas through the paper. The best way of keeping your reader with you is to use plenty of 'signposts' or transitions. These are words, phrases or sentences that mark the relationships between the different units of your text.

One use of transitions is in orienting your reader to the overall structure of your paper. Be explicit about the way your paper is organized so that your reader always knows how each piece fits into the general picture. Finish off each section with a concluding statement; begin each new section with a statement of the topic of the section.

Transitions are also used to indicate relationships between one sentence and the next and between one paragraph and the next. Sometimes the nature of these connections is apparent from the structure of the units themselves, without any words signalling the relationship. For example, a subordinate idea may be expressed in a subordinate clause. However, in order to make it easier for your reader to understand what you are saying, you should mark or signal the relationships between one sentence or paragraph and the following one. For example, when you want to follow a statement with a contrasting statement, choose a word or phrase that indicates the fact that there is a contrast between the two ideas. In this case, you would use connectives like 'but' and 'however,' or expressions like 'contrasts with' or 'differs from.' Similarly, when you give an example, use phrases like 'such as' or 'for instance,' and verbs such as 'illustrates' or 'exemplifies.'

These signals allow you to mark the path that you are taking so that your reader can easily follow. Be kind to your reader; don't make him or her do more work than is necessary.

Checking sentence structure

Good sentence structure results from:

1. constructing individual clauses properly

2. linking the clauses into larger units in ways that are grammatically and logically correct.

Some sentences, called simple sentences, consist of a single clause. For example:

```
The change in the tax laws will affect both
businesses and individuals.
```

The main thing to check in such sentences is that there is a subject and a verb, and that they agree grammatically. Other points to check for include the correct use of the following:

- definite and indefinite articles

- tenses

- placement of adverbs

Using a good English grammar book will help you with these and other problems that you might have.

Simple sentences are straightforward and are unlikely to cause you any major problems. However, you cannot write a paper consisting of only simple sentences; such writing has an abrupt, jumpy feel to it, and is considered childish for academic writing.

More complex sentences contain two or more clauses or ideas. Suppose we start with the following simple sentences:

1. The water is pumped into the holding tank.

2. The temperature of the water rises approximately ten degrees Centigrade.

3. The ice melts.

If you want to combine two or more of these clauses into a complex sentence, you have to make some choices. For example, you have to decide how much weight or importance you want to assign to each clause. Is the information in one of the clauses more important (in your view) than that contained in the others? If so, this clause should be made into the main clause and the others will become subordinate clauses. What you have then is a grammatical subordination that mirrors the logical subordination of the less important clauses.

Like other languages, English has ways of indicating that one clause is subordinate to another one. For instance, the less important clause may appear as a participial phrase or a relative clause. Thus, if you decided that sentence 2 above should be a main clause and sentence 1, a subordinate clause, you might come up with a sentence like the following:

4. The temperature of the water pumped into the holding tank rises approximately ten degrees Centigrade.

In this complex sentence two ideas are expressed. When you are checking your paper for sentence structure, make sure that the grammatical relation between the clauses in each complex sentence properly represents the logical relation that you want to convey.

It is harder to check for proper grammatical structure in complex sentences than in simple sentences, because in a complex sentence parts of the main clause may be separated from one another. For example, in sentence 4 above, the subject has been separated from the verb by the intervening 'pumped' clause. This makes it much easier to make a mistake with respect to subject-verb agreement.

What if the two clauses are of equal importance, i.e., they both seem to contribute equally to the sentence as a whole? In this case, you simply join the two sentences. For example, you can join (coordinate) sentences 2 and 3 above using the conjunction 'and.'

> 5. The temperature of the water rises
>   approximately ten degrees Centigrade
>   and the ice melts.

This sentence is perfectly grammatical. However, in this case there is actually a stronger connection between the two ideas than the fact that they both occurred. Specifically, there is a cause-and-effect relation between the two events. Thus, you should help your reader by signalling this connection, as is done in 6 and 7.

> 6. The ice melts as a result of a ten degree rise
>   in temperature.
> 7. The temperature of the water rises ten degrees,
>   causing the ice to melt.

In summary, you must think about how the different clauses in a complex sentence are logically related. Once this is clear in *your* head, you can emphasize this logical relation for your reader by choosing to coordinate or subordinate clauses and by using words like 'however,' 'consequently,' 'but,' and other conjunctions.

13.5 Last minute papers

As a foreign student, you will find it harder to write a paper in a short time than native speakers of English. But sometimes it needs to be done. Here is a strategy for writing a quick paper:

1. Work on an outline; have the structure of the paper clear in your head. Make some notes on the overall structure in case you lose your sense of what the paper is about and where it is going.

2. Write the paper according to the outline, that is, write something on each section and subsection in your outline. (You may

have to cut some pieces out of the outline if it turns out to be too much material to cover.)

3. Print the paper and make revisions, running through the checks listed on page 216.

4. Make the necessary corrections in your paper.

5. Run the paper through a spelling checker.

6. Print a copy of the paper.

7. Sit down and read the paper through very carefully.

8. Make final changes and again run the paper through a spelling checker.

9. Print the final copy. Staple the pages together and hand it in.

14

Polishing your paper

Writing a paper using a typewriter makes it easy to distinguish different drafts or versions of the paper. In contrast, when you use a computer, it is often difficult to draw a line between distinct drafts. The paper evolves change by change—sometimes letter by letter. The ease with which changes can be made sometimes becomes a disadvantage; the paper may be continually revised and never finished. In practice, however, you are often saved from perpetual revision of a paper by the deadline set by a professor.

After your paper has undergone a certain amount of revision, or when a deadline approaches, you will feel that it is time to produce a final 'good copy.' This chapter takes you through the process of producing the final copy. You can use the computer to help you polish your paper both in terms of how it is written and how it looks in printed form.

We will first cover some basic steps you can take to improve your paper so that it reads smoothly and flows properly from one part to the next. Then we will discuss certain formatting conventions that should be followed when you are preparing the final version of your paper. Following that, we will discuss some formatting 'extras' which you can add to give your paper a very professional appearance.

Before going through these areas in detail, however, let us look at a step-by-step overview of the last stages of producing a paper.

1. **Polishing your writing** Once you have the basic structure of your paper in place as described in the last chapter, you can work on polishing your writing. How to go over your paper and improve your style is discussed in Section 14.1.

2. **Formatting** After all the writing is done, you can start to think about the formatting. You can work on the basic layout of your paper, format your footnotes and bibliography, and

check any citations you made in the text (Section 14.2). In addition, you may be able to explore some finer details of format, as discussed in Section 14.3.

3. **Check spelling** Before you print out your file, check it for spelling and typing errors by running it through a spelling checker program. (See Section 9.3.)

4. **Print the paper** Print out a copy of your paper so that you can read through a 'hard copy' version of the paper.

5. **Check grammar and spelling** Read carefully through your paper, looking for grammatical errors (e.g., lack of subject-verb agreement), punctuation errors, repeated or omitted words, additional spelling mistakes not caught by the spelling checker, and any other errors that you know you tend to make.

6. **Check the footnotes and references** Look through the paper again, this time checking to make sure that the footnote calls in the text match up with the footnote bodies (Section 9.3). Check that the citations given in the text are referenced in the bibliography (Section 14.2).

7. **Take a break** If you have time, it is useful to stop working on the paper for a while. When you come back to it, you will be able to review it with a fresh perspective.

8. **Check the paper for the final time** If you have made changes, you should again check the paper using a spelling checker. Read the paper through for the final time. Does the paper have a title and your name?

9. **Print the paper** Print out the final copy of the paper and check that each page was printed correctly.

10. **Copy the paper** Make a copy of the paper for yourself. Staple the sheets of the original and hand it to the professor.

14.1   Polishing your writing

The first step in preparing a final version of your paper is to examine the paper to find ways to improve its style. Style includes aspects of writing that have to do with overall readability, rather than grammatical correctness.

The following list covers several ways to improve the readability of your paper:

1. remove wordiness

2. substitute synonyms where appropriate

3. avoid overuse of 'hedges'

4. resolve ambiguities

5. make sure that transitions are well-marked

6. check for coherence

7. check that sentences are well-balanced and flow smoothly from one to the next

8. check for consistency in style

Wordiness

Wordiness refers to text that is padded with words that aren't doing any work. Remember: a clean, simple style is highly prized by readers because it makes the content of a paper easier to absorb.

The following sentence contains a considerable amount of padding:

> Moreover, research <u>results</u> have <u>also</u> shown that <u>going over</u> and reviewing your notes a few hours after a lecture increases <u>to a great degree</u> your retention of the material <u>presented by the professor</u> in the lecture.

Removing this padding results in a much smoother sentence:

> Moreover, research has shown that reviewing your notes a few hours after a lecture greatly increases your retention of the material presented in the lecture.

Another way to get rid of padding is to choose direct, straightforward verbs rather than phrases consisting of 'empty' verbs followed by a noun. In other words, replace 'perform an analysis' with 'analyze,' 'carry out an investigation' with 'investigate' and so on. As you read through the paper, replace weak verbs with strong, meaningful ones.

Synonyms

The use of *synonyms* helps you avoid too much repetition, particularly with certain abstract concepts that you frequently need to make reference to. For example, in discussing the points made by another writer, you may use the noun 'claim.' However, it is poor style to repeat the same word too many times in close succession, and so you should use synonyms such as 'view' and 'argument.' In addition, in some cases you can alternate between using nouns such as 'view' and verbs expressing a similar meaning, such as 'maintain,' 'hold,' and 'claim.' A good thesaurus will help you find appropriate synonyms. Another way of discovering useful sets of synonyms is to see what different words are used for common concepts by authors in your field.

Hedges

Hedges are words like 'might,' 'possibly,' 'may,' and 'seems.' These words are necessary sometimes, but many students have a tendency to overuse them.

> *   Present your thesis as strongly as possible, given the evidence that you have.

Ambiguities

Ambiguities are phrases which could be interpreted in more than one way. These are hard for you as the writer to catch. You *know* what you mean. What you have to do is put yourself in your reader's position and look for places in which your writing could be misinterpreted.

Transitions

One good way of making your paper clear and readable is to glance over your paper and make sure that all transitions are clearly marked. One way of marking transitions between sentences and clauses is to use logical signposts such as 'consequently,' 'although,' 'because,' and 'on the other hand,' which show the relationship between two ideas. On a larger level, transitions are used to signal relations between points or arguments within paragraphs or subsections, for example 'Another reason . . . ,' 'In sum . . . ,' etc. Finally, transitions are needed to indicate when one topic is finished and another is about to begin. Some phrases that are commonly used to join one section of a paper to another include 'In this section . . . ,' 'We can conclude that ...,' 'We can now consider ...,' and so forth. (See Section 13.4 for further discussion of transitions.)

Coherence

Writing a paper on a computer makes it easy to make changes. However, when you make those changes your attention is restricted (by the screen) to less than a pageful of text, and so you might not realize that making the change will require a corresponding change somewhere else in the paper. Basically, you have to make sure that following the revision stage, you still have a coherent structure, and that your references within the text to different sections, diagrams, etc., are still accurate.

Flow

Next, you must assess the overall flow of your prose. Make sure that you have not used a monotonous style, either a choppy style consisting of nothing but short simple sentences, or a long-winded style containing strings of complex sentences. It is usually best to alternate longer and shorter sentences to provide a good flow.

Consistency

Finally, you must check that your paper is written in a consistent style that is appropriate for the task at hand.

> **!**   Maintaining a consistent style will be difficult, if not impossible, if you have taken pieces of text more or less directly from your reference sources.

You should also watch out for parts of your text that are hard to read because of phrases that don't fit in with the rest of the sentence or paragraph. This is a common occurrence when a text is modified and remodified until little is left of the original text. Read your paper carefully, looking for older pieces that no longer fit in.

Since checking for style is quite hard for foreign students, it will be useful if you can find an English speaker to check your paper through briefly, indicating places in the text that were found to be confusing. Be sure, however, to check it through yourself first; you want your checker to concentrate on mistakes that you couldn't find.

> **!** Be sure to use a spelling checker if you have access to one. It is important to catch as many spelling and typing errors as possible, since too many of these errors make the paper look unprofessional and may annoy the professor.

14.2   Formatting conventions for academic papers

There are certain basic conventions for the format of academic papers which you should follow in producing your final draft. These conventions concern various aspects of your paper's appearance, including:

1. setting the page format

2. citing references

3. adding a bibliography

Page format

Page format includes the following:

- setting margins

- changing the line spacing (e.g., single-spaced versus double-spaced text)

- justifying lines

- using different font styles

   Papers should be double-spaced with reasonable margins (one inch on all sides is a good standard to aim for). Altering the margins (top, bottom and side) and the spacing alters the number of pages that you produce. Sometimes you might have to reduce or expand the margins to change the number of pages in your paper. In general, though, you should be able to write a paper that approximates the length suggested by the professor. You shouldn't hand in anything that is extreme in terms of spacing or margins.

> ***** If you print out your paper on computer paper that is in one continuous sheet, out of courtesy to the professor you should separate the sheets and staple them before handing in the paper.

The other aspects of page format, that is, justification and different type styles and fonts, are matters of personal taste. Again, don't be too extreme; more importantly, be consistent.

Citing references

An academic paper invariably includes citations to other works. The style of citing references varies, depending on what your field of study is. Scientific writing tends to number the citations in the text in the following manner:

```
Studies on the behavior of mice have shown that
alcohol is potentially very addictive.  [1]
```

The number 1 refers to the number of the source work referenced in the bibliography at the end of the paper. In some styles, the number is a superscript, like a footnote call. Other formats are possible; for example, the citation may consist of the beginning of the author's name and the year of publication:

```
Studies on the behavior of mice [Blo85] have shown
that alcohol is potentially very addictive.
```

In the humanities and social sciences, references are generally cited in the text using the last name of the author and the year of publication.

```
Research has shown that alcohol is potentially
very addictive (Bloom 1985).
```

There are several variations on these basic styles. If you are writing a paper for a professor or for your colleagues, the most important thing to remember in citing references is to be consistent. One easy way to pick an appropriate style is to look in the journals associated with your field and from these, adopt the style you find the most appealing.

If you are writing for a journal, you will have to follow the guidelines set by the editors of that journal. These guidelines can be found in the journal itself or you can write to the journal to get a copy of their 'stylesheet,' or guidelines for authors.

Adding a bibliography

The format of the bibliography or list of references is even more variable than the citations given in the text. If you use the scientific style of citation mentioned above, then the references will be numbered in the order in which they are cited.

> [1] Bloom, B. Alcohol Addiction. Journal of Drug
> Dependency 15(2):101-124, May 1985.

If you have been following the humanities style, your references will look something like the following:

> Bloom, B. Alcohol Addiction. Journal of Drug Dependency
> 15, 2, May 1985, pp. 101-124.

Journal and book titles are almost always put in italics (or underlined if you are unable to produce italics on the machine you are using). There are many minor differences in style, however. Sometimes journal titles are abbreviated; in other cases, they are given in full. In addition, there are a number of ways to indicate the volume number and the date.

Your list of references will probably begin on a separate page following the text of your paper. It may be titled either 'Bibliography' or 'References.' In theory, a bibliography is a list of *all* materials consulted in the preparation of a paper, while 'references' refers to a list of works actually cited in the paper. But in practice the distinction between them is often blurred.

> ***** Remember: Be consistent in your treatment of references.

At some point in your career, you will probably want to use a computer program that will help you format your citations and bibliography. Examples of these 'bibliography' programs, which are similar to the formatting programs discussed in Section 9.3, include Bibliography (for use on IBM PCs) and Scribe.

14.3   Further formatting possibilities

The more work you have put into a paper, the more likely you are to feel that it should have a professional appearance. There are a number of ways to improve the appearance of your paper including:

1. typographic choices

2. diagrams and tables

3. a title page

4. section headings

5. headers and footers

6. fine-tuning (pagebreaks)

You should not think of adding any fancy touches to your paper, however, until you have the basic structure correct. Adding polish will not help a paper that is poorly structured; in fact, adding fancy features tends to highlight the inadequacies of a poorly written paper. If you have followed the procedures outlined in the previous chapter and produced a reasonable piece of work, then you can consider adding some of these extra features. Otherwise, spend the time revising your paper instead.

Typographic choices

Typographic choices refer to the fonts or type styles that you have available. Many word processors allow you to use at least **boldface**, *italics*, and <u>underlining</u>. In addition, you may be able to change the size and type of font (e.g. Roman or Helvetica) within your text.

If you take advantage of these features, use them sparingly and consistently in your academic papers.

Use of diagrams and tables

One advantage of writing your paper on a computer is that you can use special drawing software such as MacDraw and MacPaint to produce graphics, which can then be transferred into your text. In addition, the results of a spreadsheet program may be transferred to your file and inserted as a table.

If there are technical difficulties preventing you from inserting a graphics file directly into your text file, you will have to rely on more traditional 'cut and paste' methods.

Although well-conceived diagrams can make your paper more understandable, the time taken to produce a diagram may be considerable, even when you use a computer. You will have to assess whether the benefits of a diagram justify the time spent on it.

Adding a title page

Another possible option you can add to your paper is a title page, sometimes called a cover page. A title page is a separate page which provides a pleasing cover to a paper and helps your professor keep track of papers.

A title page should contain at least the following information:

- title of the paper

- your name

- course name or number

- date

A title page is not strictly necessary, since the above information can also be given at the top right-hand corner of the first page of your paper. However, many people feel that a title page is a more attractive way of displaying this information. In general, the more details of submission or course information are needed, the more likely you are to need a cover page.

One possible layout for a title page is shown in Figure 1. If you are writing a research paper not tied to a particular course, you might use the format shown in Figure 2. Remember to center text using the editor's centering commands rather than trying to add spaces before each line of text.

If you have numbered pages, the numbering should start on the first page after the title page; but don't worry if you don't know how to accomplish this on your word processor.

Adding section headings and headers

Some word processors will allow you to add special formatting commands that introduce section headings in your paper. For example, you might enter a command such as the following:

```
@section Conclusion
```

The result is the following section heading:

5. Conclusion

The computer numbers the sections and subsections and changes the type style so that the heading is set off from the rest of the text.

Of course, even if your word processor does not automatically create section headings, you can probably produce the same result yourself using editing commands.

```
┌─────────────────────────────────────────────────────┐
│                                                       │
│                                                       │
│   The Economic Feasibility of Extracting Oil from     │
│           the Athabascan Tar Sands                    │
│                                                       │
│                                                       │
│                                                       │
│                                                       │
│                                                       │
│                                                       │
│                                                       │
│                                                       │
│                                                       │
│                                    Jorge Perez        │
│                                  Economics 125        │
│                                  June 3, 1987         │
│                                                       │
│                                                       │
│                                                       │
└─────────────────────────────────────────────────────┘
```

Figure 1. A title page for a course paper

Adding headers and footers

Headers are becoming more common as the use of computers spreads. A header is a line of text that appears at the top of every page of the paper. You only have to specify the header once by means of a special command; the computer ensures that it appears at the top of each page. As you can see, the header at the top of this page contains the section number, section title, and page number.

The opposite of a header is a footer, which appears at the bottom of every page. Footers often contain just a page number.

You will have to judge for yourself whether section headings and headers are appropriate for the papers that you write.

```
The Economic Feasibility of Extracting Oil from
          the Athabascan Tar Sands



                  Jorge Perez
              Stanford University
                 June, 1987
```

Figure 2. A title page for a research paper

Fine-tuning the format

Fine-tuning the format of your paper is another activity that can take up a considerable amount of time (and paper). Once you have decided on the major formatting features, namely line spacing and margins, you can look through your paper to check the divisions made by the printer between pages of text. These divisions are known as page breaks.

You may want to change a page break in your text, for example, if a section heading happens to fall at the end of a page. In this case, you put a pagebreak command immediately above the section heading, so that it is shifted to the top of a new page.

> **!** Don't waste time in premature formatting of your work.

You will also use the pagebreak command (or 'new page' command) when you want to start a fresh page somewhere in your paper. For example, you may want the references to start on a fresh page. (It is much easier to use the command that gives you a new page than it is to try and pad the previous page with blank lines.)

For very fine control over your text, you can use a special formatting program such as TEX, Scribe, TROFF (a UNIX formatter, pronounced 'tee-roff'), or StarIndex (which works in conjunction with WordStar). These formatting programs allow you to use formatting commands to get all of the features so far discussed (see Section 9.3), plus the following additional features:

- a table of contents

- specially formatted environments for quoted material, examples, mathematical formulae, etc.

- an index

- non-standard characters, such as ©, ∀ and ⇒

Using these formatters produces very professional looking text, but they also take a considerable amount of time to learn and use.

Final words

Now you are on your own. You have learned many different ways in which computers can help you in your academic career. Now it is up to you to find new ways of making computers work for you. We hope that by reading this book, you will be able to avoid some of the mistakes often made by novices and will be able to take full advantage of the enormous potential of computers.

Good luck (and look after your files)!

A

Three text editors

Up until now we have looked at computing in general terms, without discussing specific computers or programs in detail. In this appendix we will give an overview of three word processing programs. The three word processors cannot always be compared directly, since they differ in so many important respects: for example, they vary in power and in mode of operation, and they are designed to run on different types of computers.

The first editor we will look at is WordStar, a popular screen editor designed for the IBM PC microcomputer. This editor can be used on many brands of microcomputers, especially those similar to the PC. WordStar is an example of a *menu-driven* editor, as explained below.

The second editor, EMACS, was developed at the Massachusetts Institute of Technology, and is widely used on a variety of minicomputers and mainframes. EMACS is a powerful *command-driven* editor which can be customized to suit the user.

The third word processor is MacWrite, the original editor designed for the Apple Macintosh. MacWrite is not a very powerful editor, but it is worth learning for two reasons: It is very easy and enjoyable to learn, and it offers new features such as *icons* and *menus* that are likely to become standard on future word processing programs. Another editor for the Macintosh is Word, made by MicroSoft. Word is similar to MacWrite, but is more powerful and incorporates a number of improvements in design.

A.1   WordStar

Perhaps the most distinctive feature of WordStar is its *menu* system. All the commands that make up WordStar can be found somewhere in its menus. Since commands in WordStar are given by choosing an option from a menu on the screen, this editor is an example of a *menu-driven* program. In WordStar, you issue a command by choosing a menu and selecting one of the options it contains. Learning WordStar involves, in part, learning which menu contains the command you require.

Opening WordStar

In general, when using WordStar you will have two disks in the disk drives: one is a WordStar program disk and the other is a disk containing your own files. Once you have the machine booted and these two disks appropriately placed, you can begin using WordStar.

Let's assume you are logged on to disk drive A. (See Appendix B.) To call up WordStar from DOS, you type **ws** to the prompt A>.

    A>**ws**

If you are logged on to disk drive B, which contains your text files, then you will have to use the **a:** prefix to indicate to the computer that the application you want is in the other disk drive:

    B>**a:ws**

When the WordStar editor has been opened, the first thing you see is a menu, called the Opening menu (or No-file menu, in older versions of WordStar). This menu contains a series of options, many of which concern file operations.

In order to open a text file, you choose **d** from the Opening menu. (Choosing a text file automatically selects the *word wrap* option, making the editor suitable for writing English text. Non-text documents are opened with the option **n**, which turns off word wrap.)

Notice that at this point there is no need to distinguish between entering a command and entering text, because it is not possible to enter text. (You are not yet editing a file.) Thus you simply type **d**, not *ctrl d*.

Next you are prompted for a file name. If you are creating a new file, you must devise a new name for it, different from the names of other files. If you want to work on a file that you created before, you just specify the name of that file. Then press the return key when you have completed the name. You should give text files the extension **txt**, as in 'paper.txt,' so that you know what type of file you are working with.

Once you have entered the name of your file, a document is opened and a new menu appears called the Main menu.

Entering text

You can now simply start typing to enter text. You will notice that the area that holds your text takes up only a part of the screen. At the very top of the screen is a *status line* which indicates, among other things, the name of the file you are working on and the location of the cursor. In the column on the far right of the text area, there are certain symbols or *flags*, which indicate different sorts of information: the beginning of the file (:), the end of the file (.), and flags to mark lines in which there is a carriage return (>).

Underneath the status line is the Main menu, which contains all the commands that you can give at this level. Notice that here, the commands are control commands, rather than plain characters. This is because you are in text mode, a level in the program at which it is necessary to distinguish commands from text to be entered in a file.

There are more possible commands than the ones that are shown in the Main menu. Commands that carry out other types of functions are contained in the menus whose titles are listed on the right of the screen. For example, commands that affect the appearance of the text on the screen, such as commands for margin settings and line spacing, appear in the Onscreen menu. To see this menu, you type *ctrl o* (for 'onscreen'). You can choose one of the commands from this menu by entering the appropriate letter. Or, you can press the space bar if you do not want to issue a command. Both these actions return you to the Main menu and allow you to continue entering text.

> **!** If you have selected the Onscreen menu, you can no longer enter ordinary text, even though the text in your file is still displayed in front of you; nor can you issue commands listed in the main menu, such as deleting a character or moving the cursor. To do these things you must return to the main menu.

Despite the fact that all the commands in WordStar are displayed in the various menus, the fact is that beginners rarely look to the menus to find the information they need. One reason for this may be that you have to know which menu to look at to find the command that you want. Here is a quick summary to help you learn where the different types of commands can be found:

Onscreen menu contains commands that alter the appearance of text on the screen and hence on paper when printed out. These include commands to alter the margin and tab settings, spacing, justification, and commands related to the ruler line.

Block menu contains commands that manipulate blocks of text. Thus commands for marking and for moving blocks are found on this menu. Also included here are commands for saving and exiting from the file, and for printing.

Quick menu contains commands that help you move the cursor around quickly. The cursor commands on the Quick menu provide for large jumps of the cursor through the file. The 'search and replace' commands are also found here.

Print menu is concerned with printing special characters and type-faces such as underlining and boldface. Note that the Print menu does *not* contain commands for printing documents; that is done from the Block menu or, more commonly, from the Opening menu.

Help menu contains commands to display useful information about various topics.

In WordStar, giving most commands is a two-step process. First, you select a menu and then you choose a command or option from the menu. For example, if you want to save your text, you choose *ctrl k* for the Block menu and then select s to save your file to disk. Once you become familiar with the commands, you can issue a single command: *ctrl ks*. (Giving commands from the Main menu is only a one-step process, since the commands are entered directly from that menu.)

Saving text

The commands for saving a file may be summarized as follows:

- save and continue: *ctrl ks* saves and lets you continue working on your file.

- save and exit: *ctrl kd* exits the file after saving.

- abandon file: *ctrl kq* exits the file, without saving the changes. (The file on the disk is unchanged.)

- save and exit WordStar: *ctrl kx* saves the file and exits Word-Star.

WordStar keeps a backup version of your files (i.e., an extra version) with the extension .bak. So, for any file you have saved more than once, there will be two versions—the latest one, and the version preceding that. The purpose of this feature is to give you some

protection from accidental deletion of your files. You have to rename
a backup file before you can open it.

> **!** If you differentiate files according to their exten-
> sions, you will lose this automatic backup to some
> extent. WordStar makes only one backup version
> for files with the same name preceding the extension.
> Thus two files called **bill.txt** and **bill.let** cannot both
> have backup files. WordStar will create only one such
> file, **bill.bak**, whose contents will be similar to ei-
> ther **bill.txt** or **bill.let**, depending on which one was
> saved most recently.

Modifying text

Moving the cursor

Moving the cursor in WordStar can be accomplished by means of
control commands. *Ctrl e* moves the cursor up; *ctrl x* moves it down;
ctrl s moves the cursor left; and *ctrl d* moves it right. Notice that
the keys 'e,' 'x,' 's,' and 'd' are arranged in a diamond pattern on the
keyboard, with the points of the diamond representing directions of
cursor movement.

The basic cursor movement commands in WordStar can be summarized as follows:

	Forward	**Backward**
character	*ctrl d*	*ctrl s*
word	*ctrl a*	*ctrl f*
line	*ctrl x*	*ctrl e*

	Beginning	**End**
line	*ctrl qs*	*ctrl qd*
file	*ctrl qr*	*ctrl qc*

One possibly confusing aspect of cursor movement in WordStar is
that the cursor cannot be moved to places in the file where there has
been no text entered into the computer. For people, blank spaces on
the screen all look alike; but WordStar distinguishes between blank
space that has been entered as invisible characters (space, tab, or
return), from blank space in which no text at all has been entered.
Thus if the cursor is at the beginning of a new line, you cannot move
the cursor to the right because there is nothing there in the file.

Scrolling

The easiest way to scroll through a file is to use the 'page up' and 'page down' keys on the cursor keypad. On some keyboards these keys are labelled 'prev(ious) screen' and 'next screen.' The command *ctrl c* scrolls the screen up, *ctrl r* scrolls down. screen..

Making changes

WordStar allows the deletion of characters, words, lines, and blocks. Characters can be deleted with the delete key, which removes the character before the cursor. Some other deletion operations are carried out as follows:

- character (at cursor): *ctrl g*

- word (following cursor): *ctrl t*

- line (following cursor): *ctrl y*

- block: *ctrl ky*

Insert mode in WordStar is activated by pressing the Insert key (often labelled INS), or by the command *ctrl v*. When insert mode is on, the word INSERT appears in the top right corner of the screen. When insert mode is off, the editor is in overwrite (or replace) mode.

Reforming a paragraph

Paragraph reform is accomplished by typing *ctrl b* when the cursor is at any point in the paragraph. The paragraph will then be reformed according to the format settings in effect. These settings, found in the Onscreen menu, include the margin settings, line spacing and justification. In WordStar, if you change any of these settings during the time you are editing, the text does not change until a reform is carried out.

Once a reform command is given, the reform continues until a hard carriage return is reached. This means, essentially, that to reform a large chunk of text, every paragraph of that text must be reformed.

If the reform does not fill in the text as you expect, it may be that you have an unnoticed hard carriage return in the middle of the paragraph or even at the end of every line. In this case you will have to find each hard carriage return and delete it. (Hard carriage returns are flagged on the right-hand side of the screen.) The best way to delete these unwanted carriage returns is to position the cursor at the beginning of the line immediately following the hard carriage return and press the DEL key.

It is possible to reform the whole file at once by using the command *ctrl qq*, which repeats whatever command is given until you hit the space bar to stop the command. Thus, giving this repeat command immediately followed by *ctrl b* will cause the file to be reformed paragraph by paragraph.

The reform for the whole file will only work if the same margin settings are used throughout the file. If you have any indented text, then you should not use this method. If you do, all your indented text will be reformed to match the non-indented margin settings.

As you might expect, such a powerful command as the repeat command *ctrl qq* is not without its dangers. For example, if you type *ctrl qq* followed by **b** rather than *ctrl b*, then the editor will place the string of characters bbbbbbbbbb in your text until you make it stop by pressing the space bar. This is a good example of a case in which it is much preferable to have insert mode turned on, since then you will not lose any text.

Marking blocks of text

To mark the beginning of a block, you position the cursor and give the command *ctrl kb*. To mark the end of a block, you again position the cursor and give the command *ctrl kk*. The block will then be highlighted in color or in reverse video.

Here are some block operations:

- delete: *ctrl ky*

- copy: *ctrl kc*

- move: *ctrl kv*

- write to a file: *ctrl kw*

Leaving WordStar

The most usual command for exiting a file is *ctrl kd*. To leave Word-Star altogether, you enter *ctrl kx*. Both these commands save the file before exiting. (See p. 240.)

Printing

Controlling the appearance of your printed document is accomplished in several ways in WordStar. The Onscreen menu contains several commands controlling such features as line spacing and justification. In addition, two other sets of commands which determine how your text will look on the printed page are print commands and dot commands.

Print commands are found in the Print menu. They include commands for changing the typeface of words (e.g., *ctrl pb* for boldface) and for printing accents (using *ctrl ph*) and superscripts (*ctrl pt*).

Dot commands, which are placed directly in your file, are commands controlling features such as margin size, page numbering, and *pitch*. These commands, placed at the left-hand margin of the page, are preceded by a dot (.) to distinguish them from your text. For example, you can set the top margin of the printed page by entering the command .mt followed by a number. The dot command must be placed at the very beginning of the line.

The actual printing out of a document is usually accomplished from the Opening menu. To print, you choose **p** from that menu and specify the name of the file to be printed. The editor then presents you with a series of questions about what print options you would like. Pressing the carriage return in response to a question will give the default setting.

Overview of WordStar

The key to manipulating WordStar with ease lies in being able to find your way around the hierarchical menu structure. As pointed out above, once you have learned the major commands, you no longer need to look at the individual menus; you can think of selecting a menu and making a choice from that menu as a single command. Once you reach this level of knowledge, you can turn off the menus so that you have more room on the screen to display the document you are working on. You do this by changing the help level shown on the help menu (*ctrl jh*). Help level 2 is very useful since it turns off the main menu (the first to be learned), but allows the other menus to be displayed when you call them up.

One advantage of WordStar is the number of add-on programs that are available to be used with it. These include MailMerge, for producing form letters; CorrectStar, a spelling checker; StarIndex, a formatting and indexing program; Footnote, which will generate footnotes; and Bibliography, which allows the user to properly format a set of references.

A.2 EMACS

EMACS is a powerful editor designed to be used on large computers, since its power requires a fairly large memory. It is a *command-driven* editor, that is, commands are entered at the keyboard and are not chosen from a menu.

EMACS has an extensive set of commands that allow the user to freely manipulate text and files in many different ways. EMACS will take longer to learn than the other editors considered in this appendix, but in return it far exceeds them in speed and capabilities. For a full account of EMACS commands, you will have to consult the manual.

In the preceding chapters, various examples of EMACS commands were written as 'escape' commands (e.g., *esc* v). In fact, these commands are 'meta' commands, but on most terminals, the escape key is used instead.

Preparing to use EMACS

EMACS is a general editor, which means it can operate in different modes depending on what you want to use it for. Assuming that you want to write papers rather than Pascal programs, you need a version of EMACS which recognizes sentences and words as important units and which has the word wrap feature.

In order to customize EMACS in the way you want, you can set up an *initialization file* (EMACS.init). For a beginner, it is best to copy someone else's *init* file rather than write one from scratch. You can always modify the copied file later to suit your own preferences once you have learned more about EMACS.

Opening EMACS

To start EMACS from the exec level, you can type **emacs** (or on some systems **edit**). There are two ways to call up a text file that you want to edit. One way is to specify the file name at the exec level when you call up the editor. Using this method, you simply type **edit myfile** (where 'myfile' is replaced by your file name). This command is appropriate whether you have edited the file previously or are creating a new one. Alternatively, you can open (or create) a file from inside EMACS. To do this, you first enter EMACS, then type *ctrl x ctrl v*, followed by a file name. This allows you to "visit" a file, i.e. to move from one EMACS file to another. When you have entered the file name (either a new file or one previously edited) and pressed return, an EMACS document is opened.

The situation is a little more complicated than this because EMACS can load more than one file at once. Different files are loaded into different buffers, using the command *ctrl x ctrl f.*

When the file is opened, the screen has three parts: a text area, a *status line,* and a command area. (See p. 57.)

Entering text

You enter text by simply typing at the keyboard. The editor is likely to be in 'insert' mode, but you can change to 'overwrite' mode if you prefer.

> **!** You may accidentally enter a minibuffer, or special storage area. When this happens, your cursor goes to a special area at the top of the screen. To exit the minibuffer, type *ctrl g.* Repeat if necessary.

Saving text

Saving text is accomplished by typing *ctrl x ctrl s.* It is also possible to set up an 'autosave' mode so that the editor automatically saves the file every so often.

> **!** Saving the file and exiting the file are two distinct commands in EMACS; there is no 'save and exit' command as some other editors have.

Modifying text

Moving the cursor

The two commands for moving the cursor backward and forward character by character in EMACS are *ctrl b* and *ctrl f,* respectively. These are easy to remember: 'b' stands for 'backward,' and 'f' for 'forward.' Two other commands, *ctrl p* for 'previous' and *ctrl n* for 'next,' move the cursor to the previous and the following line, respectively.

Commands given by means of the *meta key* often parallel the control commands. Thus *meta b* and *meta f* move the cursor backward and forward word by word instead of character by character.

Here is a summary of the most useful cursor movement commands in EMACS:

	Forward	**Backward**
character	*ctrl f*	*ctrl b*
word	*meta f*	*meta b*
line	*ctrl n*	*ctrl p*

	Beginning	**End**
line	*ctrl a*	*ctrl e*
sentence	*meta a*	*meta e*
paragraph	*meta [*	*meta]*
file	*meta <*	*meta >*

These cursor movement commands illustrate the structure of a program that is command-driven. There are relationships among the commands that help you to remember them.

Scrolling

Scrolling is straightforward in EMACS. To move forward one screen-ful, you just type *ctrl v*. To move backward to the previous screen, use the command *meta v*. When you are scrolling through the file, the screens you see overlap by one line to help you keep track of them.

Making changes

Delete operations include the following:

- character (at cursor): *ctrl d*

- word (following cursor): *meta d*

- line (following cursor): *ctrl k*

- sentence (following cursor): *meta k*

- block: *ctrl w*

A useful feature of EMACS is that text deleted by any of the above commands (in fact, text deleted in any way apart from the use of the delete key) can be retrieved. What's more, EMACS allows you to retrieve not only the last piece of text deleted, but also up to six previous deletions. To restore the last thing that was deleted, you type *ctrl y* ('y' stands for 'yank back'). If you want previous deletions to be recovered, you follow the *ctrl y* command with *meta y* until you get the piece of text you want.

EMACS has other ways of modifying text. One operation is transposition. The command *ctrl t* transposes, or turns around, two letters; *meta t* transposes two words.

In addition, it is also possible in EMACS to change a word to all upper case (*meta u*), all lower case (*meta l*), or capitalized (*meta c*).

Reforming a paragraph

To reform a paragraph, you use the command *meta q* when the cursor is anywhere within the paragraph to be reformed. The end of a paragraph is indicated by a blank line or indented text; when the reforming operation reaches either of these points, the reform stops.

To produce justified text, type *meta l meta q*.

Marking blocks of text

To mark the beginning of a block (also called a region in EMACS), you position the cursor where you want the block to begin and then type *ctrl 'space'* or *ctrl @*. The end of the block is marked by the cursor position.

Since block marking in EMACS does not show on the screen in any way, it is best to check that you have the marking correct before you carry out any operations on the block. The way to do this is to switch the marker and the cursor, which is achieved by typing *ctrl x ctrl x*. The cursor will then jump to the beginning of the block.

Commands that operate on blocks of text include:

- delete: *ctrl w*

- retrieve: *ctrl y*

- write as a file: *meta x* **write region myfile** (Again, substitute your file name for 'myfile.')

Leaving EMACS

As mentioned above, there is no 'save and exit' command in EMACS. And unfortunately, the editor gives you no warning when you leave EMACS without saving your file. This means that you have to be especially careful when exiting your file to make sure that you have saved your changes. Remember, the command to save a file in EMACS is *ctrl x ctrl s*.

Exiting from an EMACS file may be accomplished in two ways. If you want to return to the exec level, then you use the command *ctrl x ctrl z*. If you prefer to go directly to another file, you use the visit command, *ctrl x ctrl v*.

Printing

Printing an EMACS file is achieved from the exec level, and not from the editor itself. EMACS allows you to enter certain print commands, such as underlining, that alter the printed output.

Overview

EMACS is the most complex of the three editors discussed in this book. This means that the investment of time and energy necessary to become proficient in EMACS is larger than that demanded by the others. However, the returns are also greater; EMACS lets you have more control over your text and lets you do things that would be difficult, if not impossible, in the other two editors. For example, EMACS has an abbreviation mode (see p. 144) and allows you to define macros (see p. 132).

A.3 MacWrite

MacWrite, designed for the Apple Macintosh, has several novel features: it is a *window editor* and commands are given by moving a pointer to make selections from pull-down menus. (See p. 44 and 58.)

MacWrite is a very basic text editor. It is simple to use and easy to learn. Despite the lack of certain commands, MacWrite has been used successfully by students writing their doctoral dissertations.

The basic operation of MacWrite consists in many cases of using a *mouse* to mark blocks of text and to choose appropriate commands from a *pull-down menu* to operate on that block.

Experienced users find that using menus is a little slow; they prefer to give keyboard commands where possible. If you look at a pull-down menu, next to many of the commands you will see an equivalent keyboard command.

Opening MacWrite

To open MacWrite, you first insert the disk containing the MacWrite program. Next, you select the MacWrite icon. To do this, you move the pointer to the icon using the mouse, and then click (i.e., press and release) the mouse button. Then you move the pointer to the File menu, press the mouse button, and keep it depressed while moving the mouse towards you. When you do this, the various options on the pull-down menu will appear. If you want to create a new file, then release the mouse button when *open* is highlighted on the menu.

To open a file that was created in a previous session, choose *open* from the File menu. It is also possible to open files from within MacWrite by choosing *open* or *new* from the File menu.

> ***** The quickest way to open a file is to click on it twice in quick succession. This is equivalent to selecting and choosing *open* from the menu. It may take a couple of attempts to get the speed of the double click right; it should be fairly fast.

Entering text

Entering text takes place within a *window* which usually fills most of the screen. (You may change the size of the window by dragging the sizer located in the bottom right corner.) All the commands that can be given are contained in the menus whose titles (headings) are visible along the top of the screen.

The format or shape of your text can be changed by selecting different options on the ruler (also called the ruler line). Margins and tabs can be set by dragging the appropriate icons into place.

When you change the settings on a ruler line, the text under that ruler line rearranges itself according to the new settings. Since a file can contain multiple rulers, it is possible to have different margins at different places within the text (for example, you may want to indent certain paragraphs to represent quotations). Other settings which may vary for different parts of the file include justification and centering.

The appearance of text can also be changed through the use of commands in the Style menu. The possibility of selecting special type styles like italics and changing the size of the text is one of the most interesting features of MacWrite.

You will notice that the shape of the pointer changes from an arrow to an 'I' when the pointer is in the text window. The I-shaped pointer makes it easier for you to position the cursor in the text.

Saving text

To save the text you have written, choose *save* from the File menu. If you choose *quit* and you have made changes since the last save command was given, then you will be given the chance to save your changes.

Modifying text

Moving the cursor

The cursor is moved by simply moving the I-shaped pointer to where you want the cursor to be and then clicking the mouse button.

Scrolling

Scrolling in MacWrite is accomplished by manipulating the scroll bar to the right of the text window (see p. 13). There are three main options in scrolling. You can pick up the square white box (called the thumb) which is located inside the scroll bar, and drag it up or down depending on the direction you would like to scroll. This is useful for scrolling through large amounts of text, as for example when you want to move to the beginning or end of a file. Another method of scrolling, used for more limited movements, is to click on the grey area above or below the thumb. This lets you see the previous or following screenful of text. A third way to scroll, for the most limited movements of all, is to place the pointer on the arrows at the top and bottom of the scroll bar and click. This scrolls the text in small jumps.

To make it easier to be more precise in scrolling, the page number of the text on the screen is displayed within the thumb.

Making changes

Text is modified in MacWrite based on a principle of select and act. See **Marking blocks of text** below.

Reforming a paragraph

In MacWrite, paragraphs are reformed automatically as you type. However, you may have to make some minor adjustments yourself when merging two paragraphs.

Marking blocks of text

Blocks of text are selected by positioning the mouse at the beginning of the targeted text, and dragging to the end of that piece of text. Dragging consists of pressing the mouse button and then moving the mouse with the button still depressed. As the mouse moves across the text, the text becomes highlighted in reverse video.

Selecting text in this way is quite straightforward, but it takes a little practice to become proficient. One problem may be that you move off track a little, causing other text to be selected than what you are aiming for. If this happens, do not stop and start again; simply keep the button depressed and move back on course.

An alternative way to select text is to insert the cursor (by clicking the mouse button) at the beginning of the block, then move the pointer to the end of the block you wish to mark. You then click the mouse button while holding down the shift key. When the mouse button is released, the entire block will be highlighted. This is the easiest way to select large pieces of text (such as the whole file).

> * A quick way to select a single word is to place the pointer on the word and 'double click' the mouse button.

Once the text is selected, you can perform various operations on the marked block:

- delete: *cut* (from the Edit menu)

- copy: *copy* (from the Edit menu)

- change font size or style: (choose options from Style menu)

- replace: type in the new text.

> ! If a block of text is selected and you press any character key, the block will be replaced by that character. If you do this by mistake, choose *paste* from the Edit menu immediately.

Since deleted text can be retrieved by choosing *paste* from the Edit menu, it is possible to transfer text from one part of a file to another, or even from one file to another.

To move a block of text to another file, you must go through the following procedure:

1. delete the block of text

2. choose *close* from the file menu

3. choose *new* from the file menu to open a new file

4. *paste* in the deleted material

5. save the new file, giving it a name

6. choose *close*

7. choose *open* and open the original file

If you are concerned about the possibility of losing the block of text, you can *copy* rather than *delete* the text in Step 1 above. This gives you an extra copy of the block which can later be deleted.

Leaving MacWrite

To leave the editor, choose *quit* from the File menu. This will return you to the desk top.

Printing

Printing while within a document can be accomplished by selecting *Print* from the File menu. If you are working from the desk top, select (the icon of) the file and choose *print* from the File menu.

Overview of MacWrite

MacWrite has several advantages: It is simple to use, easy to learn and is very good for producing different fonts and type styles. MacWrite also allows you to import diagrams and drawings from other programs such as MacPaint.

However, MacWrite is limited in some ways. For example, you have to keep your files small, and the more advanced editing features found in other word processors are absent.

B

Three operating systems

In this appendix we will discuss some basic commands used in three different operating systems: PC-DOS, UNIX and the Apple Macintosh System/Finder.

B.1 DOS

DOS stands for Disk Operating System. Some version of DOS, either PC-DOS or MS-DOS, is widely used on IBM PC computers and IBM PC compatible computers. Several versions of DOS have been developed since it first appeared. The summary of DOS commands in this section covers only the most basic functions and so is applicable to most versions of DOS available.

Some DOS commands, such as **copy**, are loaded into the computer's memory when the computer is booted; others, such as **format**, need to be read from a file on the DOS disk.

One important feature of DOS is the use of logged disk drives. Typically, there will be two disk drives available, labelled A and B. The logged disk drive is the one which the computer will access when you give a command. The way to tell which disk drive is the logged disk drive is to look at the form of the prompt. When drive A is logged, the prompt is A>; when drive B is logged, the prompt is B>.

Suppose, for example, you gave the command **chkdsk** to the prompt A>. Then the computer will look at the disk in the logged disk drive, A, for a file called 'chkdsk.'

Disk drive A (the one on the left) is usually the logged disk drive when the computer is first booted. However, if a computer has a hard disk, the hard disk drive will usually be the logged disk drive, and the prompt will be C>.

To change the logged disk drive from A to B, you type **b:** at the prompt. The result is a new prompt, B>, which shows that drive B is now the logged disk drive.

```
A>b:
B>
```

What do you do if you have the prompt A>, and the file you want to access is on the disk in drive B? In this case, you prefix the command with b:, as shown below.

```
A>b:chkdsk
```

Working with files

To simply display your file on the screen (without editing it), you can type in the command **type** followed by a file name.

Creating files

You usually create files within applications programs.

Copying files

Files can be copied using the copy command. Examples of the command are:

```
A>copy a:test.txt b:
```

```
A>copy a:test.txt b:demo
```

```
A>copy a:*.* b:
```

The first copy command shown above takes the file 'test.txt' from the disk in drive A and puts a copy of the file on the disk in drive B, giving it the same name. The second command both copies the file and renames it, saving it as 'demo' on drive B. The last command copies all the files from disk A to disk B.

Naming files

Files are usually named when they are created in an application. Renaming files is done using the rename command.

```
A>rename junk.txt paper.txt
```

Rename changes the name of the file from 'junk.txt' to 'paper.txt.'

Printing files

Printing is usually done from an application. However, if necessary, it is possible to print from DOS using the following copy command:

> A>copy paper.txt lpr1

Deleting files

Files can be deleted by using the command **del** or **erase**.

> A>del b:junk.txt

> A>del *.txt

The first command deletes the file 'junk.txt' from the disk in drive B. The second deletes all text files from the disk in drive A.

Creating directories

To create a directory, you use the command **mkdir** or **md**.

Getting system information

To get a list of files in your current directory or logged disk drive, you type **dir**.

Disk operations

DOS has some useful disk operations. One of these is **diskcopy**, which makes an exact copy of the contents of one disk and transfers this copy to another disk. To begin this operation, you give the following command with the DOS disk in place:

> >diskcopy a: b:

Next, you remove the DOS disk, and insert the disk whose contents you wish to copy into drive A. The disk which will contain the new copy is inserted in drive B. The computer will then prompt you with 'press any key to start.' Once you press a key, the contents of the disk in A will be transferred to the disk in B. Since this is a potentially dangerous operation (you might write over the files you want to keep), it is a good idea to 'write-protect' the source disk. (See p. 50.)

Another command, **chkdsk**, tells you how much available memory you have on a disk.

Formatting a disk

New disks need to be formatted before you can use them. You must have a program called 'format' available on a disk before you can undertake a format. Assuming that you have a DOS disk in drive A, you put your new disk in drive B, and issue the following command:

    A>a:format b:

As with most commands, there are options you can specify to modify the basic command. The most important option in this case is /s.

    A>a:format/s b:

This option installs a couple of hidden system files on the disk you are formatting, making it into a *bootable disk* that can be used to boot the computer.

!   Never use the format command without specifying the disk to be formatted.

Utilities available

In addition to the file-manipulating commands discussed above, DOS supports a primitive line editor called EDLIN.

B.2   UNIX

The UNIX system, which was developed at Bell Laboratories, is gaining in popularity with academic and industrial users. It is the 'programmer's operating system;' it is powerful and has many functions. However, it operates in a 'terse' mode and is often described as 'unfriendly.'

UNIX is implemented in a programming language called C. This means that UNIX users can write their own utilities in C, which should run on any UNIX machine.

One of the advantages of UNIX is that it allows the user to run more than one process at a time. Secondary processes can run in the 'background,' while you work on another task in the foreground. Another of the many powerful features of UNIX is the ability to string several commands together.

Working with files

To display your file, you use the command **pr** or **cat** followed by the file name.

Creating files

Files are usually created in applications running under Unix.

Copying files

The copy command in UNIX is **cp**. Like all UNIX commands, it can be modified in various ways. Modifications in UNIX commands are indicated by a hyphen. Thus, you might give the command:

%cp -i notes asg/paper

The percent sign here is a prompt. The command creates a copy of the file 'notes,' which it places in the directory 'asg.' The copy is given the name 'paper.' The -i option prompts the user if the copy command will overwrite an existing file.

Naming files

Files are usually named when they are created in applications such as editors. The names of files can be changed by 'moving' them.

mv oldname newname

> **!** Remember that UNIX distinguishes upper and lower case. The following names label three distinct files: 'paper,' 'Paper,' and 'PAPER.'

Printing files

Files can be printed from the operating system by giving the commands **lpr** or **print**.

Deleting files

Files are deleted by giving the command **rm**. Once files are removed, they cannot be undeleted.

Creating directories

Directories are created using the command **mkdir**.

Getting system information

To get information about commands, you can type **man** followed by the command.

To see who is on the system, use the commands **who** or **finger**. If you want to see the files in your current directory, type **ls**; and if you want to see what processes you are running, type **ps**.

Mail

There are various mail programs that run under Unix. To enter the mail program, you type **mail**.

Utilities available

UNIX supports a large number of utilities including two editors called ed and vi, and two formatters called TROFF and NROFF.

B.3   Apple Macintosh System/Finder

The Macintosh is graphically oriented. Many commands are given by manipulating *icons* (or images) in a manner that corresponds in some sense to the way in which things are done in real life. For example, the screen consists of a representation of a 'desk top' with various objects placed upon it, including a trash can. Deleting a file involves dragging the pictorial representation of the file (an icon) across the desk top and putting the file into the trash can. Dragging an item is achieved by positioning the pointer on the object, pressing the mouse button and moving the mouse while keeping the button depressed. The button is released when the icon is where the user wants it. (This is easy once you see it done.)

The Macintosh System/Finder provides an interface very different from Unix. The extensive use of icons and menus makes it easy to learn to use a Macintosh program. However, on the negative side, the finder is rather slow and does not have as many features as other operating systems.

Working with files

Files can only be viewed from within an application.

Creating files

Files are created from within applications programs.

Copying files

On a Macintosh computer, there are two ways to copy files. One way involves making a copy of a file on the same disk. In this case, you select the file (by clicking on the icon for the file) and choose *duplicate* from the File menu. This allows you to make backup copies of the files you are working on.

The second way is to transfer the file from one disk to another. To do this, you select and drag the icon of the file that you want to copy onto the icon of the target disk.

To select more than one file at a time, you hold down the shift key while clicking on the icon.

Naming files

Files are named within an application. Files can be renamed by selecting the name under the file icon and typing in the new name.

Printing files

Printing can take place either from the desk top or from within an application. From the desk top, you select a file, then choose *print* from the File menu. Your disk must contain special files for you to be able to print.

Deleting files

You delete files by dragging the file icon to the trash can, which is usually at the bottom right of the screen.

Creating directories

The Macintosh uses *folders* as directories. A new folder will appear on the disk if you select *new folder* from the File menu. You can then drag the icons of files until they are over (or in) the folder.

Getting system information

You can get information about individual files by selecting a file and typing *command i*.

Disk operations

Disks can be copied by dragging the icon of the disk to be copied onto the icon of the empty disk.

Formatting a disk

On a Macintosh, the computer will recognize an unformatted disk and display a message (fig. 1) asking you if you want the disk to be initialized. Occasionally, the computer will give this message even when you insert an old disk. In this case, simply choose *eject* and insert the disk again.

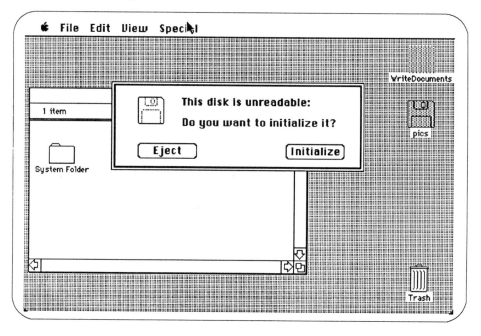

Figure 1. Initializing a disk on a Macintosh

Utilities available

Several utilities can be loaded in with the system such as a clock, calculator, note pad and even puzzles.

C

Computer commands

C.1   Editing commands

Getting started

Editing a new file   _____

Editing an existing file   _____

Saving and exiting

Save a file   _____

Save and exit   _____

Exit without saving   _____

Exit to operating system   _____

Moving around in a file

	forward	*backward*
Character	_____	_____
Word	_____	_____
Line	_____	_____
Sentence	_____	_____
Screen	_____	_____
	_____	_____

	beginning	*end*
Line	_____	_____
Screen	_____	_____
Page	_____	_____
File	_____	_____
	_____	_____

263

Screen commands

Scroll forwards _____

Scroll backwards _____

Split the screen _____

Move cursor to other window _____

Return to one screen _____

_____

Deleting material

Delete previous character _____

Delete character _____

Delete word _____

Delete line _____

Delete sentence _____

Delete paragraph _____

Delete block _____

_____

Search commands

Search _____

Search and replace _____

Query replace _____

Replace _____

Options: _____

_____

_____

_____

_____

Working with blocks (or regions)

Mark beginning of block _____

Mark end of block _____

Move block _____

Copy block _____

Delete block _____

Write block to a file _____

_____

_____

_____

_____

Format

Reform a paragraph _____

Left margin _____

Right margin
Line spacing
Justification
Ragged right
Center text
Page break

Printing

Print a file
Top margin
Bottom margin
Left margin
Right margin
Text height
Text width

Boldface
Underline
Italics
Accents

Superscript
Subscript
Page break
Header
Footer
Set page number

Other commands

C.2   Operating system commands

Working with files

File commands

    List your files (dir) _____

    Display a file on the screen (type) _____

    Copy a file (copy) _____

    Rename a file (rename) _____

    Print a file (print) _____

    Delete a file (del) _____

Subdirectory commands

    Create a subdirectory (mkdir) _____

    Remove a subdirectory (rmdir) _____

    Connect to a subdirectory (cd) _____

Disk commands (for microcomputers)

    Format a disk (format) _____

    Copy a disk (diskcopy) _____

Starting applications

    Starting an editor _____

    Starting a data base manager _____

    Starting a spreadsheet _____

C.3   Getting started

Logging on to a multi-user system (step by step)

Booting a microcomputer (step by step)

D
Answers to selected questions

Answers to Chapter 1

1. Computers seem smart in several ways. For one thing, they can hold a considerable amount of information. They are also able to process information in a way that has all the appearances of intelligence. On the other hand, computers also seem to be dumb. They can't understand English or any other human language. Typically, computers cannot learn from experience or make judgements. If you make a simple spelling mistake in giving a command (e.g., typing **fingeer** instead of **finger**), the computer acts as though you have typed something that was completely random. Human beings, on the other hand, have the capacity to interpret messages that are somewhat defective.

2. The command *Please tell me the time* has the advantage of being very English-like, but it takes a long time to type and there are numerous possibilities for making mistakes.

4. data base, interface, input

9. (a) A (b) ! (your keyboard may have something else.) (c) A (d) 1

10. To give a control command, such as *ctrl* a, you hold down the control key, and keep it depressed while you tap the a key. To give an escape command, such as *esc* a, you press and then release the escape key <u>before</u> tapping the a key.

11. Dot-matrix printers are more versatile in that they can often print graphics and non-standard characters (α, β, etc.).

Answers to Chapter 2

1. First you have to open an account. Once you have an account, you simply find a free terminal and log on.

2. Assuming that you are at a terminal, you log on by typing your name and pressing the return or enter key. Next you type your password and press the return key. (Note: when you type your password, the letters will not appear on the screen.)

5. (a) BULL (b) TELNET (c) Trailer H6

6. Some computers automatically log you out after a certain period of inactivity.

Answers to Chapter 3

1. Booting the computer is a fancy name for starting it. Often, booting consists of inserting a disk containing system files into the disk drive and then turning on the power switch. If you have a hard disk, these system files are already present in the computer and so just turning the computer on automatically boots it.

2. If your computer has a hard disk, you may be able to simply turn on the microcomputer and call up the editing program that you want. If your microcomputer doesn't have a hard disk, you will probably have to go through the following steps:

(a) Insert a disk containing a system file into the disk drive.

(b) Turn the computer on.

(c) Insert the disk containing the word processor you want to use.

(d) Call up the editing program.

You may have the system files and the word processor on the same disk, in which case step (c) is unnecessary. The order of (a) and (b) may be reversed with some computers such as the Apple Macintosh.

3. Any two of the following: keyboard, mouse, graphics pad or tablet, joystick, optical scanner, digitizer.

4. Any two of the following: monitor, printer, plotter, loud-speaker.

5. The most vulnerable part of a floppy disk is the exposed area that is read by the disk drive head. A scratch on this exposed area could result in the loss of a large amount of information.

6. Ways in which diskettes can be damaged include the following: bending, heating, magnetizing, scratching, wetting.

8. (a) A disk stores programs and data. (b) A disk drive reads data from a disk to a computer and writes data from a computer to a disk.

9. (a) saving your files (b) removing the disks (c) switching off the power.

Answers to Chapter 4

3. (a) moving the cursor to the appropriate point and (b) making the actual changes (e.g., inserting or deleting text).

4. Moving the cursor generally refers to changing the location of the cursor on a single screenful of text. Scrolling, on the other hand, is a way of moving through a file from screen to screen. During scrolling, if you move the cursor off the screen (at the top or bottom), then the screen will scroll to 'keep up' with the cursor.

5. Any two of the following: (a) using control keys; (b) using cursor keys; (c) by using a mouse; or (d) using some other special input device.

6. If there is no text following the cursor, then it makes no difference whether the editor is in insert mode or overwrite mode. Let us assume there is text following the cursor. When the editor is in insert mode, the existing text will be shifted to the right (and down) as it is displaced by the new text you type. When the editor is in overwrite mode, the existing text will disappear as it is replaced by the new text.

7. Save your work often. Make backup copies of your files.

8. Temporary memory refers to the information held in the computer. If the computer is turned off, the material in temporary memory is lost. Permanent memory refers to the information stored on magnetic material such as disks.

10. When you save a file, you are transferring a copy of the file from temporary memory to permanent memory.

Answers to Chapter 5

2. An operating system has many functions. To the user, the most obvious functions concern the management of files: deleting old files, copying, renaming, keeping files organized, and so on.

3. You usually only format a disk once: after you have bought it and before you use it to store files. If you have an old disk and you are absolutely sure that there are no files that you want on the disk, you can reformat the disk.

4. On a menu and pointer computer, you copy a file by dragging the file icon onto the icon of a new disk. On other computers, a command like **copy** or **cp** is often used.

5. On a menu and pointer computer, you might drag the icon of a file on top of an image of a trash can. On other computers, you use a command like **delete** or **erase** or **rm**.

6. (a) saving your work regularly (b) making backup copies of your files.

Answers to Chapter 6

3. A wildcard character is a special symbol, which when used in a search command will match any one or more characters in the target. The wildcard is useful when you are unsure of the spelling of the target or you are searching for several targets which have approximately the same form.

4. If the search and replace acted solely on whole words, then the only effect would be that 'on' in the first line would be changed to 'in.' If, on the other hand, the change affected parts of words, then the text would look like the following:

> All electrinic mail systems in computers share some commin characteristics. To send a message an email user logs into a terminal, writes the message, and gives a command to send the message to another user.

7. No.

Answers to Chapter 7

1. (a) communications software (b) a modem (c) a telephone. A direct wire connection may replace the modem and telephone.

2. Any three of the following: (a) to get access to software not available on your own computer; (b) to use electronic mail; (c) to get access to bboards on other computers; (d) to transfer files; (e) to use printers; (f) to search library catalogues; (g) to gain access to commercial services such as business information; (h) to access commercial data bases such as DIALOG.

3. Method 1: (a) enter mail program (b) give address (c) give subject of the message (d) write the message (e) send message (f) quit the mail program.

Method 2: (a) open file (b) write message (c) exit file (d) send the file, specifying the address of the recipient.

4. (a) enter the mail program (b) give a command to read a message, followed perhaps by the number of the message (c) read the message (d) quit the mail program.

Answers to Chapter 8

1. Data base of airline bookings; vehicle registration data base.

2. A record is cne entry in the data base. It is equivalent to an index card. A record consists of several fields, each of which contains one category of information, e.g., a name field, an address field, etc.

5. A search picks out one or more records in the data base that conform to the specifications given in the search. A sort orders all the records in the data base according to some criterion such as alphabetical order of entries in the name field.

6. A data base is like a set of electronic index cards. It is used primarily to store information. The data base manager is able to retrieve the information in a data base very efficiently. A spreadsheet also holds information, but its information is stored in the form of a large grid rather than a set of records. Spreadsheets are designed for information that is best stored in table form, such as financial information. One of the main uses of spreadsheets is in performing numerical calculations on the stored data.

7. A spreadsheet is a sheet full of cells which are labelled according to their row and column. Different headings and numbers can be entered in the cells of the grid. It also contains the equivalent of a calculator.

Answers to Chapter 9

2. A footnote call refers to the number, or other indicator, in the main text which signals the existence of a corresponding footnote. The footnote body is the actual text of the footnote. It appears at the bottom of a page or at the end of the paper or chapter.

3. (a) Write the text and enter the formatting commands using an editor. (b) Run the file produced in (a) through the formatting program. The final step is to print out the file produced by the formatting program.

4. By using powerful commands such as macros and abbreviations for the common formatting commands that you use.

6. Probably only one: sheo.

7. Because every time you write the word 'a,' as in 'a person,' it would be expanded into 'autonomous.'

Answers to Chapter 10

1. Your library may use either the Library of Congress system or the Dewey Decimal system. Some libraries use both; a few use their own system.

3. (a) Bibliographies contain lists of references that have been chosen by a researcher on a particular topic. (b) Indexes contain information about all the articles in a set of journals in a particular field, listed by topic and/or author. (c) Abstracts contain summaries of articles in a particular field.

4. First look for a card for the book in the card catalogue. You can either look up the author's name or the title of the book. When you have found the card, make a note of the call number. Find the location of the book by looking at the library's map or directory.

5. Periodicals may be listed in the general catalogue and/or they may have their own catalogue. When you have found the entry for a periodical title, you must look to see where the journal is stored. The older, bound volumes of the journal may be stored in a different place from the more recent issues.

6. You can search for books by looking in the subject card catalogue under subject names that you think are appropriate. Another strategy is to look first at a list of the headings that the library uses. If your library follows the Library of Congress system, you can look up your topic in the book of Library of Congress headings.

To find out relevant journal articles on your topic, look up the topic in an index and/or volume of abstracts for your field of study. Once you have a good journal reference, check the bibliography of the article for other articles of interest.

Answers to Chapter 11

4. (a) The OR search will give more citations because it will produce the citations under 'economics' *plus* the citations under 'Cambridge.'

Answers to Chapter 12

1. Scanning means looking at a text for some particular information. You can get an idea of the content of a book or article by scanning through it looking for the main ideas.

2. Index cards are useful because (a) they can be carried easily; (b) they are simple; (c) they can be rearranged (d) they are cheap.

3. Using a data base enables you to take advantage of the computer's storage capacity and processing power. Thus, using a data base, you can (a) store a considerable amount of data; (b) perform searches; (c) sort the records quickly; (d) sometimes transfer the stored data to your text files.

E

Glossary

abbreviation mode (noun)

A time-saving function found on sophisticated word processors such as EMACS. Abbreviation mode allows you to enter a shortened form of a word or phrase which the computer automatically 'expands' into the full word (or phrase). The user defines abbreviations for the computer as needed.

account name (noun)

The name by which the computer knows you. Your account name may be similar to your first or last name. Alternatively, it may have a completely different form, such as 'ga.gmb' or 'z.ztop.'

address (noun)

A string of characters used to send electronic mail to a user. The address usually consists of a user name followed by the name of the computer on which the account is valid. The parts of an address are often separated by symbols like @ or %. An example of an address: BARLOW@lotsa.

alphanumeric keys (noun)

The keys for numbers and letters.

ALT key (noun)

A key found on some keyboards (IBM PC, for example). It is similar in function to the escape key.

append (verb, noun)

To copy one file onto the end of another, thereby making one large file that contains both smaller files.

application, applications programs (noun)

Programs which allow the user to make use of the computer without a knowledge of programming. Such programs automatically translate the user's commands into the commands of a computer language. Some common applications programs are word processors and data base managers

architecture (noun)
The basic design of a computer.

archive copy (noun)
A backup copy of a program, file or manuscript which is stored in a safe location.

autorepeat (noun, verb)
Some computers and programs allow the user to repeat a key automatically by keeping it depressed for around half a second. Thus to produce the sequence bbbbbbbbbbbbbbbbb, the user holds down the 'b' key. Other computers have a special key labelled 'repeat' to carry out this same function.

baud rate (noun)
The rate at which information is transferred between a terminal and a remote computer linked by a modem. Modems with low baud rates (e.g. 300 baud) make working on the computer a slow process.

bboard (noun)
An electronic bulletin board. Bulletin boards are used to publicly display various types of information. They may be general or specialized, official or unofficial.

boot (noun, verb)
A term for starting up a microcomputer. Booting consists of turning the computer on and inserting the system software containing the appropriate system files. The computer then reads in the required system information contained on the disk.

bootable disk (noun)
A disk containing the system files necessary to boot a microcomputer.

break key (noun)
A key found on some computers which acts like the command *ctrl c*. Pressing the break key will often stop a program that is running.

bye (noun)
A command which stops a process. It is equivalent to **logoff** on some computers.

call number (noun)
A sequence of numbers and letters that identifies each book in a library. The call number is displayed on the spine of the book and usually inside the book as well.

caps lock key (noun)
Computers, like typewriters, have a key which can be depressed so that all the letters typed will appear in upper case. The caps lock key is pressed again to return to normal lower case typing.

card catalogue (noun)
A place where the author, title and subject cards for books are kept.

carriage return (noun)

The lever on a typewriter that moves the paper so that you can write on a new line. On a computer, carriage return refers to the key (often called 'return' or 'enter') which moves the cursor to the beginning of the next line on the screen. This key is also used to indicate that a command is complete and ready to be executed (carried out). 'Return' refers in addition, to the invisible character entered into the computer when the return key is tapped.

cell (noun)

A space for an individual piece of data in a spreadsheet. Each cell in the spreadsheet is identified according to the row and column that it occupies.

character (noun)

A character is a single element recognized by the computer or printer. There are various types of characters, including letters, numbers, symbols (e.g. & and #), and invisible characters (space, tab, return). In addition to these kinds of text characters, there are also control characters such as *ctrl c*.

citation (noun)

Bibliographic information about a single reference or source. Online library catalogues typically list references in the form of citations, including such information as author, title, date of publication, and serial information, if any.

command-driven program (noun)

A program that is controlled by commands typed in at the keyboard, normally without the presence of a menu. EMACS is an example of a command-driven program. Contrast *menu-driven program.*

command key (noun)

A special key that is used to give a command to the computer. Two common command keys are the control key and the escape key.

command mode (noun)

On some computer systems you must enter a special command mode before you can give a command. Such systems have two separate modes, one for entering data and one for giving commands.

communications (noun)

The linking of one computer with another.

compatibles (noun)

Short for 'compatible computers': computers that are similar in operation to other famous or standard computers. For example, a Compaq computer is an IBM PC compatible computer; it acts like an IBM PC and will run the same basic software as an IBM PC.

connect time (noun)

The length of time a terminal is connected to a computer. Connect time is often used as a way of determining charges.

control c (noun)

Entering this command, often written *ctrl c*, stops a program that is running and returns the user to the top level.

control key (noun)

A key which is used in combination with other keys to give commands to the computer. Often labelled CTRL.

crash (noun, verb)

When a time-sharing computer stops working unexpectedly, it is said to crash.

cursor (noun)

An indicator on the screen that shows where text that is entered will appear.

data (plural noun)

Any collection of information, either textual or numeric. Often a distinction is made between the data, i.e. the information manipulated by a program, and the program itself. The word 'data' may also refer to a set of discrete pieces of information such as numeric values. In this sense it is used in opposition to *text*, which refers to material written in a natural language such as English.

data base (noun)

A store of information organized in a set framework.

data base manager (noun)

A computer application designed for creating and maintaining data bases. Also called data base management program.

data entry (noun)

The process of typing information (often numerical) into the computer. The term is often used when entering data base or spreadsheet information.

default (noun)

A preset value that is automatically selected by the computer unless another option is specified by the user. For example, margin settings typically have a default value specified in the program itself.

DEL key (noun)

Short for delete key. A key which moves the cursor back one space and deletes the character previously occupying that position.

delete (verb)

To remove data (characters, words, paragraphs, etc.) or files. Deleted elements can sometimes be retrieved within a limited time period after deletion.

digitizer (noun)

An input device for a computer. A digitizer will take the information from a photograph, text, map or sound recording and enter it into the computer in digital form.

directory (noun)

A directory can be thought of either as a place where files are kept or as a list of the files.

disk (noun)

A form of permanent magnetic storage for computers.

disk drive (noun)

A device on a computer which reads information from and writes information to disks.

DOS (noun)

Short for Disk Operating System. A commonly-used operating system designed for microcomputers such as the IBM PC.

down (adjective)

Not working. A computer or printer that is not operational and hence not available to users is said to be down.

download (verb)

To transfer data from a large computer to a microcomputer.

downtime (noun)

The time at which a large computer is scheduled to become unavailable or down. Also, the period of time during which the computer is unavailable. Often downtime is scheduled ahead of time by the computer operators for repair or maintenance work.

electronic mail (noun)

A system for transmitting messages via computer for users of a large computer or network. Also can refer to the messages themselves.

EMACS (noun)

A powerful word processor often available on large computers.

email (noun)

Short for electronic mail. Pronounced 'ee-mail.'

enter (verb)

To send data or commands to the computer by pressing the return key.

enter key (noun)

Another name for the return key.

escape key (noun)

A special key, often labelled ESC, that is used to give certain commands to the computer.

exec level (noun)

The level at which commands are given to the operating system on certain large computers. For these computers, the exec level is the *top level*. Exec is stressed on the second syllable.

fatal error (noun)

An error occurring in the running of a program which brings the program or computer to a halt.

field (noun)
Part of a data record that holds a particular type of information. For example, fields in an electronic address book might include Name, Address, and Phone number. Each individual record will then contain information for each of those fields.

file (noun)
Text or data stored as a unit and identified by a label called the file name. Like files in a file cabinet, computer files help keep information organized in meaningful units.

file transfer program (noun)
A program for transferring files from one computer to another.

flag (noun, verb)
A marker inserted into a text. Flags can be used as placeholders, or as indicators. For example, in WordStar, the word **insert** appears at the top of the screen when the program is in 'insert mode.' For programmers, flag is also used as a verb meaning 'to mark with a flag.'

floppy disk (noun)
A form of permanent memory storage for microcomputers, generally in the form of a flat flexible disk encased in cardboard or hard plastic. Floppy disks may hold software, such as word processing programs, or data, such as a user's files.

folder (noun)
A device for grouping similar files together on a menu and pointer computer. Equivalent to the use of subdirectories on other types of computer.

format (verb, noun)
1. (referring to disks): To add (electronic) lines to a new disk so that it can be written to and read from by a computer. Same as 'initialize.' The format command is part of the operating system.
2. To alter the shape or layout of a text (e.g., a paragraph or a whole file) so that it conforms with certain settings for line spacing, margins, page length, and other aspects of its appearance on the printed page and/or screen.

formatter (noun)
A program for putting text into a specified format. Formatters are designed to allow the user to control the appearance of the printed output.

formatting program (noun)
See formatter.

ftp (noun)
The name of a file transfer program for large computers. Pronounced as individual letters: f-t-p.

function key (noun)

Some keyboards (e.g., the IBM PC) contain function keys labelled F1, F2, etc., which allow certain common commands to be given with a single keystroke. The commands represented by the function keys vary, depending on the program used.

global (adjective)

Affecting the whole file. For example, a global change will alter words throughout the file, not just those showing on the screen.

goto (noun)

A command found in some word processors that moves the cursor to a particular page. It is pronounced like the English words 'go to.'

graphics pad (noun)

An input device consisting of a stylus or pen attached to a flat pad. Moving the pen on the pad translates into movements of the cursor on the screen. Graphics pads are designed for drawing or creating graphics.

hard copy (noun)

See *printout*.

hard disk (noun)

A form of permanent memory storage for microcomputers. A hard disk, which is often mounted inside the computer, has a much greater memory capacity than a floppy disk.

hardware (mass noun)

Computer machinery such as monitors, system units, printers, keyboards, etc. Often used in opposition to *software*.

help system (noun)

An online system which provides information about commands and general program information.

icon (noun)

A pictorial representation of an object on the screen. Some objects typically represented as icons include disks, files, and printers.

idea processor See *outliner*.

init file (noun)

Short for *initialization file*. Init is pronounced with stress on the second syllable.

initialization file (noun)

A file containing settings that the user has chosen for a particular application such as a word processor or mail program. Each time the application is used, the settings in the initialization file are automatically selected. An initialization file allows you to customize a program to suit your needs by choosing the settings you prefer as default settings.

initialize (verb)

To *format* a disk. New disks must be initialized (or formatted) before they can be used.

input device (noun)

A piece of hardware designed for entering commands and/or data into the computer. The most common input device is the keyboard.

insert mode (noun)

Turning insert mode on and typing characters causes any characters that follow the cursor to be pushed to the right as new text is entered. Insert mode is the opposite of *overwrite mode*.

integrated program (noun)

A program containing several applications that work closely together. An integrated program might contain a spreadsheet, a word processor and a communications program.

invisible character (noun)

A character which the computer recognizes as a character like any other, but which appears on the screen as empty space or as a line break. The invisible characters are tab, space, and carriage return.

iterative search (noun)

A search of an online catalogue in which the result of a search is further defined by the use of AND, OR, and NOT.

job (noun)

Logging on to a time-sharing system starts a job. The job consists of your set of interactions with the computer from the time you log in to the time you log out. It is possible to have more than one job running at once.

joystick (noun)

An input device that gets its name from the joystick (i.e. control stick) in an airplane. The computer is sensitive to the movements of the joystick; thus commands can be given by manipulating the joystick.

justification (noun)

A toggle found on some word processors which, when turned on, makes the right margin of the text straight.

justify (verb)

To make the right margin of a text straight rather than ragged. The text in this book, for example, was justified using a formatting program.

key (noun)

Keys are the button-like parts of a keyboard designed to be pressed or tapped with the fingertips. Characters are entered into the computer by pressing keys.

keyboard (noun)

An input device containing several rows of *keys*.

kill (noun, verb)

Short for **kill job**. This command is often equivalent to logging off the computer. It stops the job that is running.

light pen (noun)

An input device shaped like a pen. The computer screen is sensitive to a beam of light emitted by the pen. Commands are given by pointing the tip of the light pen at particular areas on the screen.

line editor (noun)

An editor in which data can only be entered or modified by calling up individual lines in the file. This type of editor is less flexible than the *screen editor*, since with a line editor the cursor is not freely moveable throughout the file.

load (noun)

A measure of computer use at any particular time. A high load on a time-sharing computer means that there is a high demand on its processing capacity.

load (verb)

The computer loads software or data by transferring information from files stored on permanent storage devices, such as disks, into the computer's temporary memory. Same as *read*.

log in See *log on*.

log off (verb)

To end a session on a time-sharing computer. Also log out. The command for this function is often **logoff** or **logout**.

log on (verb)

To start a session on a time-sharing computer. Also log in. This function is often performed using the commands **logon** or **login**.

log out See *log off*.

low-level (adjective)

A description for instructions which are closer to the representations that the computer uses to carry out its tasks, rather than to the forms of instructions which the user employs. Examples of low-level instructions include assembly language and machine code.

Macintosh (noun)

A microcomputer made by Apple which uses a mouse as an input device.

macro (noun)

A shortcut for giving a complex command. For a command requiring several keystrokes, it is possible to define a macro which acts as a kind of abbreviation. Thus the same command can be given with only one or two keystrokes.

MacWrite (noun)

A word processor for the Macintosh computer.

mainframe (noun)
A large, time-sharing computer that supports numerous users simultaneously.

menu (noun)
A table or list of options that the user can choose from. The options represent the possible commands that the computer can carry out at the level at which the menu is available.

menu and pointer computer (noun)
A type of computer having an arrow-shaped indicator on the screen which can be used to select options from a *menu*. The term is used in this book only.

menu-driven program (noun)
A program that is controlled by selecting options from a menu. Contrast *command-driven program*.

meta key (noun)
A key found on some keyboards which is used in giving commands. It is similar in function to the escape key.

microcomputer (noun)
A small computer containing a microprocessor on a single chip. An example is the IBM PC. Microcomputers are in general designed to be used by a single person, although some powerful versions exist which can support several users at once.

minicomputer (noun)
A time-sharing computer of medium power such as a VAX or a DEC 20.

modem (noun)
Short for MOdulator-DEModulator. A device for making a connection between a terminal and a remote computer over telephone lines.

monitor (noun)
The part of the computer or terminal which contains a screen on which data is presented to the user. A monitor is somewhat similar in appearance to a television set. Other names for it are *visual display unit* (VDU) and CRT (cathode ray tube).

mouse (noun)
An input device which can be used to position the cursor on the screen or to give commands. The mouse is manipulated by moving it across a surface and by 'clicking', or pressing its button(s).

multi-user system (noun)
A computer that can support more than one user at the same time. Time-sharing computers are the most common type of multi-user system.

network (noun)
A group of computers linked together by a direct wire connection. Networks allow direct communication between computers and the sharing of resources such as printers.

numeric keypad (noun)

A group of number keys arranged for easy entry of figures.

numlock key (noun)

The key which switches a numeric keypad from cursor arrows to numbers or vice versa.

online (adjective)

Refers to the existence of a live connection between a central computer and some peripheral hardware. For example, for a terminal or printer to be online, there must be a functioning electronic pathway that links it to the main computer.

online library catalogue (noun)

A catalogue of library materials stored in a computer data base.

operating system (noun)

Software that manages the storage and retrieval of information on the computer. The operating system is responsible for the various 'housekeeping functions' of the computer: keeping order among files and programs, managing the computer's resources (including peripherals) and scheduling its operations.

optical scanner (noun)

An input device used for transferring text directly from a printed page into a computer.

outliner (noun)

An applications program designed to allow the user to write text in the form of headings and subheadings. Changes in the organization of an outline are very easy to accomplish using these programs, which are sometimes called idea processors.

overwrite mode (noun)

When the computer is in overwrite mode, the characters typed are entered on top of existing text, which makes that text disappear. This is the opposite of *insert mode,* which shifts old text to the right instead of replacing it.

pagebreak (noun)

A command which orders the printer to start a new page at the point in the file at which the command is given. Can also refer to the actual break between lines of text from one page to the next, in which case it is usually written as two words (page break).

password (noun)

A sequence of characters, known only to the user, which serves to positively identify the user to the computer. Passwords provide protection for the users' files and prevent unauthorized use of the user's allocated computer time and disk space.

path (noun)

A record of the connections between different levels of subdirectories in UNIX and other operating systems.

peripherals (noun)
Hardware components other than the central system unit of a computer. Common peripherals include monitors, keyboards, printers and hard disks.

permanent storage (noun)
Devices for storing data or software on magnetic material. Permanent storage is independent of the flow of electricity through the computer. Some common forms of permanent storage include floppy disks, hard disks, and tapes.

personal computer (noun)
A small computer designed to be used by one person. Also called a *microcomputer.*

pitch (noun)
The number of characters per inch on printed output.

plotter (noun)
An output device connected to a computer which draws lines and graphs.

pointer (noun)
An image, often in the form of an arrow, which appears on the screen of a menu and pointer computer. The pointer can be used to give commands by selecting choices from a menu. Its placement on the screen is often controlled by manipulating a mouse.

print command (noun)
A command used in a word processing program to alter the form of printed text. Typical print commands control features such as bold face and underlining.

printout (noun)
The paper version of a file, produced by a printer.

process (noun)
A program running on a computer.

processor (noun)
The unit at the heart of the computer which carries out computations. In a microcomputer this is called a microprocessor.

program (noun)
A set of instructions written in a computer language such as Pascal or Lisp.

program (verb)
To write a series of instructions in a programming language that makes the computer do something.

programming language (noun)
A type of code used to give instructions to a computer. Programs can be written in many different programming languages, for example, BASIC, Pascal, Prolog or Lisp. It is not possible to program in English because computers cannot interpret natural languages.

prompt (noun)

A special character (e.g., @, >, %) that appears on the screen to indicate that the computer is ready to receive a command. On many computers, the form of the prompt changes depending on what program is being run.

prompt and cursor computer (noun)

A computer that presents the user with a prompt followed by a cursor. The user gives commands to the computer by typing at the keyboard in response to the prompt. (This term is used in this book only.)

proportional spacing (noun)

A method of printing characters in which the size of the character determines how much space the printer assigns to it on the line. For example, with proportional spacing the character 'i' is given less space than a 'w.' Some devices produce only non-proportional spacing. Typewriters, for example, give every character the same amount of space regardless of its size.

pull-down menu (noun)

A menu on a Macintosh which is displayed only when the pointer passes over the menu bar and the mouse button is depressed.

read (verb)

The computer reads data or software by transferring it from a magnetic storage medium, such as a disk, to the computer's internal memory. Same as *load.*

record (noun)

A set of information about an individual item stored in a data base. A record is organized into a set of fields representing the different classes of information stored. For example, for a data base which stores information about local restaurants, each restaurant will be given its own record. Information about location, type of food, etc. will be stored in fields on the record.

reform (noun, verb)

A word processing command which causes the text to fit between the margins. When the reform command is given, lines of text which are too long for the margin will be divided, and lines that are too short will be added to.

return key See *carriage return.*

run (verb)

To run a program is to make the computer execute (carry out) the instructions contained in the program. If some of the instructions are written incorrectly, the program may not run.

scan (noun, verb)

To look at a list of titles or headings. For example, you might enter a command to scan your mail. What you see then is a list containing just the heading of each message.

screen (noun)
> The special glass front of a monitor on which data is displayed.

screen editor (noun)
> An editor that allows free cursor movement through the file. Data may be entered or modified directly once the cursor is moved to the appropriate place in the file (see *line editor*).

scroll (verb)
> To move previous or later parts of a file into view on the screen. It is possible to scroll through a file, screenful by screenful.

scroll bar (noun)
> The part of a *window* that allows you to scroll through a file.

search (verb, noun)
> A command that locates a particular string of characters in a file. Also, the process of carrying out a search.

search and replace (verb)
> A command which finds instances of a particular string of characters in a file and replaces them with a different string of characters.

software (mass noun)
> Programmed instructions that make the computer carry out desired tasks.

sort (noun, verb)
> To put the records in a data base in a particular order. For example, a data base might be sorted in alphabetical order of the name *field*.

spelling checker (noun)
> A program that searches through a text file for spelling and typing mistakes.

spreadsheet (noun)
> An applications program that stores a set of data in grid form and allows the user to carry out calculations on the data.

stacks (noun)
> The place in the library where books for general circulation are kept.

status line (noun)
> A line on the screen that displays information such as the name of the application in use, the name of the file, position of the cursor, etc.

switch (noun)
> A physical or software item that has two or more positions or values. A command may be modified by a switch. For example, on some word processors, the print command may be modified with a switch specifying information such as choice of printer.

symbolic character (also **symbol**)

One type of character that the computer recognizes. Symbolic characters include mathematical symbols (+ %) and punctuation marks (, ! :). In other words, symbolic characters include all those characters which are neither *alphanumeric* nor *invisible.*

synonym (noun)

A word with a meaning very similar to the meaning of another word. For example, 'leap' is a synonym of 'jump.'

system unit (noun)

The hardware component of a microcomputer that contains the microprocessor.

tab key (noun)

A key which allows the cursor to jump to preset tab settings. Pressing the tab key enters an invisible tab character into the computer.

tapes (noun)

A form of permanent storage. Information is coded magnetically on a long strip of electromagnetically sensitive material.

temporary memory (noun)

Memory that relies on a continuous flow of electricity for its maintenance. If power is lost or there is a break in an electrical connection, then the information in temporary memory is lost. Sometimes called temporary storage. Contrast *permanent storage.*

terminal (noun)

A keyboard and monitor that are connected to a remote computer by wires.

time-sharing computer (noun)

A computer that divides its processing power among numerous users at once. The computer devotes small packets of time to each user; all users, however, appear to have continuous access to the computer.

toggle (noun, verb)

A special kind of switch. A toggle has only two values, 'on' and 'off.' Some toggles have keys to represent them, for example, the *caps lock* and *numlock keys.* Other toggles are menu controlled, like *justify* in WordStar.

top level (noun)

The level at which commands are given to the operating system. When you log in, you enter the top level. You leave the top level when you run a program or application.

touch screen (noun)

An input device found on certain computers. Commands may be given to the computer by touching different parts of the touch-sensitive screen.

truncation (noun)

A technique used in searching an on-line library catalogue. In a truncation search, only the stem of a word (i.e., the main part) is specified as the target. This causes similar words to be found by the search as well. Also called a stem search.

undelete (verb)

To retrieve text that has been deleted.

UNIX (noun)

An operating system in use on VAX and other computers.

up (adjective)

Available, functioning; the opposite of *down*.

upload (verb)

To transfer information from a microcomputer to a large computer.

upper case (adjective, noun)

Capital letters. THIS SENTENCE IS WRITTEN IN UPPER CASE.

utilities (noun)

Certain small programs that give information or carry out simple tasks. Some examples are: sorting or alphabetizing programs; clocks and calendars; notepads. Utilities are usually convenient additional services which are included as part of larger software packages.

VDU (noun)

See *visual display unit.*

vi (noun)

A text editor designed for use with the UNIX operating system. Pronounced as individual letters: v-i.

visual display unit (noun)

The part of the terminal or computer that contains the screen. Commonly abbreviated as VDU. Also called a *monitor* or CRT.

window (noun)

A rectangular box that appears on the screen to give information or display data. Windows are often controlled by the user; they can be opened and closed, moved around, and changed in size or shape. More than one window can appear on the screen at once.

window editor (noun)

A word processing program such as MacWrite that operates in a window environment. The text files of these editors are displayed in windows.

word processor (noun)

An applications program that allows the user to write text.

word wrap (noun)

A convenient feature available on many word processors. Word wrap automatically moves words to the following line when the right margin has been passed. This means that the user does not need to enter a return at the end of each line; the return key needs to be pressed only at the end of a paragraph.

workstation (noun)
A small powerful computer with a large graphics screen.

write (verb)
To transfer data from the temporary memory in the computer to an electronic medium, such as a disk, for permanent storage. The opposite of *read*.

write-protected (adjective)
Write protection on a disk prevents the disk drive from *writing* to the disk.

wysiwyg (adjective)
Pronounced 'wizzy-wig.' (What You See Is What You Get.) Some computers and word processors will show you on the screen what your document will look like when it is printed out. You can see *page breaks*, boldface type, etc., directly on the screen.

Index

ORDER FORM

Please send me the following Athelstan titles on Computers
and English as a Second Language. I understand that if I am
not completely satisfied, I can return the material within
30 days for a full refund.

Quantity	Title	Unit Price	Total Price
____	Working with Computers (hardback) (ISBN 0-940753-07-3)	@$23.95	____
____	Working with Computers (paperback) (ISBN 0-940753-08-1)	@$15.95	____
____	Computers and ESL in Higher Education (booklet)	@$2.25	____
		Subtotal	____

Shipping: $1 per first book,
$.50 for additional copies;
$.25 per pamphlet.   ____
Californians: Please add sales tax.   ____

TOTAL ORDER   ____

INDIVIDUALS: must prepay with check or money order.
INSTITUTIONS: seı d purchase order

Name _____

Address _____

_____

_____ Zip _____

Country (outside U.S.) _____

____Please add my name to Athelstan's mailing list.

ATHELSTAN   P.O. Box 6552-W, Stanford, CA 94305.
Tel. (415) 285-0''34

ORDER FORM

Please send me the following Athelstan titles on Computers and English as a Second Language. I understand that if I am not completely satisfied, I can return the material within 30 days for a full refund.

Quantity	Title	Unit Price	Total Price
_____	Working with Computers (hardback) (ISBN 0-940753-07-3)	@$23.95	_____
_____	Working with Computers (paperback) (ISBN 0-940753-08-1)	@$15.95	_____
_____	Computers and ESL in Higher Education (booklet)	@$2.25	_____
		Subtotal	_____

Shipping: $1 per first book,
  $.50 for additional copies;
  $.25 per pamphlet.   _____
Californians: Please add sales tax.   _____

TOTAL ORDER   _____

INDIVIDUALS: must prepay with check or money order.
INSTITUTIONS: seɪ d purchase order

Name _____

Address _____

_____

_____ Zip _____

Country (outside U.S.) _____

___Please add my name to Athelstan's mailing list.

ATHELSTAN   P.O. Box 6552-W, Stanford, CA 94305.
Tel. (415) 285-0′′34